Heavy Metal Music
and the Communal Experience

Heavy Metal Music
and the Communal Experience

Edited by
Nelson Varas-Díaz and Niall Scott

LEXINGTON BOOKS
Lanham • Boulder • New York • London

Published by Lexington Books
An imprint of The Rowman & Littlefield Publishing Group, Inc.
4501 Forbes Boulevard, Suite 200, Lanham, Maryland 20706
www.rowman.com

Unit A, Whitacre Mews, 26-34 Stannary Street, London SE11 4AB

British Library Cataloguing in Publication Information Available

Library of Congress Cataloging-in-Publication Data

Names: Varas Díaz, Nelson, editor. | Scott, Niall W. R., editor.
Title: Heavy metal music and the communal experience / edited by Nelson Varas-Díaz and Niall Scott.
Description: Lanham, Maryland : Lexington Books, [2016] | Includes bibliographical references and index.
Identifiers: LCCN 2016023392 (print) | LCCN 2016024640 (ebook) | ISBN 9781498506380 (cloth : alk. paper) | ISBN 9781498506397 (Electronic)
Subjects: LCSH: Heavy metal (Music)--Social aspects.
Classification: LCC ML3918.R63 H44 2016 (print) | LCC ML3918.R63 (ebook) | DDC 306.4/8426--dc23
LC record available at https://lccn.loc.gov/2016023392

Printed in the United States of America

Table of Contents

Heavy Metal Music and the Communal Experience

An Introduction

Nelson Varas-Díaz and Niall Scott

To the unfamiliar eye the relation between metal music and community might seem like a contradiction. After all, how can community emanate from practices that to outsiders seem to foster loudness, extremity and violence? Those individuals who have enjoyed this musical genre at some point in their lives will probably have a very different appreciation of metal music and its culture in terms of community. In fact, many aspects of metal music point toward the importance of community as part of its practices. Some salient examples can be provided just to illustrate this argument. These include shared experiences (e.g., concerts, listening to music together), dress codes (e.g., use of recognizable band shirts), behavioral expectations (e.g., protection during mosh pits), use of collective information outlets (e.g., magazines, websites), and jointly discussed significant events (e.g., death of a musician). The central idea is that when these experiences are shared and valued by many persons, they can provide individuals with a sense of meaning and purpose that allows them to come together as a community. Although this may sound simple enough, it is actually quite a complex process. Beyond being a mere association of people, the complexity involves processes that concern exploring the expanse and the limits of the metal community and even dealing with paradoxes where although the music may be held in common, values such as political, artistic, and ethical ones can be extremely diverse. Yet these are all held together under the banner of "metal."

Defining community is difficult and full of challenges. Scholarly work has addressed a plethora of concepts to define what a community is and how it functions for the individuals that compose it. For example, scholars have addressed the role of geography in community formation. This perspective fosters the importance of physical closeness and face-to-face interaction in the process of building a collective narrative or identity. Other scholarly work has focused on the functions of the community.

These approaches tend to highlight individuals' investment into a collective group depending on how that experience works for their benefit and well-being. Academic work has also addressed how communities are "imagined" or conceptualized in order to provide its members with a sense of longevity and historicity that transcends their current moment. Finally, scholarly work has also highlighted the importance of shared values or worldviews, emotional connectedness, and social support in bringing people together as a community. What these approaches have in common is the underlying notion that community, in its many interpretations, is the final output of collective consciousness and collaboration. In this process, individuals usually identify some benefit in belonging to a group that at times surpasses their quest for individuality. The formation of communities in relation to metal music echoes this proposition. This volume not only builds on interdisciplinary research on community, but also offers some new insights into community formation and cohesion in metal music culture that on the surface, as mentioned above, resists straightforward treatment in terms of community.

Scholars who study metal music as a social phenomenon have begun to systematically address the issue of community in their research. This research has addressed how communities are formed (e.g., musical scene formation) (Wallach and Levine 2012), their diverse manifestations throughout the world (Riches and Lashua 2014), interpretations of their communal practices (Scott 2014), inclusion of diverse members (e.g., women, members of the LGBT community) (Hill 2011; Snell 2014; Clifford-Napoleone 2015), and variables that predict their cohesiveness (Varas-Díaz et al. 2015), among other issues. These research ventures are a reflection of the importance placed on the communal experience in metal music. Just as important, research has documented how on many occasions the idea of community can clash with the notions of individuality and resistance to social conformity that are so important to metal music (Venkatesh et al. 2014). It should come as no surprise that for some individuals enmeshed in particular metal subgenres the notion of community seems like an uncomfortable contradiction. How can individuality and community be simultaneously celebrated? This is just one example of the challenges of understanding the notion of community in metal music.

In this edited volume we aim to delve even deeper into the notion of community in metal music. We do so by highlighting that community formation is not a mere outcome that individuals aspire to achieve in order to feel cohesion with others, but rather a life-long process full of contradictions, negotiations, and tensions. In this scenario, community is not always equivalent to the unproblematic sense of togetherness that seems to permeate most conceptualizations on the subject. It is in fact a constant process in which such a sense of togetherness is present, but simultaneously challenged by issues of inclusion/exclusion, changes in the demography of its members, uncomfortable practices of those already on the inside its borders, and constant interaction with other groups in which metal communities coexist. Part of this challenge occurs in the boundary changes of the metal community that are influenced by negotiations concerning musical genre, while other challenges concern the ruptures and coalescences occurring within metal culture.

We have divided the book into five sections. Taken collectively the chapters focus on how the communal experience in metal is conceptualized, positively experienced by many, fraught with tensions for others, and how it is constantly expanding and proposing new challenges for its members.

ENTERING THE COMMUNAL AND CONCEPTUALIZING COLLECTIVENESS

In this first section of the book the authors address how the notion of community in metal music can be theoretically conceptualized. This is done with a clear understanding of the importance of the communal experience and its potential benefits, but without neglecting the implications of communal idealization frequently found in research on community. Furthermore, they delve into the process through which communities centered on metal music are formed from an early age, their potentially protective function for young people, and the process through which a sense of togetherness is frequently achieved via simple acts like hanging out.

Deena Weinstein addresses the complexity entailed in conceptualizing communities in general, and the metal community in particular. She provides a definitional and conceptual framework to approach the possibility of metal and community, supplemented with her phenomenologically grounded insights in the metal music festival event. She highlights how communal formation is guided, among other things, by shared values, mutual identification, interaction, solidarity, and boundaries. For her, depending on how these factors are combined, metal communities can be labeled as ideal, diminished or mythic. The differences are important since they allow individuals within the community to conceive and describe the collective from different perspectives ranging from very realistic conception of their self-selected group, to more idealized versions that sometimes border on the unreal.

Niall Scott addresses the apparently paradoxical constitution of the communal in metal music. Using Aristotle and Kant's work as theoretical cornerstones for his analysis, he examines the tension of the communal experience as one that highlights our constitution as social entities, while simultaneously exploring those individualistic instances in which the communal is unwarranted. Through an analysis of music videos, song lyrics and musicians' speeches rooted primarily in the works of the bands

Slipknot and *Machine Head*, the author argues how the issue of community in metal music is better understood as an ongoing paradox rather than a simple process of togetherness and harmony.

Esther Clinton and Jeremy Wallach explore the process of communal formation via a phenomenological approach, focusing on the idea of "hanging out and talking metal." Using examples from their research in Indonesia they focus on the concept of *nongkrong*, which is used to describe the process of being together and hanging out. Although they highlight this regional idea, their argument applies to a very common experience for fans of metal throughout the world that frequently share spaces (e.g., concerts, bedrooms, schools) and use their time to talk about metal music. Their phenomenological approach allows them to place this process in perspective by highlighting the importance of the subjective experience of those that engage in it. Their beliefs and emotions become central aspects of the process of being together and exchanging ideas about music, and the world in general, while developing collectivity.

STRENGTHENING COMMUNITY

In this second section of the book authors explain how the communal experience in metal music is strengthened via shared experiences that can bring together individuals across the world. Specifically, they describe how the musical and visual narrative created by international bands can serve as a bonding agent for the communal experience. They also explore how young metal fans use community as a protective strategy and the complex process through which their safe havens are formed. One analysis explores more tribal association of fandom exemplifying cohesion, whereas the other brings out themes of metal community providing a response to alienation and exclusion from other social groups.

Toni-Matti Karjalainen documents the process of community formation in metal via fans' identification with the Finnish band *Nightwish*. Through acquired narratives from fans from thirty different countries he describes how the music, lyrics, and overall aesthetics developed by this band allow individuals from different parts of the world to have a personal connection with the ensemble, while also fostering collective experiences which are essential for community formation. Particular attention is provided to the formation of the communal experience via appreciation of one particular album in the band's catalogue: *Imaginaerum*.

Paula Rowe's contribution to the book addresses the formation of metal communities at an early age. Her qualitative work with adolescents in South Australia highlights the processes through which young people who appreciate metal music begin to establish notions of collectivity in relation to the music. This process, which begins with the simple act of listening to music, can subsequently turn into a sense of belonging to a collective that provides some sort of protection from outside threats (including bullies). She emphasizes how social exclusion from other more traditional adolescent groups plays an important part of community formation among young metal fans. Her work exemplifies how metal music, and the communal experience surrounding it, can be a strategy for survival in a very difficult developmental stage.

COMMUNITIES IN CONTEXTUAL INTERACTION

In this third section of the book authors explore how metal communities are contextual. That is, they are in constant interaction with their surroundings and other communities. The researcher presented here challenges the notion that metal communities are socially isolated entities.

Nelson Varas-Díaz, Sigrid Mendoza, and Eric Morales document the process of community formation in the Caribbean region via ethnographic research on the islands of Cuba and Puerto Rico. They use a multi-method approach with qualitative interviews and lyric/image analysis to explore how communities in the region interact with their context. Their results show how musicians in the Caribbean have examined their racial, ethnic, and national roots to transform their traditional interpretations and reveal their darker and morbose sides, which are more directly linked to metal music expectations. Their work is an example of how metal communities, although closed to some outsiders, are in fact porous and in constant interaction with other groups and their environments.

TENSIONS WITHIN THE COMMUNAL EXPERIENCE

In this fourth section of the book authors explore tensions within the communal experience. Some of these tensions emanate from discussions over subjects that are addressed in the music and by members of the community, which are deemed as extreme and in some instances as hate speech. Other tensions arise from critical conceptualizations of the metal community that question essentialist notions of collectivity and focus on how it can be a byproduct of myth and storytelling. With a strong focus on black metal the authors use their insights to move the metal community toward critical boundaries that delineate possible normative limits to the collective group: what ought not to be tolerated.

Vivek Venkatesh, Bradley J. Nelson, Tieja Thomas, Jason J. Wallin, Jeffrey S. Podoshen, Christopher Thompson, Kathryn Jezer-Morton, Jihan Rabah, Kathryn Urbaniak, and Méi-Ra St. Laurent address the issue of online hate speech in the black metal scene. They do so via an innovative methodological approach that aims to fuse the social sciences and humanities. Using corpus-assisted critical discourse analyses the authors document the presence of specific keywords in black metal related discussion boards. They document how participants frequently tackle and discuss issues related to racism, nationalism and hate speech in these forums. Their findings are important as they shed light on how communities are sometimes fraught with tension over hate speech toward particular groups and how these are challenged/tolerated/fostered.

Karl Spracklen addresses the imaginary aspects of community formation within the black metal scene. Applying Bruno Latour's Actor Network Theory to his analysis, he specifically explores how the "second wave" of black metal in Norway, made infamous/famous for church burnings and murder, has become part of a narrative among metal fans that serves as a myth-making process. The constant telling and retelling of the stories surrounding this "second wave" of black metal serves as a key component of a sense of belonging among the members of the imagined community. Spracklen challenges the more essentialist notions of community by addressing how it can also be a product of storytelling and myth-making.

EXPANDING THE COMMUNITY BEYOND PREVIOUSLY THOUGHT BORDERS

In this fifth and final section of the book authors explore the ever-expanding nature of the challenges faced by a growing community. As metal music continues to develop and be an ever-present staple of underground culture, members of the community will age and become ill. Exploring how their fans and peers will address this growing sector of the community is an important endeavor for the future of metal. Finally, as the metal community continues to grow and more diverse actors coexist within its borders communication between them is important. Both issues highlight the changing nature of the metal community and the challenges posed for its members.

Keith Kahn-Harris explores the concept of care within the metal community. This might seem contradictory in light of metal music's more individualistic and transgressive tendencies. Still, he proposes that care is an important aspect in metal music and provides examples of how members of the community have shown support for others who have become terminally ill. The proposed reflection gathers importance as he explains how the aging process of members in the metal community (e.g., musicians) will inevitably foster new considerations on how they care for each other in times of need.

Finally, Brian Hickam provides us with an in-depth analysis of how the metal community has grown to include a wide variety of actors that go beyond musicians and fans. Through the use of systems theory he explains how these actors, including now scholars in Metal Music Studies, interact with each other to form the larger metal community. He proposes that in this ever-growing and pluralistic scenario strategies must be developed in order to communicate with each other for the benefit of the larger metal scene. The use of metaphors is proposed as a mechanism to establish a conversation on shared meanings between all members of the metal community.

We hope that the chapters included in this book serve to continue a vigorous discussion on metal music and community. For those who are part of the metal music scene, both locally and globally, the importance of community related issues has been ever present. We expect that the chapters included here echo the experiences of long time metal fans, while highlighting both the benefits and tensions entailed in community formation. We are hopeful that academia will continue to expand its views on metal music and those who enjoy it. Finally, we would like to thank Sigrid Mendoza, Kadriel Betsen, and Kayra Fuster for their help in the final process of developing this collection, and the University of Puerto Rico for supporting the academic conference in 2014 that shares the title of this book.

REFERENCES

Clifford-Napoleone, Amber. 2015. *Queerness in Heavy Metal Music: Metal Bent*. New York: Routledge.

Hill, Rosemary Lucy. 2011. "Is Emo Metal? Gendered Boundaries and New Horizons in the Metal Community." *Journal for Cultural Research* 15 (3) (July): 297–313. doi:10.1080/14797585.2011.594586. www.tandfonline.com/doi/abs/10.1080/14797585.2011.594586.

Riches, Gabby, and Brett Lashua. 2014. "Mapping the Underground: An Ethnographic Cartography of the Leeds Extreme Metal Scene." *International Journal of Community Music* 7 (2): 223–241. doi:10.1386/ijcm.7.2.223.

Scott, Niall. 2014. "Seasons in the Abyss: Heavy Metal as Liturgy." *Diskus* 16 (1): 12–29.

Snell, Dave. 2014. "'The Black Sheep of the Family': Bogans, Borders and New Zealand Society." *International Journal of Community Music* 7 (2): 273–289. doi:10.1386/ijcm.7.2.273.

Varas-Díaz, Nelson, Eliut Rivera-Segarra, Carmen Medina Rivera, Sigrid Mendoza, and Osvaldo González-Sepúlveda. 2015. "Predictors of Communal Formation in a Small Heavy Metal Scene: Puerto Rico as a Case Study." *Metal Music Studies* 1 (1): 87–103. doi:10.1386/mms.1.1.87.

Venkatesh, Vivek, Jeffrey S Podoshen, Kathryn Urbaniak, and Jason Wallin. 2014. "Eschewing Community: Black Metal." *Journal of Community & Applied Social Psychology* (April). doi:10.1002/casp.

Wallach, Jeremy, and Alexandra Levine. 2012. "'I Want You to Support Local Metal': A Theory of Metal Scene Formation." *Popular Music History* 6 (1) (May 14): 116–134. doi:10.1558/pomh.v6i1/2.116. www.equinoxpub.com/PMH/article/view/14440.

Part 1

Entering the Communal and Conceptualizing Collectiveness

ONE

Communities of Metal

Ideal, Diminished and Imaginary

Deena Weinstein

Community has always been part of metal in some form or other, and it still is. The question is what kind of community are we talking about? I had been interested in the metal community long before I was consciously interested in the phenomenon of a metal community. I recall being in Calgary, Canada, in September 2013. The event I attended was officially called a Festival, the Noctis Festival, and it had conference presentations during two days. Bands and visiting presenters (mainly academicians and metal journalists) stayed in the same hotel, meeting one another in the lobby, and at formal and spontaneous parties. At the evening concerts, a shuttle-ride away from the hotel, were hundreds of metal fans, most of whom were from the region, although a good number came from Edmonton, Vancouver, Winnipeg, and other Canadian locales.

I'd spoken to dozens people one on one, in groups of three to five, and earlier in the day to a roomful. All of the people were fans of metal — some of them were also metal musicians performing at that festival, others were metal musicians not yet ready for prime time. Another set of metal fans was what I call metal mediators — those who wrote about metal (in academic or popular outlets), who were associated with indie metal labels, or were metal DJs, metal visual artists, metal concert promoters, and managers of metal bands.

I walked from the backstage area into the audience around 10:30 one night, moving around until I could find one of those special spots in which the bass sounds resonated against my sternum. Backstage people were mentioning the great responses to each band's set, and walking among the crowd I could see, not merely hear, their enthusiasm. I kept running into people with whom I'd spoken with earlier, a few whom I'd known for years, some who seemed to know me from appearances in metal documentaries, and the majority merely fans. Their words and visual greetings to me made the music coming into my ears even more exciting. Between two songs, when the cheering stopped but before the band started again, I fell out of the moment in which I'd been suspended for who knows how long (certainly I didn't have any sense of time's passing) and realized that I was in, as I exclaimed to several sets of people later in the evening, a "real metal community"—one that was south of heaven, perhaps, but definitely heavenly. Sure the great music we heard was part of the pleasure, but we weren't talking only about the music. Speaking informally during the day with participants, including those manning tables presenting their record label's releases, or other metal paraphernalia, some of them independently used that phrase "real" or "great metal community" to characterize the event.

On the flight back to Chicago I realized that my experience at the Noctis Festival was comparable to the ones I'd had at many of the Milwaukee Metalfests I had been to, and various metal concerts I had attended in and around Chicago. My pleasure in Calgary and in remembering the experience there was augmented by those many similar memories.

When I told my husband about the Calgary experience, I kept enthusing: "It was a real, a genuine, metal community." What I and those using the term metal community in Calgary meant intrigued me. And why did we each preface it with adjectives, especially "great," "genuine," and "real"?

All of the mediators of the festival and members of bands playing on stage were fans, generally big fans, of metal. Some of the mediators played in bands too, although not at the festival, and some of the band members on the festival stage worked as mediators at other times, like the drummer in *Witch Mountain* who is a booker of bands in Portland, Oregon.

Mediators invited to the festival for the daytime conference, visual artists involved with album covers and posters, metal journalists, and video documentarians were also avidly enjoying the music, and were indistinguishable from "mere" fans or band members not then on stage. And these "mere" fans interacted with one another and with band members and mediators as equals in their metal fandom. Part of that fandom was expressing their pleasure at being with other metal fans. The other part of their pleasure was listening to the music while headbanging in time to it, arm-thrusting with clenched fists or horns at key moments, and yelling and clapping approval to each performance. Of course they also displayed their metal fandom visually—some in full metal gear straight out of central casting, some sporting metal-worthy tattoos or patches, and most wearing a metal T-shirt.

"Mere" fans also served as metal mediators in conversation with other fans. They were impromptu metal critics describing concerts they had seen, putting forth their views on some album, and adding some arcane knowledge about a band to their conversation. Interpreting their metal discourse and iconography as displays of "cultural capital" misses much of its impetus and its impact. Those fan activities and self-presentations were co-constitutive of the festival and the participants recognized their roles.

When I was asked to speak at the Heavy Metal and the Communal Experience conference in Puerto Rico in 2014 I was enthused; I recalled the Calgary experience under the term metal community and I wanted to grasp that term more deeply.

METAL COLLECTIVITIES

When I returned to Chicago from Calgary, I was eager to explore the concept of "music collectivities" in order to place the notion of community, as the participants in the conference/festival had meant it, in the context of extant discourse in popular-culture and particularly in popular-music studies. It was a welcome opportunity to be invited to the Puerto Rico metal conference, where I was to speak on the nature of the metal community, a presentation that was the initial statement of the ideas that appear in the present chapter.

In my exploration of the literature on music collectivities, I found that none of the definitions and interpretations fit the Calgary experience precisely, although all of them were useful in illuminating some aspect of the social organization of music and some of them described kindred phenomena to what was meant by "community" at Calgary. The various terms for getting a handle on metal collectivities make up a discursive formation in Foucault's phrase (1972). All of them deal with the same problem, yet do so in different and at times contradictory ways. Studying the discourse formation of music collectivities led to my account of the metal community, presented next, that more closely approaches the collective structure of the Calgary experience than the alternatives, although each one of the alternatives is appropriate to the scope and problems that it addresses.

At first, my exploration of the literature on music collectivities did not proceed in a systematic order. I shuttled back and forth among the alternative concepts, building up understandings of each one in relation to the others. Through that process, a typology emerged that was divided into concepts that were partial in terms of the totality of the Calgary experience and those that were more comprehensive and approached more closely what I was trying to get at.

Many of the debates over the superiority of one interpretation of music collectivities over others can be resolved by paying attention to the circumstances, including the eras in which they were used, and the problems that the different interpretations are addressing. It is not a matter of trying to clear some concepts of music collectivities from the discursive field, but to ascertain the range of applicability of each and to assess its fit to the ideas growing from my experience and understanding of what the "community" meant at Calgary. My discussion here will work from the partial concepts of music collectivities to the more comprehensive ones, leading to the concept of community that I have constructed to fit the experience I seek to understand.

It is only fitting to begin with the concept of music collectivities, especially in metal and punk, that today is generally used as a baseline, subculture. Formulated in several works by academicians related to the Birmingham Centre for Contemporary Cultural Studies (CCCS), subculture was embedded in a perspective which provided a left contestational alternative to establishment sociology, adopting a Gramscian judgment on the significance of culture (Hall and Jefferson 1976). The CCCS cultural sociologists, working within the restrictive environment of the reaction against the blocked liberation movements of the 1960s, turned to culture in search of resistances to Western capitalist hegemony. They challenged the then dominant view that popular culture is always an instance of manipulation of a docile mass by a predatory elite, which doubtless has wide applicability, and identified areas of culture where popular initiatives were present that contested elite values and sometimes confronted them.

The concept of counter-culture had emerged in the 1960s. In the succeeding reactionary period, the CCCS deployed the concept of subculture, referring to a group whose values, beliefs, and styles are at variance with those of the wider culture in which it is embedded. Among the most important of the contestational subcultures identified by the CCCS were music subcultures. They saw youth subcultures in Britain as the result of what the French sociologists Ernesto Laclau and Chantal Mouffe called dislocation. "A structural dislocation thus emerges between 'masses' and 'classes,' given that the line separating the former from the dominant sectors is not juxtaposed with class exploitation" (2001, 56). They saw British working-class youth, having suffered diminution of their life-chances, adjusting to their new situation ideologically.

Metal music and its linguistic, visual, and lifestyle accompaniments constituted one of those adjustments, although the CCCS didn't analyze the British heavy metal subculture. Andy Brown (2003) analyzes the reasons why metal was marginal, if not "invisible" to the CCCS. Others, like

Weinstein (1991, 97–143), used CCCS to describe that portion of heavy metal fans who were subcultural.

One can dispute the specific sociology of culture put forth by the CCCS without devalorizing the contribution that it made to legitimizing the study of marginalized movements by showing their independence of the hegemonic cultural apparatus. Those movements could be studied for themselves and not merely as expressions of, as Louis Althusser (1971) put it, the Ideological State Apparatus. Indeed, the CCCS sociologists identified positive functions that subcultures served for the members and their challenges to the hegemon. The CCCS cut through the Marx-Weber polemics in Britain—subcultures were neither ideological expressions of the "state" apparatus nor deviations from the general social norm; rather, they continued the radical democratic legacy of the counter-culture, although they did not engage in political mobilization (Hall and Jefferson 1976).

Metal subcultures do still exist, probably more so outside the post-industrial west than in areas where they once were active. Metal music itself has fragmented, and importantly, music fans too have changed in character and dispositions, affecting sociological interpretations of music collectivities.

Building on the work of the French sociologist Michel Maffesoli (1996), who had theorized the concept of *tribus* (tribes) to identify looser and more fluid groups than subcultures, Andy Bennett coined the term neo-tribe to refer specifically to music collectivities. Still working within a partial understanding of music collectivity emphasizing the youth audience, Bennett framed his discussion as a conceptual critique of subculture from a "late modern" or "postmodern" perspective. Based on his study of dance music in Britain, Bennett argued "that the music and stylistic sensibilities exhibited by the young people involved in the dance music scene are a clear example of a late modern 'sociability' rather than a fixed subcultural group" (1999, 599).

For Bennett, the key distinction between subculture and neo-tribe is a loosening of social cohesion in the latter that follows from an individualistic orientation of its "members": "the term *group* can . . . no longer be regarded as having necessary permanent or tangible quality, the characteristics, visibility and lifespan of a group being wholly dependent on the particular forms of interaction, which it is used to stage" (1999, 605). The neo-tribe registers a change from a resistance formation to an opportunity for play-acting by individuals whose identities have been de-linked from an enduring group to which, most importantly, they are committed. The neo-tribe disperses the subculture; it is a means for individuals to immerse themselves in a temporary identity corroborated by others, to perform an identity in public, to consume it and then to move on in their drift through what Jean-Francois Lyotard (1984) called the "archipela-goes" of culture.

There obviously cannot be a metal community, however community is defined, if those who orient themselves to the music and the other components of its culture constitute a neo-tribe. The concept of neo-tribe is an indication of a threat to community from a mentality that figures engagement to cultural forms as identity-play rather than as intrinsic to identity formation, if not its core. The phenomenon to which Bennett refers might be applicable to British dance music audiences/fans at the time that he studied them; it has limited use, if any, to characterize the "collectivity" of metal, which has not yet and perhaps will not become fully postmodernized, although it is more variegated and fluid than is a subculture.

Although subculture and neo-tribe are polar opposites along an axis of commitment to a group, they have in common a nonexclusionary emphasis on youth groups that are the audiences/fans/consumers of music. They do not include in their concepts of music collectivity the full range of actors who were present at Calgary, not only the appreciators, but the creators and mediators, too; and they do not acknowledge that the appreciators are not only young. Nonetheless the concepts of subculture and neo-tribe are useful for illuminating aspects of the concept of community toward which I am building. Subculture highlights the commitment to a collectivity that is essential to the idea of community that will be developed here, and neo-tribe shows deep structural/de-structuring factors that threaten a metal community.

Passing over the divide between partial concepts of music collectivities and more comprehensive interpretations, many scholars, some of whom will be mentioned, have attempted to rectify the limitations of the discourse's emphasis on youth and audience. Sharing some of the reservations about received concepts that have been adumbrated in the present discussion, David Hesmondhalgh addresses "the relationship between music and the social (2005, 33)," drawing on Steve Neale's expansion of the concept of literary genre to suggest that "genre" could serve as an orienting concept to clarify social relations. Neale, according to Hesmondhalgh, "broke through" the restrictive definition of literary genre as a grouping of texts "to see genres as systems of orientation, expectations, and conventions that link text, industry, and audience" (2005, 32).

It must be said at the outset that it might be misleading to appropriate and expand a term so deeply entrenched in cultural discourse as "genre" is, and use it to cover social processes; but that is simply a semantic observation. Hesmondhalgh does come closer to the concept of community sought here, but his statement of the problem he addresses involves a split between music and social processes that then has to be sutured with contrived mediations. Hesmondhalgh (2005, 33) references Jason Toynbee (2000) in his rejection of "expressivism" (music is simply an "index of the social") on the grounds that "communities and genres are "complex," and are "porous" (see Varas-Díaz, Mendoza, and Morales in this volume) and "subject to outside influences." However, what is the alternative to "expressivism"? Hesmondhalgh does not adopt the opposite "culturalist" thesis that musical forms constitute music collectivities. There must, then, be interaction between the two that Hesmondhalgh does not specify.

Returning to the Calgary experience, the music functioned neither as an independent nor a dependent variable; it was an integral part of the event, both the currency in a series of exchanges, and the focus of those exchanges, indeed, their raison d'etre. There was no problem of relating "music to the social," a concern that harks back to nineteenth-century debates between materialists and idealists over the causal efficacy of ideas. To put the matter simply, both are parts of the mix.

A second, more developed, comprehensive, and widely deployed concept of music collectivity is expressed in the term "scene." During the reign of the term "subculture," Will Straw (1991) proposed the term scene to underscore the relationship of local to more global music-making activities. More recently the term has become a staple of popular-music studies. Jeremy Wallach and Alexandra Levine have provided a succinct and precise definition of scene that is totalized as a mode of consciousness rooted in social practices in a locality: "for 'scenic consciousness' to be achieved, a minimum number of scenic institutions must exist: a record store, a hangout (which could be the record store), and at least one all-ages venue (i.e., not a bar that prevents minors from entering) that can be used on a regular basis by local bands" (2001, 121).

Scene comes closest to the concept of community sought here. As Keith Kahn-Harris notes, it straddles the boundary between "an emergent feature of everyday interaction and a construct of the researcher" (2007, 22). It includes artists, mediators, and audiences, relating to one another in an organizing process through facilities (institutions). With appropriate substitutions for Wallach and Levine's list to cover a conference/festival, Calgary was a "scene," albeit a brief one, but it was more than that. The participants at Calgary didn't refer to the gathering as a "real scene,'" because there was an internal solidary dimension to their experience. The scene sets the stage for community with a "communitarian," not simply a "scenic," consciousness.

Scene is also too rooted in locality to function as a general term for music collectivities, such as what I explicitly call the metal community. Attempts to expand the definition of scene beyond territorial locality have not been entirely convincing, such as the positing of virtual scenes, which remain separate from local scenes. There has been no conception of a "meta-scene" that would tie the two together. Is there a metal scene in general? It would be a stretch to always answer that question in the affirmative, given metal's fragmentation along musical and ideological lines. The quest for a metal collectivity must look in another direction, and, surely, that is not to deny the applicability of scene to the root phenomenon that it names.

Having gone through the typology of the concepts proposed and used to characterize music collectivities in recent theorization, none of them is fully adequate to describe the Calgary experience. The term that participants at the festival used, "community," remains the most precise one, although that term has been defined in a multitude of ways.

Community, as the designation of the metal music collectivity proposed here, is inclusive of all the actors that constitute the sociocultural process of metal artists, mediators, and audiences. It also involves an articulation of the relations among those actors that can be defined as a transaction. That transactional community will be specified in the discussion of the forms of metal community after laying the groundwork for it in a roughly consensual definition of community as it has come to be used in sociology.

FEATURES OF COMMUNITIES

Despite the different meanings of the term community, from premodern tribal societies and small towns to professions, and the metal community, all have basic features in common. The first characteristic is that its members share a set of values. If it is a total society, those are values about fundamental aspects of life, many of which are codified in a religious institution. The values in subcommunities that focus on some occupation, leisure pursuit, or interest more or less relate to the wider community's core values. In both types of community, total and partial, the values define what is morally right and wrong, what is beautiful and ugly, and what is true and false. This is what is called the culture of the community; it dictates the appropriate and inappropriate content of a particular community, its codes of conduct, art, belief systems, and traditions.

Knowing that you share values with another person gives you a sense of trust in them. You know what you can expect from them, and this knowledge makes you more likely to interact with them. Additionally, you tend to identify with those with whom you share values. Interaction among members is not just another feature of a community, but the *enactment* of shared values and identification.

Along with sharing values, mutual identification and interaction, a fourth feature is solidarity. Solidarity is an emergent feature, a resultant of sharing values, mutual identification, and interaction among members. Solidarity is a structural resultant, but is also a cognitive recognition of that resultant sometimes called a "consciousness of kind" (Giddings 1904). Other terms that reference the sense of solidarity are camaraderie and "communitas" (de Burgh-Woodman and Brace-Govan 2007). (In a sense, the feeling of solidarity is the antithesis of the experience of alienation.) As an emergent feature of community, solidarity is instrumental to community, constituting it, and maintaining it. But it is also consummatory, what John Dewey (1934) calls a value in and of itself.

Solidarity tends to feed back into each component that creates it — enhancing shared values (and also the knowledge that they are shared), strengthening identification with one another and with the resulting community itself, and increasing interaction among members of that community. It generates commitment. This understanding of community as a process sees it as a self-reinforcing virtuous cycle.

A final feature of communities is that they have boundaries. Like the previously mentioned features, boundaries too vary, from nearly impermeable to highly porous. Boundaries are emergent in highly solidary communities. But boundaries can also create solidarity within the community when they are imposed by powers outside it. If all your immediate neighbors have fenced off their property, you don't have to build a barrier to demarcate your yard and keep out those you don't want there. Most communities require some level of boundary maintenance (Nagel 1994). Boundary maintenance also involves socializing strangers who want to enter the community, teaching them the values, including the behaviors, of members. Enculturation is most effectively done by people who are already acquainted with the "stranger," such as older relatives and good friends. For music communities, individuals who appreciate the music before entering the community would have more incentive to integrate into the community than those who were unfamiliar with that style of music. At concerts, "newbies" learn how to appreciate metal, although many form some idea from watching concert videos.

THREE TYPES OF METAL COMMUNITIES

The utterances of the phrase metal community, mine and others in Calgary, were prefaced by some adjective: "real," "true," "perfect," "ideal," some of which I have discussed above. Why were those modifiers necessary? Using those adjectives implied, consciously or not, that not all metal communities were at the same level or type of fulfillment. If this one was real, true, perfect, or ideal, it meant others were less real, less true, less than perfect, less than ideal. That is, actual metal communities may be in some ways deficient, flawed. One can imagine some scale that ranks metal communities from "perfect," through all levels of deficiency, to not really a metal community at all. I'll greatly simplify those differences by dividing them into two types.

Those that have all of a community's five features (shared values, mutual identification, interaction, solidarity, and boundaries) described above, each one fully realized, will fall under the *ideal metal community*. The term ideal is taken from Max Weber's ideal-type analysis, "the con-

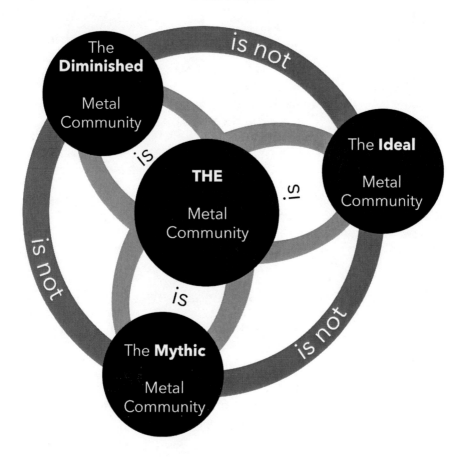

Figure 1.1.   Types of metal communities.

struction of certain elements of reality into a logically precise conception"
(Gerth and Mills 1958, 59), in which the term ideal does not mean best or
some unattainable ideal of perfection, but refers to some example exhibit-
ing all of the definitional features of that phenomenon. Thus a bicycle
that has its seat stolen is still a bicycle, and a guitar without strings is still
a guitar, but neither one is an ideal-type of bicycle or guitar, respectively.

Those examples that fall short of maximizing each of those five variables, and this type has far more instances than the other, I'll call the
diminished metal community. There are many reasons for the various types
of diminution, and these reasons are so prevalent that ideal-typical metal
communities are, when they are not very short lived, rather rare.

A third type of metal community is *not* a real community at all but an
imagined one. This *imaginary metal community* will also be referred to here
as a *mythic metal community*. This third type of community is widespread,
perhaps now more than ever.

Metal community, whether ideal, diminished or imaginary, have as their cultural centers metal music. This begs the question, a topic of discussion among metalheads ever since the term heavy metal came into popular usage, of whether or not the music of some given band, or even a whole style of music (like glam metal a.k.a. "hair metal," or nu-metal) should be considered metal at all. Any of the three types of community can be focused on some subgenre or particular style.

Listening and joining in to perform and appreciate music together, especially when its rhythm and tonal qualities (and melodies too) are familiar to all who also react to that music together physically (head banging, arm thrusting, singing along, playing air guitar), and in addition, watch one another's reactions (seeming to feel just what they are feeling), enhances the pleasure, but also by itself provides a strong feeling of solidarity. When those songs are celebrations of the metal community itself, the sense of solidarity is increased. Some of the better known anthemic songs are: *"Denim and Leather"* (Saxon 1991), *"Metal Heart"* (Accept 1985), *"Whiplash"* (Metallica 1983), *"United"* (Judas Priest 1980), *"Heavy Metal Maniac"* (Exciter 1983), *"Heavy Metal (is the Law)"* (Helloween 1985), *"In Union We Stand"* (Overkill 1987), and *"Metal Command"* (Exodus 1985). They function much like the songs of nation states (national anthems), union workers, social movements (*"We Shall Overcome"* for the Civil Rights Movement in the United States), and many of the Christian hymns sung at church.

Ideal Metal Community

The ideal metal community can be understood using the term subculture discussed earlier. The ideal-typical community occurs when the musicians and the various mediators (what Keith Negus [2002] refers to as cultural intermediaries), who were once just metal fans, emerge as specialists from that subcultural audience and continue to maintain their subcultural status. Certainly some of the band members and mediators earn money from their activities in the community, but that is not their primary motivation.

The ideal metal community is enacted in this situation because each of the definitional features of a community (shared culture, identification, interaction, solidarity, boundaries) is maximally fulfilled. Each member shares the values and adheres to the norms, expressing their passion for metal.

An ideal metal community is rare and fragile, for reasons that will be made clear shortly. Yet it has been actualized at various times and places over the past thirty-five years or so. Most examples are very short lived — at single metal concerts and festivals. The Calgary festival described earlier, which lasted only three days, is one such example. In those intense

face-to-face groupings, the features of this ideal-type are readily identified.

Musical values like appreciating virtuosity are expressed not only in
the performed sound produced by the musicians on stage, but in their
occasional dramatic enactments of the difficulty of making that music,
like the looks of concentration on their faces. It is also articulated in the
care that the technicians give to the sound in the venue and in setting-up
and maintaining the band's instruments. Of course the appreciation of all
for the quality of the music is palpable—for example, heard in their
screams, sing-alongs, and clapping; seen on their faces with expressions
of sheer pleasure and their frantic headbanging; and felt in the gentle
scrum of a mosh pit.

The fan participants identify with one another, in part because they
are all there to share the same musical experience. Of course, the fact that
they tend to wear similar clothing, minimally metal T-shirts, and tend to
present themselves to others in a similar way also makes identification
with one another easier. Watching the guitar solo while playing air guitar, or singing or mouthing the words along with the singer, show that
fans are identifying with the band. In the ideal metal community fans
identify with musicians, rather than idolize them.

All interact with one another, whether in brief face-to-face discussions
between sets, in addresses that one or more of those on stage make to the
audience, and in the audience's reactions to musical peaks and utterances
from the stage. Band members feel themselves to be members of the
community—they go into the audience to catch sets by other bands, and
hang with fans—rather than remaining cloistered backstage. Mediators,
such as those selling merchandise or serving as security, see fans and
bands as equals, and treat them accordingly. No one is ripping anyone
else off or feels ripped off by others. Fans willingly and proudly support
the bands and mediators by buying tickets, merchandise, beer, and the
like. Importantly, it is through the nonverbal interaction, in which all are
aware of the others' appreciation of the music, that each one intensifies
their own appreciation of it, and that feeds back to all, a virtuous cycle of
maximal excitement. One can also see activities like moshing or head-
banging in unison as ritual interaction that enhances solidarity for the
different segments of the audience.

The solidarity felt by all at a concert results from the expression of all
of the values of metal and the maximization of interaction and identification with one another. One has a sense of being at one with the metal
community while also feeling fully oneself; the strong emotions of pleasure can be freely expressed and there is no alienation, rather there is the
feeling of being accepted. If the ideal metal community is enacted at a
concert, the venue itself forms the spatial and temporal boundaries of the
experience, and when the concert is over and all have departed in different directions, the temporary community no longer exists.

Concerts are the short-lived mayflies closest to the ideal metal community. However there are instances of the ideal-type that have lasted for several months and even several years, surfacing throughout metal's long history, in different parts of the world as local metal scenes. Many, including the best known of them, were organized around an emerging or newer style of metal.

During the late 1970s, local scenes began to arise, some of which were, for a time, ideal-typical metal communities. In a local scene, all members of the transaction, fans, musicians, and cultural intermediaries, are based in the same city (although there are touring bands and recorded music by those outside the community, distributed by those outside the community too). Fans serve as many of the mediators, putting out fliers for shows, working as roadies or sound technicians at concerts, designing T-shirts and making copies of recordings to sell, and so much more. Some of them make some money for their meditating efforts; many do those jobs without financial remuneration. "Scene musicians and ancillary creative people often cannot support themselves entirely from the music. They typically take low-skill service jobs in the community and depend on money and other support from partners, family, and friends." (Lena and Peterson 2008, 703). These scenes also have had minor but crucial types of mass mediators, all locally based, from metal radio shows to local "zines." It is not clear in the age of mass broadband and Wi-Fi Internet access that local scenes are any longer fully possible.

The San Francisco thrash scene in the first part of the 1980s, also known as the Bay Area thrash scene (Epstein 2009; Fellezs 2016; Port 2011; Wagner 2011; Weinstein 2013), probably was an example of an ideal metal community. It resembled and was influenced by the hardcore punk scenes that arose in San Francisco (and elsewhere, such as in southern California), in the late 1970s and early 1980s. In each of those scenes, for a time, fans formed bands, bands were fans, mediators joined bands, and some fans and musicians became mediators of one sort or another.

Local metal communities of the ideal-type cannot be absolutely insular—their members need to have heard some metal recordings and possibly seen touring metal bands from elsewhere perform in concert. That is, they have already been "metalized" from the outside. Some of the local bands in the community will probably wish to perform elsewhere and are helped to do so by local mediators that send the band's music, via tape, CD, or Internet, to those in other locales. Even the most DIY scene also relies on technology created elsewhere, from musical instruments to the late 1970s inexpensive four-track cassette recorders.

A key mediator of the San Francisco thrash scene was the Rampage Radio program, the metal specialty show broadcast to the Bay Area from the University of San Francisco's radio station, KUSF. One might argue that the "Bay Area Bangers," a local name for the local metal community, was created, at least in part, by this late-night show. The heavy dose of metal provided by DJs Ron Quintana and Ian Kallen featured newer recordings from what would become known as the New Wave of British Heavy Metal (NWOBHM) bands. When asked how the scene started, Gary Holt, guitarist in *Exodus*, said that the radio show was responsible, adding, "They totally got us into the New Wave of British Heavy Metal thing—everything from Tygers of Pan Tang to Venom to Budgie to Diamondhead to Angel Witch." (Epstein 2009). Holt's one-time co-guitarist, Kirk Hammett, also recalled the show:

> Rampage Radio came on at some ungodly time—it started at 1 or 2 in the morning. By the time it came around, me and my friends were all drunk. I remember the first time I heard a Venom song—it was "Live Like an Angel, Die Like a Devil" and it literally sounded like someone dragging a shovel across the pavement. I was like, Oh, my God, this is a sound I've never heard before! It's kinda shitty—but I like it! After two bottles of vodka, it sounded beautiful to our young, unjaded ears. (Epstein 2009)

Another mediated interaction that helped to constitute the San Francisco scene was the metal 'zine started by DJ Quintana, which connected fans and bands both inside the Bay Area and beyond. He was originally going to call the publication *Metallica* until a metalhead friend of his from Los Angeles, Lars Ulrich, convinced him that *Metal Mania* was a far better name.

Those mediators helped to construct and recruit members to the community, but the "scenic consciousness" is best experienced at live performances. Bands like *Exodus* were able to play to their face-to-face community in a variety of small venues including Ruthie's Inn, the Stone, and the Mab. The latter had been famously used by the hardcore punk fans going to see local fave, the *Dead Kennedys*. However it also became famous as the location where the then Los Angeles based band *Metallica's* live set was taped, and that tape eventually resulted in their getting a recording contract and album release (Weinstein 2013).

Other scenes, like the Norwegian black metal one centered around Euronymous and his Helvete record store in Oslo (Moynihan and Søderlind 1998), also appear to fall under this ideal community.

Diminished Metal Community

There are so many ways in which a metal community can fail to achieve the ideal form, or if it has done so, to maintain it for more than a very short time. Each of the five features of a community may not be ideally achieved, but falling short of the ideal can happen in greater or lesser degrees. If just one or two members of the community are in it for the money, or to be able to hang with their friends despite not being into the music, the community would be diminished from the ideal only slightly. On the other hand, if a critical mass of members were like those one or two, the community would be a long way from ideal.

Numerous metal communities only fall short of the ideal type because one key mediator, key in that they have the capital to make contracts and get municipal permissions, are not committed metalheads. They may never have been so, merely seeing metal as a market from which to profit, or their passion for metal was overshadowed by their passion for money. Band members too may go commercial, sell out, playing music that they recognize as inferior in order to please a larger audience, one broader than the metal community in which they began, to earn more money.

Some of those who were once fully committed metalheads may replace that primary identity with one with their profession or family, yet, for reasons of habit and/or nostalgia, do not leave the community. People can and do, change their musical tastes, but when their jobs (as musicians or mediators) are central to metal, withdrawing is difficult. What sounded good at sixteen may be hard to take at forty (although judging from those in attendance at long-in-the-tooth metal bands' concerts, age has not diminished their enthusiasm for the music).

Interaction is crucial to an ideal-type metal community, so going to concerts and festivals, or frequently hanging out informally with other metalheads, encourages increased self-identification with metal and identification with other metalheads. Mediated interaction by tape-trading via mail or cyber-communications, rather than face-to-face, provides, all things being equal, weaken community bonds. Socializing new community members into the culture too is more efficient and certainly more effective when done in person—and is least effective when done on one's own. On the other hand, mediated forms of interaction (e.g., the Internet), maintain communication among metalheads in the time between attendance at events.

Despite the profusion of blogs, websites, Facebook and Wikipedia pages, and the like devoted to metal, from which anyone can learn about it, it is not clear that the Internet has enhanced direct interaction in metal communities. Fans can more easily pass as metalheads, and bands and mediators can have others create their cyber-messages. If direct interaction plays less of a part in the social relations sustaining a metal community, that community becomes diminished.

Solidarity weakens when a segment of the community has "issues" with the demographics of another segment, be it their race, gender, social class, ethnicity, or religion. On the other hand, if the metal community is made up of a single demographic that is seen as inferior by the mainstream society, the solidarity of that community is strengthened. When political and religious leaders stir up moral panics against metal, metal communities feel more solidary.

In the past, when metal had a pariah status, maintaining boundaries was not problematic. However, in the current century in post-industrial societies, boundaries have become incredibly porous for several reasons. One is the impact of the Internet. Trusting in another's commitment to metal without face-to-face interaction, indeed without knowing if the other's presentation of their age, location, gender and anything else is accurate, is difficult online where it is far easier to pass oneself off as a member. The widespread discovery of once obscure metal communities breaches their boundaries. "The proliferation of black metal across the Internet and a recent surge of extreme metal memoirs and zine collections have denied it the subcultural obscurity that fans once prized," says Ross Hagen (2014, 230). To reestablish boundaries they have resorted to creating "illegible band logos and 'leetspeak'" incomprehensible to poseurs or the uninitiated.

A second boundary-busting activity is the result of some of those semi-extreme bands like *Metallica* and *Ozzy Osbourne* that became more mainstream-friendly at the start of the 1990s. Other bands joined in on the successful audience-enlarging model. Some new fans might have gone on to become metalheads, but most were merely fans of these bands and had some of the fashion and little to any of the knowledge of the metal culture. When the author spoke with a few dozen women at Ozzy's show (at the Aragon Ballroom in Chicago on November 3, 1995), each of whom said they had dragged along their boyfriends or came with other female friends, all but two knew that Ozzy had been in a band named *Black Sabbath*.

Today well-known metal bands are playing to non-metal audiences at general rock festivals like the Reading Festival, Lollapallooza, Glastonbury, and Bonnaroo. Such moves may recruit people into metal, letting most of them think that metal is just like other types of rock except for some musical differences. But the fact that festival organizers today want to have metal bands on their bill is due to changes that diminish metal communities—the rise of omnivores and neo-tribes.

Omnivore rock fans that were noticed by researchers in the 1990s (Peterson 1992; Bryson 1996) have altered the previous assessment of metal. Whereas once, in Bryson's terms, they were into "Anything but Heavy Metal," in the current century, metal, in post-industrial societies at least, has become cool. Fans of all types of music now like metal too. It was once "seen as decidedly beyond the pale of refined tastes, [but metal is] now consumed more by the highly educated" (Warde, Wright, and Gayo-Cal 2008, 164). Omnivores tend to like many different styles of popular music, and are neither committed to nor very knowledgeable about any of them. So called "weekend warriors" may cursorily pass muster at a concert, but their various "faux pas" leave committed metalheads unable to trust or identify with them. The larger the segment of omnivores, the less solidarity. The presence of Bennett's neo-tribes is a bit less disruptive of the solidarity of metal communities, yet they too give away their lack of depth in the culture and their temporary status as metalheads.

Despite conditions marking diminution, when metal fans, bands, and mediators have internalized the metal code, they are able to fit into communities far from home. This allows for the proliferating globalization of metal festivals. Festivals are temporary communities that transcend a fixed location. It is possible to constitute them because of an ideological continuity within individuals who are not in the community at the time and that ideological persistence is often reinforced by media.

The festival provides a means by which new members are recruited and socialized into the community. That process has been described for bluegrass festivals by Robert Gardner (2004, 167):

> Festivalgoers indicated that their attraction to and continued participation in bluegrass festival settings stemmed from the overriding sense of inclusion, even when they traveled alone to a new or unfamiliar festival. Veteran members of the festival circuit were eager to demonstrate their relative expertise by walking a "newbie" through the unfamiliar sights, sounds, and rituals of the setting, which made the transition between newcomer and experienced festivalgoer a smooth one. Across multiple festival sites, participants passed down a set of long-established interactional norms and practices that organized the behaviors of both new and veteran attendees. As is common when entering any new scene or subculture, newcomers were introduced to and slowly socialized into the nuances of each festival site and its unwritten rules or norms by the more experienced.

Festivals like that in Calgary, or Hellfest in France, Wacken in Germany, and so many more, demonstrate that "a rooted locale is not a necessary condition for community participation. By establishing consistent sets of rituals and norms across the mobile festival circuit, participants cultivate the vital ingredients for a stable, enduring community to flourish" (Gardner 2004, 175). Introjection is a functional alternative to direct interaction when a community is not critically diminished.

Mythic/Imaginary Metal Community

It is the code in their heads that allows metal fans, those who have become metal mediators of one type or another, and metal musicians to participate in many metal communities, both ideal and diminished. And it is in our heads where the perfection of the metal community exists—an ideal yet imaginary metal community. Unlike the other two types of communities this one only exists in our imaginations.

This mythic imaginary ideal metal community is the ideology, the belief in an ideal-typical metal community when that ideal-type is not actualized. The imaginary metal community functions like those myths that keep people loyal to nationalities, nations, religions, corporations, and so many other groups.

Helping to establish the imaginary metal community is the metal media: metal journalists, metal video documentarians, band biographers, sometimes aided by academic writers. They idealize diminished communities and their participants. Their products are full of musicians, fans, and mediators giving their nostalgic reminiscences. Those anthemic metal songs celebrating metal and its community that were referred to earlier are also involved in the imagined ideal metal community. Such media provide even the youngest metalheads with a nostalgia for that which they never experienced and that perhaps never existed, what I've described elsewhere as constructed- or neo-nostalgia (Weinstein 2014). Hesmondhalgh, while focusing only on subcultures, acknowledges this imaginary too, when he asks: "Are they now mainly nostalgic and highly self-conscious recreations of a lost era of collectivity?" (Hesmondhalgh 2005, 30).

The imaginary ideal metal community is actualized in individuals' subjectivity, like any beliefs, ideologies, or myths. That is, it is real in its consequences. Just because the imaginary ideal metal community is not actualized, is only in one's imagination, or in a collective imagination, does not mean that it has no impact on the real world.

Among its other effects, the imaginary ideal metal community serves as the rose-colored glasses that allow members to evaluate the diminished, albeit typical, metal community in a far better light; it serves as hype, as advertising, that attracts new members into metal communities; and it may also serve as a blue-print from which to create another exemplification of the ideal-type. It may even serve as a justifying ideology, a deterrence machine in Baudrillard's term (1994) against hypercapitalist competitive individualism.

Metal communities, especially in the ideal form, and more so when they are actual rather than imaginary, provide some mitigation of the negative effects of living in the modern world.

We enjoy its freedoms and individualization, but not the feeling of loneliness, of otherness, that we are all strangers to one another. They function much like ethnic, religious and national communities, but with far better music and far better structure. Metal communities are transactional, not authoritarian.

When we spoke of the great, ideal, perfect metal community in Calgary we were talking about this imaginary ideal.

REFERENCES

Althusser, Louis. 1971. "Ideology and Ideological State Apparatuses." In *Lenin and Philosophy*, 127–88. New York: Monthly Review Press.

Baudrillard, Jean. 1994. *Simulacra and Simulation*. Ann Arbor, MI: University of Michigan Press.

Bennett, Andy. 1999. "Subculture or Neo-Tribes? Rethinking the Relationship Between Youth, Style and Musical Taste." *Sociology* 33 (3): 599–617. doi:10.1177/S0038038599000371.

Brown, Andy. 2003. "Heavy Metal and Subcultural Theory: A Paradigmatic Case of Neglect?" In *The Post-Subcultures Reader*, edited by David Muggleton and Rupert Weinzierl, 305–26. Oxford, UK: Berg.

Bryson, Bethany. 1996. "'Anything but Heavy Metal': Symbolic Exclusion and Musical Dislikes." *American Sociological Review* 61 (2): 884–99.

de Burgh-Woodman, Hélène, and Brace-Govan. January 2007. "We Do Not Live to Buy: Why Subcultures Are Different from Brand Communities and the Meaning for Marketing Discourse." *International Journal of Sociology and Social Policy* 27 (5/6): 193–207. doi: dx.doi.org/10.1108/01443330710757230.

Dewey, John. 1934. *Art As Experience*. New York: Minton, Balch and Co.

Epstein, Dan. 2009. "The History of American Thrash." *Revolver Magazine*, February 17, www.revolvermag.com/content/history-american-thrash.

Fellezs, Kevin. 2016. "Voracious Souls: Race and Place in the Formation of the San Francisco Bay Area Thrash Scene." In *Global Metal Music and Culture: Current Directions in Metal Studies*, edited by Andy R. Brown, Karl Spracklen, Keith Kahn-Harris, and Niall W. R. Scott, 89–105. New York: Routledge.

Foucault, Michael. 1972. *Archeology of Knowledge*. New York: Harper.

Gardner, Robert Owen. 2004. "The Portable Community: Mobility and Modernization in Bluegrass Festival Life." *Symbolic Interaction* 27 (2): 155–78.

Gerth, Hans Heinrich, and Charles Wright Mills. 1958. "Introduction: The Man and his Work." In *From Max Weber: Essays in Sociology*, edited by Hans H. Heinrich Gerth and Charles Wright Mills, 1–74. New York: Oxford University Press.

Giddings, Franklin H. 1904. *Studies in the Theory of Human Society*. New York: Macmillan.

Hagen, Ross. 2014. "'Kvlt-er Than Thou': Power, Suspicion and Nostalgia Within Black Metal Fandom." In *The Ashgate Research Companion to Fan Cultures*, edited by Linda Duits, Koos Zwaan, and Stign Reijnders, 223–35. Burlington, VT: Ashgate.

Hall, Stuart and Tony Jefferson. 1976. *Resistance Through Rituals: Youth Subcultures in Post-War Britain*. New York: Holmes and Meier.

Hesmondhalgh, David. 2005. "Subcultures, Scenes or Tribes? None of the Above." *Journal of Youth Studies* 8 (1): 21–40. doi:10.1080/13676260500063652.

Kahn-Harris, Keith. 2007. *Extreme Metal: Music and Culture on the Edge*. Oxford, UK: Berg.

Laclau, Ernesto and Chantal Mouffe. 2001. *Hegemony and Socialist Strategy: Towards a Radical Democratic Politics*, 2nd ed. New York: Verso.

Lena, Jennifer C. and Richard A. Peterson. 2008. "Classification as Culture: Types and Trajectories of Music Genres." *American Sociological Review* 73 (5): 697–718.

Lyotard, Jean-Francois. 1984. *Driftworks*. New York: Semiotext(e).

Maffesoli, Michel. 1996. *The Time of the Tribes: The Decline of Individualism in Mass Society*. Thousand Oaks, CA: Sage.

Moynihan, Michael, and Didrik Søderlind. 1998. *Lords of Chaos: The Bloody Rise of the Satanic Metal Underground*. Venice, CA: Feral House.

Nagel, Joane. 1994. "Constructing Ethnicity: Creating and Recreating Ethnic Identity and Culture." *Social Problems* 41 (1): 152–76.

Negus, Keith. 2002. "The Work of Cultural Intermediaries and the Enduring Distance Between Production and Consumption." *Cultural Studies* 16 (4): 501–15. doi:10.1080/09502380210139089.

Peterson, Richard A. 1992. "Understanding Audience Segmentation: From Elite and Mass to Omnivore and Univore." *Poetics* 21: 243–58.

Port, Ian S. 2011. "Author Brian Lew on the Early Days of Metallica and the Bay Area Thrash Metal Scene." *San Francisco Weekly* (December). www.sfweekly.com/

shookdown/2011/12/07/author-brian-lew-on-the-early-days-of-metallica-and-the-bay-area-thrash-metal-scene.

Straw, Will. 1991. "Systems of Articulation, Logics of Change: Communities and Scenes in Popular Music." *Cultural Studies* 5 (3): 368–88. doi:org/10.1080/09502389100490311.

Toynbee, Jason. 2000. *Making Popular Music: Musicians, Creativity and Institutions.* New York: Oxford University Press.

Wagner, David. 2011. "Fans, Bands Tout Bay Area's Thrash Metal Legacy." *The San Francisco Chronicle.* www.sfgate.com/bayarea/article/Fans-bands-tout-Bay-Area-s-thrash-metal-legacy-2393272.php.

Wallach, Jeremy and Alexandra Levine. 2001. "'I Want *You* to Support Local Metal': A Theory of Metal Scene Formation." *Popular Music History* 6 (1/2): 116–34. doi:10.1558/pomh.v6i1/2.116.

Warde, Alan, David Wright, and Modesto Gayo-Cal. 2008. "The Omnivorous Orientation in the UK." *Poetics* 36 (2–2): 148–65.

Weinstein, Deena. 1991. *Heavy Metal: A Cultural Sociology.* New York: Macmillan.

———. 2013. "Metallica Kills." In *Please Allow Me to Introduce Myself: Essays on Debut Albums,* edited by George Plasketes, 149–55. Farnham: Ashgate.

———. 2014. "Constructed Nostalgia for Rock's Golden Age: 'I Believe in Yesterday.'" Volume 11 (1):19–36. volume.revues.org/4314.

DISCOGRAPHY

Accept, 1985. *Metal Heart* [CD]. Portrait.
Exciter, 1983. *Heavy Metal Maniac* [CD]. Shrapnel.
Exodus, 1985 . *Bonded by Blood* [CD]. Torrid/Combat.
Helloween, 1985. *Walls of Jericho* [CD]. Noise Records.
Judas Priest, 1980. *British Steel* [CD]. CBS.
Metallica, 1983. *Kill 'Em All* [CD]. Megaforce.
Overkill, 1987. *Taking Over* [CD]. Megaforce.
Saxon, 1981. *Denim and Leather* [CD]. Carrere.

TWO

Absurd Communities of Misanthropic Paradox Destruction

You Play and We'll Destroy the House!

Niall Scott

In this chapter, I wish to explore some conceptual issues regarding metal and community. Community is one of those words that is widely used and applied to a range of social contexts, but quite hard to pin down. Metal too is notoriously difficult to define. To discuss community in the context of metal music and its culture then will require some concessions to the multiple ways in which community can be conceived. I will first briefly discuss issues concerning the defining of community, then move on to explore some aspects of community as understood in Aristotle's writings and Immanuel Kant's political philosophy as a means of illuminating and clarifying problematic issues in speaking of metal and community together in one breath. To explore the nature, or even the very possibility of metal and community, one can approach it from a purely theoretical perspective, or one can simply satisfy oneself by going out and observing metal culture in practice at music events for example; or do empirical work on certain questions pertaining to the subject as is presented in other chapters in this volume. I would like to present something somewhere in between and look into the notion of how community might be understood in the context of metal, by delving into conceptual offerings from Aristotle's and Kant's ideas on community and using these to unpack three examples from the world of metal music and its culture. The first is an example from metal's audiovisual realm: *Slipknot's* song and accompanying video *Duality*. This example, I think, illustrates

23

both what a metal community might look like, but also throws up some of potential problems and expands on paradoxes found in Kant's work which can be read to challenge the very idea of metal as a community. The second one comes from *Machine Head's* front man Robb Flynn, who delivered a lengthy speech during their performance at Bloodstock in 2012. Flynn opens up a way of treating the metal community as both creative and destructive supporting the unifying impact of metal music, but my own reading of its reliance on a destructive force. Indeed the title of this piece is in part inspired by a story Rob Flynn, the *Machine Head* front man tells of their early origins, where he recounts the band being invited to play at a friend's house, who hated his landlord. He retorted to the band "You guys play and I'll destroy the house."[1] The final example is a simple one, an expression of the range that the metal community covers as illustrated in contrasting song lyrics and gives focus to apparent paradoxes in the metal community as seen from a dualistic perspective.

Zygmunt Bauman in his short study on community refers to the term *community* not just having a meaning, but also a feel (Baumann 2000) and this has an impact on how it is used and understood. He further suggests that in general community is experienced as a good thing, in the sense of it conveying feelings of warmth, trust, acceptance, and safety. John Bruhn (2011, 12), although maintaining that the term is hard to define and claiming that there is no "single agreed upon definition," points out that community implies relationships that go beyond the casual and tends to identify a group with "common goals, values and, perhaps a way of life that reinforce each other, creates positive feelings and results in a degree of mutual commitment and responsibility" (12). Bruhn in a footnote goes on to cite Hillary's perspective of uncovering ninety-four different definitions for community, but holds that three features can be distilled from them—that community has a locale, features common ties, and involves social interaction (Bruhn 2011, 13 see fn 5). For metal, if the idea of community is applicable to its culture though, one could claim immediately that locale is not a strong feature, as it is now a global movement (see Wallach, Berger, and Greene 2011), although its origins are tied to place (for example, the Home of Metal project celebration of Birmingham and the Black Country in the United Kingdom as an originary place in metal's history; see homeofmetal.com/). Furthermore, the notion of social interaction, although present is a problematic and contestable feature in metal culture, especially in the more extreme subcultures of metal, such as black metal where misanthropy is given voice.

Looking into the history of the concept of community, Gerard Delanty takes the enlightenment idea of community to "refer to a more immediate world of meaning, belonging and everyday life" (Delanty 2003, 2). However Nisbet in his well-known 1969 study of community treated community as something that was (is) being lost and overcome by the modern stress on individualism. He sees the term community being discussed at the same time with the terminology of decay, destruction, and disintegration. He also notes that at the time of his writing, and I think relevant to the present study, that "in all the social sciences the various synonyms of alienation have a foremost place in studies of human relations. Investigations of the 'unattached', the 'marginal', the 'obsessive', the 'normless', and the 'isolated' individual all testify to the central lace occupied by the hypothesis of alienation in contemporary social science" (Nisbet 1969, 15). This concern and language speaks to the heart of metal's lyrical subject matter and discourse. There has even been a special issue of the journal *Metal Music Studies* devoted to the theme of marginalization (Hill, Lucas, and Riches 2015). Metal culture, arguably can be seen as acting as a critic of this age, in concert with Nisbet's assertion that prophets of the age are addressing loss of community in the context of a "sick culture." He writes: "Is it not extraordinary how many of the major novelists and poets and playwrights of the present age have given imaginative expression to themes of dissolution and decay of class, family community and morality" (Nisbet 1969, 8). Metal gives voice to these frustrations: People=Shit as *Slipknot* misanthropically proclaimed.

Some authors when discussing popular music cultures instead of using the term community prefer to speak of *scenes*—for example, Rajko Muršič's (2011) study on Slovenian metal or Rosemary Overell's (2014) study of Australian and Japanese grindcore. She uses the term "scene," but also in the context of belonging in these specific metal scenes. Interestingly though, "belonging" is an important term in defining community. Holly Kruse's look at music communities in the context of indie rock/pop and college radio uses the term scene when discussing alternative music identities as "a field of relations that shift over time, but clearly is not an entirely fluid space" (Kruse 1993, 40). However, in discussing community and music in education, Wayne Bowman prefers the term community, which he describes as "fluid porous negotiated affairs; dynamic patterns of human interaction" (Bowman 2009, 109) thus very similar to the idea of a scene, but with the concession to fluidity. Some of these seemingly contrasting ideas can work in favor or with metal culture, some against. The reasons for this will emerge when expanding on the three examples I give. From this very brief sketch though, it can be seen that where there are different perspectives in managing the complex and contested field of community, these are likely to manifest themselves in any study of the possibility and plausibility of metal and community.

In trying to define community, one can find a range of approaches in the history of philosophical thought and I aim to present two thinkers who can maybe shed light on understanding the paradoxical features of metal and community. Aristotle looks to a ruling part to identify a principle by which one can hold a collection of things in common. Immanuel Kant in his writings on political philosophy, looks to reciprocity, attraction and repulsion between parts that holds a group of things in common. Recognizing that community is notoriously difficult to define even at a conceptual level, the notion of community in the context of metal is fraught with perceived paradoxical relationships, the most noteworthy being that of individualism juxtaposed to a strong sense of belonging and identification with metal's communal expressions. Some of these paradoxes generate problems precisely with the conceptual ideas of what defines community. In terms of definition, these lay the foundations to which real instances of communities ought to conform. Using these two positions it may be possible to develop a notion of community on Metal's own terms.

ARISTOTLE AND COMMUNITY

At its most basic level, the term community describes the attainment of a certain kind of social formation. In the opening of Aristotle's *Politics* (1961) we encounter the term for community *koinonia* as simply referring to a group of individuals holding something in common. Regarding community, Aristotle maintains that:

> In all cases where there is a compound, constituted of more than one part but forming one common entity—whether the parts be continuous [as in the body of a man] or discrete [as in the relation of a master and a slave] a ruling element and ruled can always be traced. This characteristic [i.e., the presence of ruled and ruling elements] is present in animate beings by virtue of the whole constitution of nature, inanimate as well as animate; for even things which are inanimate there is a sort of ruling principle, such as to be found for example in musical harmony. (Aristotle, *Politics* [1254a] 1961)

This treatment of community in its simplest and broadest form is based, for Aristotle, on the assumption that humans are fundamentally social beings, but his interest does not concern this matter *per se*. Rather, Aristotle is concerned with what is involved in the formation of the political community. However if this in its simplest form, is all there is to the issue in defining community, then understanding metal in terms of community would be blissfully straightforward and uncontentious. Sharing a passion for the music in common with other individuals for example, would satisfy this basic definition. However more detailed attempts at definition become rather difficult as is evident in discussions of community, both concrete and abstract in the context of political theory.

Although the idea of submission to a ruling element can counter the anarchic autonomy of the individual in metal culture, it is important to recognize a certain degree of surrender to the demands of what a community delineates at the same time as facilitating certain practices. To identify as a follower, fan, or participant in metal culture, to identify as a

"metalhead" or "headbanger" or even within a sub group in metal culture, to call oneself a maggot (as *Slipknot* fans choose to), is to make a
claim about one's identity and exclude other identifiers. Such a claim
including oneself as part of a group even where voluntary, involves giving up a part of one's autonomy and allow oneself to be ruled by an
identifying principle or feature of the group one has decided to be a part
of. As Bowman recognizes:

> To identify oneself as a member of a community, a society or social
> collective, then, is to always concede a degree of autonomy—to agree
> to yield some of one's otherwise unconstrained independence, one's
> imagined freedom to do whatever one pleases in consideration for the
> greater good of the collective. It is also to delimit and demarcate one's
> personal identity. To be a member of a community "X" is to voluntarily
> accede to the normative ways of acting and interacting that typify that
> community. It is to become, oneself and in some degree an "x" rather
> than or in addition to a "y" or a "z." (Bowman 2009, 110)

An area in metal where autonomy is conceded is arguably found in the
acceptance and participation in the extreme metal world, with its "gate
keepers" and "taste makers," as Sturm (2015) calls them, the connoisseurs
and the scene elitist fans patrolling a scene where the fringe fan group
"struggle to mesh with the dominant literacy and capital that shape the
extreme metal community. When rebuffed, their response is usually a
critique of the close minded and elitist attitudes that prevail there"
(Sturm, 2015, 21).

In being rebuffed from a patrolled community boundary based on
knowledge and the accumulation of the relevant cultural capital of such a
community, there are opportunities to sacrifice autonomy in order to be
able to join, but also reject such demands and assert one's autonomy.
Community needs to have space for such assertion to happen. Nonetheless the tension between acceptance and conformity on the one hand and
space to assert difference on the other is a real problem for the stability of
community—so how can both fragmentation and assimilation be maintained in the idea of community in metal? We turn to Kant to address this
problem.

KANT AND COMMUNITY

Kant's ideas on community combine his political and moral philosophy.
His ideas are very much embedded in his definitions of what a human is
as a sociable creature who finds him/herself as straddling a tension between being in solitude and being in relationship with others. In the
selection of short articles he wrote compiled as *An Idea for a Universal
History with a Cosmopolitan Purpose*, he refers to the success of human
social order as stemming from an antagonism, which he defines as "the

social unsociability of men" (Kant 1992, 44). He expands on this antagonism as the tension held between humans wanting to associate together
in community, but as soon as they do, this is countered with a tendency
to want to break these associations up.[2]

Kant ideas also find themselves emerging in a scientific context, where
the notions of attraction and repulsion coming from Newtonian physics
were gaining credence. In this approach, Kant conceived of community
but without the idea of a ruling part governing over others—be it a ruling
principle, person or institution, that featured strongly in the ancient
Greek mindset seen in Aristotle. On this very point, Susan Shell writes
that Kant's notion of community is not one of dominion, but rather reciprocity among coequal parts (Shell 1993, 118). Regarding the antagonism
and tension, Kant wrote:

> This propensity is obviously rooted in Human nature. Man has an
> inclination to live in society, since he feels in that state more like a man,
> that is, he feels able to develop his natural capacities. But he also has a
> great tendency to live as an individual, to isolate himself since he also
> encounters in himself the unsocial characteristic of wanting to direct
> everything in accordance with his own ideas. (Kant 1992, 44)

Kant however thought that we had a strong obligation to develop and
engage in community too, as it was for him the site in which we as
humans could most fully flourish and develop our talents and abilities.
Developing one's talents is seen as a moral duty by Kant, argued for in
his *Groundwork to the Metaphysics of Morals* (Kant 2005). Because of this
relationship, Gehrke (2002) argues that Kant's position leads to maintain
the development and sustaining of community as a moral duty. This may
though be a bit much to pursue for the metalhead, the idea that one has a
moral obligation as a metalhead to develop and sustain community.
However, there is something useful in Kant's treatment of community
insofar as it is *in* community humans can explore both what we share and
our express our differences: "our differences that separate us are also
critical to community" (Gehrke 2002, 15). Thus for Kant, community is
not just built on that which is held in common, as Aristotle's definition
provides, but also a place where one's individuality and autonomy can
have expression. We could not have only uniformity in community or
else we would find ourselves in a state of singularity, with no position
from which to judge and account for difference, including the boundaries
of community. For metal this means that we need to know where the
metal community ends to be able to recognize its difference, but this is
not a stark rigid border. It is very much a contested arena. Consider
metal's fluid edge in music generated by, for example, *Faith No More* and
The Red Hot Chilli Peppers on metal culture's fringes. These bands arguably represent affiliation with metal's sound, aesthetics, and fanbase, but
also spread out into other musical genres, such as funk and rap music.

Yet it is one fraught with tension: community expresses the state of being with other humans as a social state that on the one hand we cannot bear, but also a state that we cannot bear to leave. In articulating this position, Kant quite accurately captures a crisis point in community which is useful I think in deepening what community can mean in the context of heavy metal culture. Let us now move on to discuss three examples that exemplify the problems and apparent paradoxes thrown up by these ideas on community.

DUALITY, ASSOCIATION, AND DESTRUCTION

Slipknot, a nine man outfit founded in 1995 and originating from Des Moines, Iowa, are one of the more significant heavy metal bands to emerge from the so-called nu-metal era of the 1990s. Their spectacular live shows sees them dress in masked outfits arguably paying homage to the visual traditions in North American horror film aesthetics and their lyrical content focuses on misanthropic, socially critical, and negative themes. *Slipknot's* iconic video accompanying the song *Duality*, from their 2004 album *Vol. 3: (Subliminal Verses)* opens with a focus on a bare-chested teenager who surges forward with a throng of fans to the opening lyric "I push my fingers into my eyes." The crowd runs toward a house, where the band is already playing inside, engulfed by more headbanging fans, and break in through the windows. As the song progresses, the crowd wells, and both outside and inside the house is torn apart with bodies piling through windows, coming in through collapsed ceilings and partition walls. A moment of calm descends when Corey Taylor, the lead singer repeats "All I've got, all I've got is insane" building to a crescendo and the rhythmic mayhem continues to a sudden cut where we are left with the image of the same teenager from the beginning drenched in sweat and water.[3] The video shot by Tony Petrossian and Marc Klasfeld was to reflect a scene which they described as: "it will be like nine sardines on PCP gnawing at each other as they bounce around their tiny tin can" (Wiederhorn 2004). Wiederhorn goes on to write that "In actuality it was more like a demolition crew with no tools trying to obliterate everything as quickly as possible" (ibid.). The damage was not limited to the house—Wiederhorn goes on to describe how the fans forgetting the motto "safety first" were injured by broken glass. Yet on the other hand he recounts a teenage English fan who having flown out to be part of the shoot had no place to stay, as he was underage and could not check in alone to the local hotel, and was put up by Corey Taylor.

With the mixture of exuberant aggression and destruction, combined with a scene of a coming together around the music, can this video be a paradigmatic example of what the metal community is? It features many of the common elements of metal music culture and its practice: loud distorted guitar based music, the physicality of moshpit behavior, head-banging, a band and fans, linking to the gig and or festival event, even tropes of masculinity and aggression among other things are present to the viewer. If so, then what kind of community is being represented here? At the basic level of having the music in common, then things are straightforward, this image that *Slipknot* presents us is simply one of many that shows metal at its most exuberant, energetic, and expressive. Aristotle's ideas of having the music in common and the willingness to submit to a principle and sacrifice part of one's autonomy in the process would appear to be adequate.

However, one of the key problems that the Duality video exposes is the paradox of coming together and rejection, an association and disassociation of bodies. This paradox concerns the contrast between the social forces of fandom and association with the music at the heart of coming together on the one hand and the physical behavior that seems to indicate a desire for individuality and isolation on the other. It is a paradox that aligns closely with Kant's ideas of the unsocial sociability of man. How can such a vision of interaction be supportive of a vision of community? This is not just limited to *Slipknot's* video in the metal world. For example the individualism and misanthropy promoted not only in *Slipknot's* general theatrical negative vision, but also in some quarters the problems encountered of racism and sexism, discussed in detail by Vivek Venkatesh et al. in this volume, in the subgenre of black metal, which may rail against any discussion of community or human social relationships at all.

A second example of metal and community I offer for consideration comes from *Machine Head's* performance at the Bloodstock festival at Catton Hall in Derbyshire, UK, in 2012. *Machine Head*, from Oakland in California were founded in 1991. Their music spans a range of metal sounds, but is largely rooted in the tradition of thrash metal. Together with *Slipknot* they are considered one of the pioneering bands of the so-called New Wave of American Heavy Metal movement (Sharpe-Young 2005). The small festival is a family run venture which has been active since 2001 catering to a wide range of metal subgenres but tending to focus on new talent and some of the more extreme metal offerings. Introducing the title track from their latest release, *Unto the Locust* (2012), *Machine Head's* lead singer Robb Flynn declared:

> What is a locust? A locust could be a friend, it could be a lover, it could be a brother, it could be your parents, it could be a corporation and it could be a religion, but its effect when a swarm of them comes, is to devour everything in its path, and then they fly away, and leave you in the aftermath. Bloodstock do you know something like that? Maybe we all share something in common tonight. [4]

Although the locust's devouring power can easily be read, as Flynn does, as a metaphor to criticize institutions in capitalism, I think it can be gloriously applied to metal in a different way. That is, to treat the metal community as a swarm of locusts. The devouring activity of the locust here can also reflect the metal community in association with its sonic quality—the all-consuming sound of metal music combined with its culture. Seeing a group of metal fans assemble and congregate at an event, say a gig or festival, is akin to witnessing a swarming event. Flynn tempered the introduction to this song though by deciding roughly an hour into *Machine Head*'s set to deliver a serious and lengthy oration on music and belonging in metal culture. It can be found roughly fifty minutes into the Youtube recording of the concert. He expresses gratitude to being able to play to people who are fans of the music, but come from 7,000 miles away from where they live in California. He moves away from the locust metaphors of destruction to maintain that "Music is that release—but you know it isn't like that for everybody all the time." He goes on to criticize those who listen to monotonous background music, but then says, "Then you meet other people . . . like all of the fuckin' diehards that are here at Bloodstock and you're a different breed, you know that? You're a different fuckin' breed of person . . . and you probably fuckin' know that and you may have known that all your life." He goes on to pool together the different bands that have played the festival over the weekend: "We all fuckin' unite under that fuckin' sound, that is the fuckin' power of music." Then, introducing the song *Darkness Within*, he exhorts the crowd to sing along as loud as they want, "Be louder than the band if you want to. . . . Let's all become one voice tonight."

The unity presented here by Flynn is both a generating of the sound (of *Machine Head*) and simultaneously destroying it. I mean this in the ambiguous sense in which the original recording is destroyed in the public festival performance and its unification in one voice, replacing it with a new version but also the more colloquial slang sense of "destroying" it meaning in American slang something done really well and enjoyed.

The third example comes from a simple observation based on the sentiments expressed in the lyrics of two metal songs. There is quite a tension to be found between communal sufficiency in *Warlock's* anthemic *All We Are* with the choral chant "All we are, we are all / We are all, all we need" (Pesch and Baldasarre 1987)[5] on the one hand and the late Pete Steele of *Type O Negative's* outcry in *We Hate Everyone* containing the lyric: "Hate hate, hate, hatred for one and all / no matter what you believe" (Steele 1993)[6] on the other. This example presented the question of how do we make sense of lyrical utterances that appear to contradict each other in their sentiment, but coexist happily under the unifying banner of "metal"? Again I think we can understand this from the theoretical perspectives presented earlier. Wayne Bowman's reminder regarding community as fluid, porous, and negotiated is valuable precisely because it removes any kind of structural arrangement from the understanding of community as well as physical location. Instead, this fluidity, for example being able to negotiate the space exemplified in the contrasting lyrical expressions above and yet still fall under the unifying banner of "metal," is interpreted in Bowman's understanding that communities (and for our purposes here too, the metal community) exhibits "patterns of human interaction grounded in practices-habitual ways of (inter)acting that exert significant normative influence, yet lack attributes that are intrinsic, inherent or essential" (Bowman 2009, 110). So it would be mistaken to see either misanthropic or collective utterances as intrinsically inherent or essential to the metal community. But it is Kant's insight into the tensions present in community that hold community together. These lyrical expressions are perhaps best seen as outworkings of and giving voice to the unsocial sociability of the metal community's participants. Furthermore, *Slipknot's* duality gives a visual insight into this tension, as does *Machine Head's* example of unity in voice at a festival tempered by the destructive metaphor of the locust.

METAL AS A PARADOX DESTROYING COMMUNITY

The idea of a ruling principle as per Aristotle's ideas on community for the notion of community in the context of metal culture is something that may well be both embraced and resisted. It can be embraced where the ruling principle is that of the unifying concept "metal." Here metal is the unifying banner under which all that relates to the music and its culture is subsumed. Whether or not a case can be made for this banner carrying normative weight would require further investigation. The difficulty with metal as a unifying principle, just like the term community, is that it is notoriously difficult to define—rather we need a combination of theoretical definition and the experience of the metal culture at events, gatherings, in lyrics, and audio visual output to build a picture of the possibility of metal as a community. I concede that some might disagree with the language of there being a ruling principle to which the member of the metal community submits as counter to the individual freedom championed in metal. We might also not want to entertain the notion of community in the sense of it being obligatory to promote in the Kantian sense of the word as mentioned before. It would be difficult to argue for an obligation to not only join a metal community nor speak of its internal associations in such a manner—these are rather voluntary.

However, I do think that the insights provided by Kant and Aristotle are useful. An understanding of community that is required, I argue, for metal is one that would identify both the unifying principle (but not perhaps not *ruling* principle) of metal as well as a grounding idea that captures its paradoxes. These capture the tensions we find in metal, those tensions of collective experience and misanthropy that allow for interactions on the one hand, but maintain that dogged sense of individual autonomy on the other. We can understand the metal community as having a grounding that allows for a community to be able to embrace strong social relations supported by terminology such as sisterhood, brotherhood, even love on the one hand yet extreme misanthropy on the other without contradiction. Indeed where Delanty presents a history of modern ideas of community as being bound up with the social, and creatively, even experimentally, opposed to the state the image presented in *Slipknot's* video, although depicting a gathering, would arguably also be treated and exemplifying the antisocial. On deeper reflection, it speaks to what Susan Shell's reading of Kant on the reciprocal nature of community and its grounding as "substances that are mutually dependent without ever breaching one another's internal integrity" (Shell 1993, 122). For Kant this grounding principle is God; for our purposes, we can treat the grounding principle as Metal.

In conclusion then, metal is in a position to exaggerate the very problems that lie at the heart of understanding what community means in the paradoxes and problems it sheds light on. Weinstein's chapter in this volume develops some ideas about how the metal community can possibly be imagined; here I hope I have successfully drawn attention to some experimental thoughts that capture the idea of metal and community in its messiness, ripe with tensions.

It is possible I think to marry these ideas regarding community into a view that suits metal down to the (under) ground. The idea of the metal community can offer a different perspective bringing together elements of Nisbet's recognition of the language of loss and marginalization in community, with metal functioning as a ruling principle from Aristotle and the tensions expressed in Kant's unsocial sociability of man. We have themes of unity, belonging, sacrificing and element of autonomy, sitting it would appear alongside themes of destruction, misanthropy, and seeking out solitude and difference. One thing I suggest is this: the metal community is one that destroys itself at the moment of its incarnation as *Slipknot's Duality* video suggests as does the theme of destruction in *Machine Head's* coming together as a band. The combination of the metaphor of the locust as devouring and the unifying exhortation that followed suggest the possibility of reading heavy metal community as one that generates a unifying sound which is consumed at its inception is reminiscent of Jacques Attali's (2011) comments on noise making meaning and order but also reaching a catastrophe point. The metal community functions at its most meaningful when it remains at a perpetual peak; it is a community that is arguably committed to a state of being attractively repulsive, an absurd community built on misanthropic paradox destruction.

NOTES

1. The example comes from personal communication with the music journalist Dom Lawson, but is also be found toward the end of their performance at Bloodstock in 2012 at Catton Hall in Derbyshire, UK, available on YouTube. See below in footnote 3 for further details.

2. I have given a more detailed treatment elsewhere of Kant's notion of the unsocial sociability of man in the context Metallica's lyrics and his theories of evil, moral philosophy in a chapter entitled "The Unsocial Sociability of Humans and Metal Gods," *Metallica and Philosophy: A Crash Course in Brain Surgery* ed. by William Irwin (2007)

3. An account of the shooting of the video "Duality," the destruction of the house and consequences for its owners and band is described at: www.blabbermouth.net/news/report-slipknot-s-duality-video-cost-nearly-half-a-million-to-produce/ (accessed on 09/0/15).

4. www.youtube.com/watch?v=6BCX0GOSqzU, fifty minutes into the YouTube clip.

5. *Warlock* was a German heavy metal band from Dusseldorf founded in the early 1980s. Fronted by the iconic Doro Pesch, *Warlock's* success came through a combination of her powerful vocals and tours supporting *Judas Priest* and *W.A.S.P.* Doro continues to perform material by *Warlock* to this day.

6. *Type O Negative* is best described as a gothic and doom metal band. From Brooklyn, New York, and founded in 1989, the band folded after the tragic death of singer Pete Steele in 2010. The band's lyrical themes frequently explored the darker sides of the human psyche.

REFERENCES

Aristotle. 1961. *The Politics of Aristotle*. Trans. Ernest Barker. Oxford: Clarendon Press.

Attali, Jacques. 2011. *Noise, The Political Economy of Music*, Minneapolis: University of Minnesota Press.

Baumann, Zygmunt. 2000. *Community: Seeking Safety in an Insecure World*. Cambridge, UK: Polity Press.

Bowman, Wayne. 2009. The Community in Music. *International Journal of Community Music*, 2 (2–3): 109–128.

Bruhn, John G. 2011. *The Sociology of Community Connections*. Dordrecht: Springer.

Delanty, Gerard. 2003. *Community*. London: Routledge.

Gehrke, Pat J. 2002. "Turning Kant Against the Priority of Autonomy: Communication Ethics and the Duty to Community." *Philosophy and Rhetoric*, 35 (1): 1–22.

Hill, Rosemary, Lucas Caroline and Riches, Gabby 2015. "Metal and Marginalisation: Researching at the Edges of Exteriority." *Metal Music Studies* 1 (3): 295–302.

Home of Metal. n.d. homeofmetal.com/ (accessed 29/02/2016).

Kant, Immanuel. 1992. "Idea for a Universal History with Cosmopolitan Purpose." In *Kant, Political Writings*, edited by H. Reiss, 41–53. Cambridge, UK: Cambridge University Press.

Kant Immanuel. 2005. *Groundwork to the Metaphysics of Morals*. Laura Denis, (ed) Ontario: Broadview.

Kruse, Holly. 1993. "Subcultural Identity in Alternative Music Culture." *Popular Music* 12 (1): 33–41.

Muršič, Rajko. 2011. "Noisy Crossroads, Metal Scenes in Slovenia." In *Metal Rules the Globe*, edited by J. Wallach, H. M. Berger and P. D. Greene, 294–312. Durham, NC: Duke University Press.

Nisbet, Robert, (1969) *The Quest for Community: A Study in the Ethics of Order and Freedom*. Oxford: Oxford University Press.

Overell, Rosemary. 2014. *Affective Intensities in Extreme Music Scenes Cases from Japan and Australia*. London: Palgrave Macmillan.

Pesch, Doro, and Baldasarre, Jospeh. 1987. "All We Are." *Warlock, Triumph and Agony*. Vertigo records. CD-ROM.

Sharpe-Young, Garry. 2005. *The New Wave of America Heavy Metal*. New Plymouth, New Zealand: Zonda Books.

Shell, Susan Meld. 1993. "Commerce and Community in Kant's Early Thought." In *Kant and Political Philosophy*, edited by James Booth and Ronald Beiner, 117–54. New Haven: Yale University Press.

Steele, Peter T. 1993. "We Hate Everyone." *Bloody Kisses*. Roadrunner records. CD-ROM.

Sturm, Damion. 2015. "Elitist Aesthetics: Extreme Metal Fans a Taste-Makers and Gate-Keepers." In *Music at the Extremes: Essays on Sounds Outside the Mainstream*, edited by Wilson, S. A., 13–29. North Carolina: McFarland.

Wallach, Jeremy, Harris M. Berger, and Paul D. Greene. 2011. *Metal Rules the Globe*. Durham, NC: Duke University Press.

Widerhorn, Jon. 2004. "Slipknot's Maggots Destroy Iowa Home." *MTV News*, March 29. www.mtv.com/news/1486022/slipknots-maggots-destroy-iowa-home/ (accessed November 27, 2015).

THREE

Talking Metal

The Social Phenomenology of Hanging Out

Esther Clinton and Jeremy Wallach

Hanging out and talking about music is a kind of co-performance. As such, it depends on what phenomenologist Alfred Schutz[1] calls "a mutual tuning-in relationship" (2004, 210) and, like music itself, can foster a deep (if sometimes ephemeral) sense of community among its participants. Schutz, himself an accomplished musician (Wagner 1970, 36), understood the experience of successfully tuning in on both temporal (about which we will say more later) and musical levels. Often it is hard to recall the specific content of music-related hangout sessions. That's not a coincidence since a truly satisfying hangout session is often accompanied by heightened states of consciousness that make things hard to remember (even without the aid of recreational substances). Yet such experiences are frequently also recalled as profoundly meaningful and pleasurable, and it is hard to think that the elaborate social networks of music fandom could exist without them.

To explore matters further, we turn to studies of heavy metal music fans as well as (judiciously) our own personal experiences as metalheads. Heavy metal fandom is one of the most extensively documented genre-based music cultures in the world as a result of the robust expansion of academic metal studies over the last decade (see Hickam 2014). This allows for provisional hypotheses that we believe could be extended to other kinds of music, particularly those with deeply passionate listeners. However, the following analysis focuses on metalheads—a subcultural affinity group found on every inhabited continent.

"Hanging out and talking metal"—a specialized type of engaged metamusical conversation—is central to scenic cohesion and fundamental to the entire concept of heavy metal community, a notion that is taken quite seriously, at least as an ideal, throughout the global metal scene. Hangout sessions, which often take place between metalheads who have just met or don't know one another well, are complex, multilayered social events that play crucial roles in scenes' economies of desire and prestige at local, national, transnational, and global levels. However, while previous studies of heavy metal communities have traced the circulation of transgressive and mundane subcultural capital in scenes (following Kahn-Harris' 2007 seminal formulations) and examined their social functions (Wallach and Levine 2011), what is needed is an _experience-centered_ approach that recognizes the quality that Émile Durkheim called "collective effervescence" ([1912] 1995) as key to metal community cohesion.

We start this chapter with an investigation into the mechanisms of intersubjective encounter between metalheads using Alfred Schutz's social phenomenology. This method allows us to examine the micro-level interactions that give rise to metalheads' feelings of solidarity while hanging out together. We then describe how heavy metal is experienced in Indonesia, and how this can illuminate hanging out in metal culture more generally. We conclude by offering our "unified theory" of hanging out as the experiential anchor of the community ethos in global metal culture.

A PHENOMENOLOGICAL INVESTIGATION OF HANGING OUT AND TALKING METAL

The central idea of phenomenology is relatively simple (in contrast to its subsequent elaborations). First, that human consciousness is always consciousness _about_ something and never unanchored and second, that scholars need to focus on the nature of human experience and "bracket out" questions of objective truth and knowledge. Schutz adroitly explains the consequences of such bracketing: "What remains of the whole world after this bracketing? Neither more nor less than the concrete fullness and entirety of the stream of our experience containing all our perceptions, our reflections, in short, our cogitations" (Schutz 1970, 59). By focusing on thought through the lens of experience, phenomenology seeks to reduce experience to its most fundamental characteristics.

Typically scholars who use phenomenology as a method in their research begin their work with a lengthy historical overview of the approach, starting with Edmund Husserl and then following with later phenomenologists such as Martin Heidegger, Jean Paul Sartre, and Maurice Merleau-Ponty. Such a ponderous exercise does much to obscure an already complicated approach. Since this information is readily available (an excellent overview can be found in Berger 1999, 1–30), we present a very streamlined version here. [2]

Phenomenology, it seems to us, involves a method that, because of its focus on embodied experience, is ideal for examining what goes on in a standard hangout session. There are other reasons that phenomenology is uniquely suited to addressing the hanging out experience. For one thing, this approach adheres to a strictly agnostic position with regard to the question of "truth." So, for example, the question of whether or not the heavy metal community "really" exists is beside the point in phenomenological research. Phenomenology stands at the cusp between "modernist" and "postmodernist" modes of inquiry in that it accepts the subjective nature of human knowledge and experience, while at the same time posits that there is a world out there within which human experiences occur.

So, for example, folklorist David Hufford (1982) uses phenomenology in his study of "the old hag," the term for a phenomenon that occurs when people wake from sleep and find themselves temporarily unable to move though fully mentally alert. The medical explanation is basically that your brain wakes up before your body does, and Hufford does not dispute this. However, Hufford is interested not so much in how the "old hag" experience medically happens, but in how people who have had the experience make intellectual sense of it. Ultimately he concludes, based on the fact that people from many different cultures perceive the "old hag" as a supernatural force (usually malevolent) holding them down and preventing them from moving, that such an experience affects the person's understanding of both the natural and the supernatural.

Phenomenology is the perfect method for Hufford's project because it allows him to focus on subjective experiences and relieves him of the responsibility of deciding whether there is or is not a supernatural element to the experience. Schutz acknowledges phenomenology's focus on subjective (as opposed to empirical) information: "In certain quarters the phenomenologist is held to be a kind of crystal-gazer, a metaphysician or ontologist in the deprecatory sense of the words, at any rate a fellow who spurns all the empirical facts and the more or less established scientific methods devised to collect and interpret them" (1962, 99). Because it accepts subjective experiences, phenomenology offers the best method for understanding the many important experiences that do not lend themselves to objective, quantitative interpretation. It's not that phenomenological scholars aren't interested in understanding what "really" happened, it's that they believe that the best way to understand human experience is to *bracket* the question of truth and allow people's experiences to speak for themselves.

Of course letting experiences "speak" is no easy matter. The deep intellectualist focus in phenomenology (attested to in the extended Schutz quote above about bracketing) naturally leads to an emphasis on language, since we can only precisely access others' experiences through language. Obviously such a focus on language requires the scholar to admit and even try to understand the communal elements of existence. After all, although we all bring some idiosyncrasies to our personal language use, the languages we use existed before we were born and will continue to exist after our deaths. Ferdinand de Saussure,[3] writing about the same time as the early phenomenologists, famously explained language as being based on convention alone, not on some intrinsic relationship between the sign and its meaning. Phenomenology accepts this communal basis (what Schutz calls "intersubjectivity") to both language and thought (Schutz 1970, 55, 58, 163–177).

As philosophers, Husserl and his followers, including Schutz, were deeply interested in how people think about their existence and experiences. Their work seeks to explain how and why people think what they think, a worthy enterprise indeed. We, however, are not philosophers; one of us is a folklorist and the other an anthropologist. We are therefore more interested in understanding how culture influences (one could even say "determines") what and how we think. This brings us specifically to Schutz who, as already mentioned, was primarily interested in expanding the ideas of phenomenology so that the approach would be able to address how humans behave in groups, which led to his focus on intersubjectivity and language. Schutz recognized that the world in which an individual thinks and experiences is a cultural one, and that the individual must be able to conceive of other people as thinking, feeling beings whose actions and thoughts potentially influence herself.[4] He saw this as the primary question for sociology: how and why do people live successfully in groups (Wagner 1970, 34)? As a phenomenologist, he was particularly interested in how people *experienced* group membership.[5]

So why anchor our present argument in phenomenology? It seems to us that, for whatever reason (a topic beyond the scope of the present chapter), anthropology and sociology are rarely able to accept, never mind truly comprehend, subjective issues such as belief and emotion, both of which are central to our current topic. Phenomenology, because it brackets the "truth" of a person's experience, allows scholars to focus on their subjective experience and therefore provide valuable insight into beliefs and emotions. Schutz's work expands phenomenology to explicitly include culture; he sought to combine Husserlian phenomenology with a more sociologically oriented focus on the social world. He used the German term *lebenswelt*, literally "life-world" but usually translated into English as "everyday life" or "ordinary life" and he understood that such examples of what we would call "worldview" are culturally specific (Schutz 1970, 204). Since we are chiefly interested in metal culture, the emotional basis of hanging out, and how this influences people's belief in metal community, Schutz and his style of phenomenology seem good starting places.

Like many phenomenologists before him, especially Husserl and Heidegger, Schutz was particularly concerned with human perceptions of time. Essentially phenomenology argues that there is an objective external time that is measured by clocks (so, for example, such-and-such an event lasted thirty-five minutes), but this is not people's personal experience of time. In fact time is particularly subjective and complex because, although it is always moving forward, we can only "see" it retrospectively. Schutz argues that differences in how people experience time are one of the main reasons that individual experiences are unique, an issue that makes social relations challenging.

INTENTIONALITY AND ITS DISCONTENTS

There is, however, one way in which even Schutz and phenomenology are inadequate to our current needs to discuss the role of hanging out and talking metal in the metal community. This problem is the emphasis on intentionality, a central idea in phenomenology and one that was particularly important to Schutz (1970, 125–28). Within phenomenology intentionality has a specific meaning—what actors are hoping to accomplish through their actions. In Western culture more generally, there is a tendency to devalue activities like hanging out because they seem to lack utilitarian intentions.

The idea of utilitarian goal-related action, elaborated in Max Weber's depiction of the Protestant ethic (1930) is, we argue, particularly Western and American-centric. Weber explains that Protestants (particularly American ones) believed that their lives should be goal-oriented. This worked in both a short-term sense (a focus on acquiring money, for example) and in a long-term sense (in which it is tied to the need to present oneself as pious). And indeed, much action and thought is goal-directed. For example, I (Clinton) am typing this paragraph in order to explain a piece of our larger argument, which will be fleshed out with other paragraphs that explain other pieces of the argument until they become a unified argument that will become a chapter in this book. The goals in writing a book chapter are also fairly obvious—the desire to say something new, to participate in academic discourse, and (more gauchely) to strengthen one's academic position, including one's standing in the University.

However, must all action be truly goal-oriented? Part of the confusion rests in exactly how the term "goal-oriented" is used. What about cases where the goal is personal pleasure? Yes, doing something because it makes you happy could indeed be seen as an example of goal-orientation, but in the United States we rarely do see it that way.

Thus, a truly culturally sensitive inquiry into hanging out would necessarily recognize the cultural specificity of the valorization of goal-directed behavior to the exclusion of alternatives. Such an approach would have to take account of the centrality of hanging out for creating pleasurable experiences of social solidarity among metalheads around the world (i.e., hanging out is valuable for its own sake). Ultimately a theory of metal sociality should also address the remarkable rise and transnational spread of the field of metal studies itself (see Hickam 2014 for an overview). Though this field involves only a tiny handful of individuals, its avoidance (for the most part) of the usual posturing, bitter outsize conflicts, and fissures that accompany the expansion of academic fields is notable. Might it have something to do with a shared metal "stance" (to use Harris Berger's terminology) that underlies interaction?

HANGING OUT IN GLOBAL METAL CULTURE

It is the main contention of this essay that everyday hanging out, by which we mean unofficial and unstructured but sustained social interaction, is the social glue that makes the affirming, supportive communal experiences of heavy metal possible, even more than concerts and other singular, spectacular events.[6] Concerts are not ideal spaces for many kinds of socializing—although there is a strong sense of community at a concert, verbal communication is minimal and necessarily tends to be formulaic (such as head-banging in unison and expressing appreciation of the music through applause and cheering; see Scott 2012 for a discussion of nonverbal embodied expression in metal). Before and after concerts and during intermission verbal communication can and does occur, however. For example, people often comment on one another's T-shirts; sometimes these comments are as simple as saying "nice shirt" in passing, but also as complex as asking if the wearer has seen the band or concert depicted on the shirt and/or comparing previous concert experiences. Since metalheads usually own a lot of band shirts and carefully choose the right shirt to wear to a specific concert (metalheads who go to concerts together often discuss who is wearing what T-shirt before they go so that there won't be duplication or bands from very different subgenres), one of the primary places such conversations occur is at the "merch" tables, where band shirts, patches, banners and the like are sold.[7] Metalheads don't tend to be casual fans, so it's a good bet that the other people at a concert are serious enthusiasts and fans of the band(s).

Like concert attendees and sometimes *as* concert attendees, ethnographers around the world benefit from the hanging out ethos of metal, though in the latters' case, it functions as a stepping stone for their research. This means that their hanging out activities in the field, unlike most of their companions', are explicitly goal-oriented. We suggest that that's one reason why they usually don't try to theorize them as such (another is the teleological bias of Western epistemology, a topic we leave for another day). But the affinity created through talking metal is crucial to their success as ethnographers, and this is perhaps most poignantly illustrated in Donna Gaines' portrayal of 1980s headbangers in Bergen County, New Jersey, where hanging out was nothing less than a youth survival tactic (Gaines 1998).

In *Teenage Wasteland: Suburbia's Dead End Kids*, Gaines describes her sojourns to Bergenfield, New Jersey in the aftermath of the suicide of two local metalheads on the night of March 10, 1987. As one would expect given the fact that the late 1980s were the height of anti-metal hysteria, many puzzled (and, to be fair, deeply concerned) adults blamed the music. Gaines, herself a *Motörhead* and *Led Zeppelin* fan, wasn't convinced, so she went to Bergenfield to meet metalheads and get to know them (something the anti-metal hysterics seem never to have done).

The following passage describes Gaines' first meeting with some local young people and how they begin to trust her and accept her as someone who "gets it."

> Bobby's friend [Gaines uses pseudonyms throughout the book as requested by the people she was working with] spots my Ace of Spades lapel pin. "You like Motorhead [*sic*]?" "Ah, yeah . . . I mean . . . like . . . Lemmy's god . . . " Off guard and completely disoriented, I [Gaines] answer a guy with clumpy layered hair. (58)

Her description of their first meeting continues:

> More talk about music. We compare favorite bands. I ask if they like Metallica. Heads bang back and forth and we play air guitar "Batterr-reee!" Nicky figures yeah, if I like Motorhead [*sic*], I'd probably like Metallica. We are now at a regional hardcore—heavy metal—thrasher convention. What goes on next is a rock and roll version of "Paisan . . . landsman . . . you like Anthrax?" You sniff out cultural heritage. Then you talk. This is the centerpiece of suburban street culture. . . . But music subcults are esoteric. You either know or you don't; you can't fake it. (59)

Finally she explains the effect of this metamusical discourse:

> By now we have established lineage, and favorite bands in common. . . . We agree on Motorhead [*sic*] and Suicidal Tendencies [a thrash metal band from California] and that is enough to establish an understanding. (59–60)

Gaines was talking to "street kids" in Bergenfield. She soon learned that many of them had known the suicide victims and all of them had been interrogated repeatedly by adults. They had no reason to trust Gaines, to expect that she would understand or accept them. However, once a shared musical heritage was established, these kids were willing to accept an adult from the outside. One of the kids actually told Gaines,

"Look, if you just hang out, you'll see everything you'll understand what's going on" (66).

This is a prime example of the power of hanging out with other "insiders" in building community. Because Gaines shared some of their musical tastes (as discussed in her autobiography [2003] 2007), she was accepted as someone who would be willing to consider them people rather than problems, as so many of the other adults around them did. This might account for the concern among metalheads that someone could be, to use Gaines' term, "faking it"—people who misrepresent their musical tastes could be equally disingenuous about their values or self-representations. In the following passage Gaines explains what hanging out means to young people:

> Serious politicos have always gotten annoyed by the idea that kids see their "right to party" as a crucial issue. How can American kids be preoccupied with such trivial issues? But the kids understand their right to party as their right to create, express, and commune. It is a crucial political question for young people. The right to produce and express yourself through culture is essentially a First Amendment issue; it is no less sacred than the freedom of speech, the press, or to assemble peaceably—rights most young people do not fully enjoy. (206)

We agree with Gaines that hanging out provides an important social space in which to meet like-minded people, establish and reinforce friendships, and that it is creative and essential to people's (particularly young people's) well-being. After all, most metalheads become fans of the music as children or teenagers.[8]

Evidence of the importance of hanging out for metalheads isn't limited to the United States and Europe (see, for example, Baka 2015, Elliott and Barron 2015).[9] In his overview of popular music in the Middle East, *Heavy Metal Islam*, Mark LeVine writes that "Egyptian metalheads are one of the most closely knit groups of people I've ever met" (2008, 86). Lena and John Resborn's book of photographs of Southeast Asian metalheads and punks, *Labour of Love and Hate* (2012), includes an interview with Fah, a Thai metal musician and bar owner. He tells the Resborns that, after his band *Carnivora's* performance the night before, he ended up at "an afterparty together with some Germans and some Finnish guys who were so excited to find metal in Bangkok that they had to bond in beers until 4 a.m." (12). Such all-night drinking and socializing sessions, prime examples of what we mean by the term "hanging out," are metal community staples worldwide.

In his excellent book on Turkish metal (*Turkish Metal: Music, Meaning, and Morality in a Muslim Society*), Pierre Hecker (2012, 7–8) reflects on his own positionality in the field:

All in all, the place and atmosphere reminded me of similar places where I had spent much of my youth. In other words, I felt like I was coming home. . . . Though I was a stranger, I felt familiar with the field—the music, the settings, the social practices, and even many of the experiences reported to me during the research. Many of the actors were of a similar age to me (or only slightly younger), had been socialized into metal through the same albums and, in a few cases, had even visited the same festivals in Holland and Germany. Two of my later interviewees, who had been involved in global tape trading, had even been in contact with metalheads in France and Israel, whom I knew personally from participating in the global metal underground.

Hecker's comment about "coming home" brings to mind Schutz's observation that "'To feel at home' is an expression of the highest degree of familiarity and intimacy" (Schutz 1970, 297).

Hecker also includes numerous quotes that attest to the importance of hanging out and hangout spaces for the Turkish metalheads he met. In the following, a young woman reminisces about a specific hangout in Istanbul: "Back then, there was no other rock bar besides the old Kemancı, which was under the bridge. Actually, it was small and totally run-down, where you used to sit on barrels, and there were these kinds of trays on them [instead of tables]." But after sharing this rather unappealing image, she goes on to say, "We used to listen to heavy metal there, and all the metalheads who listened to that kind of music—this was only a handful of people—they used to come to the old Kemancı under the bridge. . . . It had a super atmosphere, although it was totally run-down. It was a dive, but the atmosphere was great. . . . It was like family" (quoted in Hecker 2012, 73).

It is easy to take for granted, but it is a similar shared metal-ness that allowed, for example, Ben Olson to interact with different factions of the Hawai'i metal scene (Olson 2013), Rosemary Overell to hang out with Japanese grindcore fans (Overell 2014), and Marco Ferrarase to converse with members of Malaysian Borneo's traditionalist black metal scene (Ferrarase 2015). And the list goes on; but as valuable and enlightening as ethnographic studies of metal scenes are (and we need many more of them!), they tend to provide us with evidence of the variety of metal socialities in the world and the ability of a sense of metal-ness to travel to the furthest extremes of the planet without necessarily revealing *how* such travel is possible and the processes through which metal scenes are formed in the first place. What is the affective motor that gives rise to a scene? An Indonesian metalhead would have an easy answer to this question: *anak metal ya suka nongkrong bareng-bareng*—metal kids like to all hang out together.

THE INDONESIAN ART OF *NONGKRONG*

During Wallach's Indonesian research (2008), local metalheads gave hanging out (*nongkrong*) and socializing (*pergaulan)* as central reasons for their involvement in the underground music scene. These are core Indonesian concepts that go far beyond the scene itself, but they help us understand how to approach the metal community from a perspective that doesn't start with the atomized individual pursuing goals. Specifically, the centrality of hanging out (*nongkrong)* in Indonesia provides a useful vantage point from which to consider the importance of the hang-out session in metal culture.

Other anthropologists have noted hanging out's importance to Indonesian youth. The following comes from Brent Luvaas' landmark study of Indonesia's DIY/indie scene. Luvaas characterizes hanging out in places like Yogyakarta's Reddoor distro as:

> involv[ing] a kind of continual sociality, an emphasis on being part of the group that goes well beyond what an American observer like myself can readily relate to. The Reddoor kids spent hours a day together, and long alcohol-lubricated nights together. They had little sense of a personal or private life apart from the group, *nor did they want one.* They minimized time alone, often complaining about having to go home. The group was their life, and even in the wee hours of morning, breaking from the group took overcoming some serious inertia. (Luvaas 2012, 77; emphasis added)

One of this chapter's authors has termed this "emphasis on being part of the group" an "ethic of sociality" (Wallach 2008). Another American ethnographer in Indonesia, ethnomusicologist Julia Byl, puts it this way, in her depiction of drinking sessions at street side watering holes in Medan:

> It was difficult to opt for quiet and solitude at night, because the sounds of someone's merrymaking almost always made it through the slotted windows. . . . The palm wine stand is a roadside stall that offers camaraderie, libation, relaxation, and a little, mostly innocent, vice [i.e., small-stakes gambling]. (2014, 173)

None of these examples specifically pertains to metal culture, though metal is a component of the DIY cultural movement written about by Luvaas. Perhaps the best description of the "art of *nongkrong"* comes from an article in *The Jakarta Post* by Tasa Nugraza Barley (2009), an Indonesian graduate student studying in the United States:

> What is nongkrong anyway? It's pretty hard to explain, really. It's so hard that I don't think Oxford English Dictionary has that word in English. "To hang around" might be the right expression in English for nongkrong, while a friend of mine thinks that "to chill out" is the right translation. For Indonesians, nongkrong simply means "to meet and talk, and smoke for some." But nongkrong is basically about talking,

specifically talking with people we're close to. But what do we talk about? Based on my experience of being an Indonesian for more than 20 years, we Indonesians talk "nothing" when we nongkrong. And that's why it's so exciting. "Nothing" here doesn't mean that we don't talk about anything at all, but it actually means that we talk about nothing important. Yes, we talk and talk for hours about things that aren't really important. (2009, n.p.)

It is worth reiterating that none of the above authors were discussing metal fans in Indonesia. However, the centrality of hanging out has been noted in research on Indonesian metal culture specifically in studies by Baulch (2007), Wallach (2008) and most recently in an extraordinary article by Kieran James and Rex Walsh (2015, 42–43), who examine the vast underground metal scene in Bandung, West Java. They interview local band members who describe a scene where participants, united by a shared metal "vision" (or, we suggest, following Berger, shared "stance") support one another, with more experienced bands helping younger ones along. "The [shared] vision extends to the metal community, which includes not only one band but all bands, and hence the ethical obligation extends beyond one's own band to the community" (2015, 42).

This shared vision is, of course, an ideal (see Weinstein's chapter in this volume), and the authors are quick to point out the exclusionary and hierarchical tendencies in the actual practices of the Bandung scene, which include the dominance of older brutal death metal bands and the marginalization of power metal and black metal. These gaping chasms between real and ideal are the norm in metal scenes (for instance, Wallach quickly realized what a letdown it would have been for his new Indonesian friends if they were to find out how fractious, cutthroat, and fragmented the metal scenes in the West really were—including the famous ones like Tampa and Oslo—compared to the ones they built themselves). In spite of these chasms, however, scene members have meaningful experiences that cause them to believe in heavy metal community, and "wishful thinking" or self-delusions are not explanations for the persistence of these beliefs, they are put-downs.

A more rigorous method is required to understand the persistence of belief. Previously, Wallach used the Indonesian culture of *nongkrong* to understand the vibrancy of the Indonesian metal scene. Now we want to use the *nongkrong* concept to understand the lived intensity of worldwide metalhead culture, to add it to our reading of Schutz's social phenomenology.[10]

A UNIFIED THEORY OF HANGING OUT

It is precisely the noisy presence of multiple others who simultaneously command attention that constitutes the most formidable challenge for phenomenology, which was initially focused on the self's sterile intellectual encounter with a passive object and only then has worked gingerly outward toward the inevitable social reality of human existence. Yet phenomenology, with its insistent focus on subjective experience, provides us with the key to our theory of hanging out.

Metalheads' intimate subjective experience of fellowship enters consciousness as a result of a shared stance toward metal and its lessons for living. This perception of "stance-in-common" animates interaction (Berger 2009). Schutz (2004) uses the term "intersubjective time-processes" to describe how people's different time senses coincide when they are engaged in certain communal activities, and he specifically mentions talking together, playing music together, dancing together and making love together. We would add hanging out to this list.

Intersubjective time-processes are important because people achieve the highest degree of mutual understanding when their senses of time coincide. Schutz explains that:

> this sharing of the other's flux of experiences in inner time, this living through a vivid present in common, constitutes . . . the mutual tuning-in relationship, the experience of the "We," which is at the foundation of all possible communication. (Schutz 2004, 210)

In other words, Schutz believes that sociality is possible because sometimes, under certain conditions, people transcend their individuality through achieving a mutually acknowledged recognition of each other's subjective humanity by sharing a vivid present.

Such experiences of a mutually shared vivid present are, like many experiences of hanging out, difficult to fully recollect after the fact. We argue that this is because, as in the case of religious/spiritual experiences, for example, the emotional effect can only be felt in the moment—when the moment ends, so does the specific feeling of community.

Philosopher David Carr, himself an eminent phenomenologist, in an essay titled, *Alfred Schutz and the Project of Phenomenological Social Theory*, has criticized Schutz's ideal as too mild-mannered to capture the emotional intensity of actual social interactions (Carr 1994). Carr's critique of Schutz's social phenomenology hinges on what he views as the atypically mild, moderate contexts of Schutz's preferred hypothetical examples, the conversation and the string quartet. Carr contends that in more emotionally heightened, extreme circumstances, relationships of mutual in-tuneness are less salient to social encounters. At first, we found this to be a formidable critique; after all, metal provides its listeners with emotionally heightened experiences and is generally considered to provide a more intense experience than string quartet music. Upon further reflection, though, we began to wonder if Carr is a musician (as Schutz in fact was).[11] No matter how loud they are, a successful metal ensemble needs to play in a tightly synchronized fashion, every bit as coordinated as an effective string quartet. A metal performance is more akin to an intense conversation where the parties are truly listening to one another than a shrill, contentious argument where communication has broken down. Schutz's social phenomenology may in fact be (probably is) inadequate as a model for social relations when dialogue has failed, but as a model for successful musical performance and a satisfying hangout session, the kind of bonding between strangers that keeps you up all night,[12] it holds up.

From the Indonesian example we might grasp the fact that the fundamental feature of the hangout session is not the "content" of the communicative gestures exchanged back and forth, but the pleasure derived from the fact of sharing within a common temporal context. Furthermore, in a context where sociality for its own sake is valued, it becomes possible to appreciate not only what the dominant occidental cultural order loses with its fixation on individual achievement at the expense of communal solidarity, but also why the metal underground has been so successful and long-lived in Southeast Asia despite extremely limited financial rewards for even the most stalwart and accomplished scene members.[13]

T-SHIRTS AND TALK

Metalheads the world over have figured out how to create instant heavy metal community away from gigs, even in the complete absence of heavy metal music—the metal T-shirt. Since the early 1980s, heavy metal T-shirts have been among the most important circulating meaningful objects in global metal culture (Berg et al. 2015; Donahue 2011). At his presentation opening the University of Puerto Rico's symposium on heavy metal and the communal experience, Nelson Varas-Díaz (2014) demonstrated how T-shirts signal communal allegiance, using videos by local metal band *Tavú* and a local salsa group in which members were wearing one another's shirts, signaling an allegiance to a Puerto Rican music community that transcends genre. The Indonesian case is similar, and in an October 2014 presentation at the College of Musical Arts at Bowling Green State University Wallach showed a video by *Gugat*, a Bandung group that wore shirts with *Slayer* and *Burgerkill* logos on them, the latter band being Indonesia's and Bandung's most famous metal outfit. Thus both global and local metal allegiances were signaled.[14]

As we saw in the previous discussion regarding concert behavior, T-shirts are more than just an invitation to dialogue, they are an *incitement* to dialogue, to heavy metal communion. When the Indonesian metal band *Seringai* opened for *Metallica* at its August 2013 concert in Jakarta, the band members knew it would be a challenge to catch the headliners' attention backstage. Their solution was to "let the T-shirts do the talking," according to guitarist Ricky Siahaan (pers. comm. October 9, 2014) by wearing shirts of bands they knew the guys in *Metallica* liked and would comment on.

While hanging out unquestionably constitutes an arena of contestation and an opportunity to display one's subcultural capital, that's not all it is; in fact *if* that's all it is, the hangout session quickly becomes tedious. The key ingredient, so to speak, is the pleasure one feels in the company of likeminded others. This pleasure, unlike that gained from the status bump resulting from the successful deployment of subcultural capital, is not derived from competition. Popular culture, including heavy metal (and to suggest that metal is anything other than popular culture is wishful thinking[15]) traffics in Romantic fantasy. That is one of its crucial functions in the modern world. What critics of popular culture fail to appreciate is how credible those fantasies become when they acquire a social dimension, and the utopias they promise begin shimmering in real spaces and times, maybe even palpable for a fleeting instant. Which brings us back to metal.

The single most comprehensive set of studies on the positive, supportive activities of metal community is led by Nelson Varas-Díaz and his research team (Varas-Díaz and Rivera-Segarra 2014; Varas-Díaz et al. 2014; 2015). Their unprecedented longitudinal study of the Puerto Rican metal scene provides strong empirical evidence for what cultural insiders have known for decades but often could not persuade outsiders to accept: "Our results evidence the importance of the communal experience among metal fans in Puerto Rico. Core scene members scored high on sense of community . . . demonstrating its importance for LMS [Local Metal Scene] members" (Varas-Díaz et al. 2014a, 98). Varas-Díaz et al. continue, "These results highlight the positive implications of community formation for members of the LMS and stress that the group cohesiveness formed extends beyond mere entertainment and *includes instrumental support in times of need*" (98–99, emphasis added). Such claims seemed so farfetched prior to the existence of independent empirical support in part because there doesn't seem to be anything particularly community-affirming about listening to music (let alone music about violence, death and destruction) if one accepts the standard western view of listening as an individualized, discrete, goal-directed activity. This is the paradigmatic assumption of most music theory, philosophical treatises on music (other than Schutz's), and a surprising number of sociological and psychological studies of music listeners. Once again, not only are the social foundations of all musical behavior elided, the act of listening is sequestered and impoverished by this assumption (and distinctly "unmetal").

Metal, as a recorded popular music artifact, is an unconsummated possibility. The necessarily social process of its production must be met by a social process of reception that unites listeners into cohesive collectivities. The experience of listening to metal is not meant to be contemplative and solitary; it is rather one of shared affective overdrive (Wallach, Berger, and Greene 2011) that compels the listener to share her reactions with co-listeners, with others who *get it*. In this way the music *catalyzes* community, even where there was none before, even at times across seemingly unbridgeable gulfs of nationality, religion, race, gender, class, sexuality and dis/ability.[16] Participants encounter each other in a shared temporal framework and realize they hold in common a metal stance on music and the world and through that recognition see each other as thinking, feeling beings. Hanging out, then, promotes not just metalhead identity and community but human fellowship.[17]

REIMAGINING METAL COMMUNITY

In Anderson's classic formulation (1983), the simultaneity of consumption is an abstract realization that accompanies individuated acts of reading novels and newspapers. We propose instead to view cultural reception (such as listening to metal) as a concrete, interactive social process, which leads to a conception of community along different lines than Anderson's imagined one. We maintain that the hangout session itself, an affective, overdriven extension—a *spillover*, if you will—of the metal music performance, makes the vision of a polyphonic, diverse, sometimes dissonant collectivity conceivable. In other words, metal's imagined community is rooted in the lived experience of not only listening to the music but talking about it while hanging out with other metalheads.

It is easy to claim, as many detractors have, that assertions regarding heavy metal communities are exaggerated or overly idealistic. But this is not the same thing as stemming from false consciousness. To dismiss such claims outright is not to be hardheaded and logical, it is to commit a logical *error* of false equivalence. We have demonstrated the experiential mechanisms that underlie feelings of communal belonging in metal scenes. We have also suggested that experience has its own validity and cultural researchers (especially metal scholars) must take it seriously.

NOTES

1. In German, Schütz's name is spelled with an umlaut. We follow most English-language sources, including the *Stanford Encyclopedia of Philosophy*, in omitting the umlaut, though admittedly it's not very metal to do so.

2. The scholar most identified with bringing phenomenological approaches into ethnomusicology and folklore, Harris M. Berger, is well known in metal studies circles for his groundbreaking research on heavy metal music and culture. In a series of articles and monographs that often draws on metal music case studies, Berger argues that experience is the irreducible unit of analysis for the meanings of expressive culture (Berger 1997, 1999a, 1999b, 2004, 2009; Berger and Fales 2005). In a future work we hope to apply Berger's theories more directly to our line of research.

3. Interestingly, when Schutz discusses semiotics, he refers not to de Saussure but to Dewey and James. This is particularly striking given Schutz's European origins.

4. We use the female pronoun to protest phenomenology's too frequent use of male pronouns as gender neutral (or, given the approach's extensive use of the male pronoun, the assumption that only males are conscious), found in both Husserl and Schutz.

5. Schutz's thought and writing, though deeply influenced by phenomenology and particularly Husserl, was built on multiple influences, including Weberian and Durkheimian sociology, Malinowskian anthropology, and the theories of American pragmatists Dewey and James.

6. See Riches, Lashua, and Spracklen (2014) for an account of the metal gig as a spectacular event in a modified Debordian sense. There are many communities in metal that only exist in cyberspace, and others where the Internet sustains metalheads' personal relationships during periods of physical separation. We leave it up to the reader whether or not our arguments are applicable to these cases; in this essay, we focus on face-to-face communities.

7. For more on the importance of T-shirts in metal culture, see Donahue 2011 and Berg, et al. 2015; on customized denim "battle jackets" see Hellyar-Caldwell 2015.

8. In summer 2014, Anna Baka interviewed metalheads at central European metal festivals about when they became fans of the music and what they valued about it. Out of fifty-two interviewees, sixteen, or almost 30 percent, became fans as children; thirty, or almost 60 percent, became metal fans as teenagers; and only six, less than 12 percent, became fans as adults (Baka 2015).

9. Elliott and Barron (2015) performed a quantitative analysis of why people attended Download Festival, a British music festival that specializes in hard rock and heavy metal held in Leicestershire, in 2014. An astonishing 72 percent of informants strongly agreed that they went to the festival "To be with friends," almost half again as many as those who strongly agreed that they went to the festival "Because it is stimulating and exciting" (51.5 percent). It is also worth noting that the potential answer "Because it is stimulating and exciting" does not specify what about the festival is stimulating and exciting. For many festival goers, the stimulation and excitement may be as much in hanging out with the other people at the festival as in seeing the bands.

10. To be sure, others have trod before us a similar, if not identical, path. The most significant scholar to interpret Indonesian cultures with an approach derived from Schutzian social phenomenology was of course none other than Clifford Geertz (1973). And Steven Feld first made a name for himself in American ethnomusicology by (among other things) combining Geertzian cultural anthropology with a Durkheimian emphasis on collective sentiment (1982). While no one has previously discussed sociality, experience, and collective affect in the context of global metal culture to our knowledge, many of Feld's most prominent students, not to mention Feld himself, have extended his insights, developed in the context of ethnographic research in a smallscale Papuan society, in the realm of popular music (see Feld 2012, Fox 2004, Meintjes 2003, Porcello 1998, Samuels 2004). There are many reasons for this; we would suggest that one explanation for this relatively smooth transition from small-scale musicking to mass-mediated grooves is the similarity of affective investment entailed in the social and musical practices under investigation. Returning to the source, as it were, of Schutz's writings allows us to confront a perennial issue in metal community, albeit one that both Geertz and Feld in their most famous work manage to sidestep through their adherence to an impersonal, superorganic anthropological culture concept. Anthropology has since moved well beyond this paradigm and embraced heterogeneous, dynamic, contestatory models, and we argue that metal culture is one of the most fertile sites in the modern world to investigate the productive, unresolvable tension between individual freedom of expression and the ties of communal belonging that characterize all contemporary complex stratified social formations.

11. We also wonder if Carr, an eminent phenomenologist in his own right, mistook Schutz's deliberate, precise writing for "mildness." It seems to us that there is a lot of passion and interest behind Schutz's deliberate writing style. But proving such a contention is beyond the scope of the present essay.

12. There is even an Indonesian word meaning "to stay up all night talking": *begadang*.

13. A notable exception is Bandung scene veterans *Burgerkill* who have risen from the DIY underground to rock star status in their own country and, more recently, to international acclaim (Hutabarat and Kusumah 2015; James and Walsh 2015; Luvaas 2012, 53).

14. Perhaps the most striking article of clothing (to Indonesian as well as foreign viewers) in the Gugat clip is not a T-shirt at all but the Muslim headscarf worn by singer Acie, the sole female in the group. This garment signifies membership in the *umat* (Indonesian for the worldwide Islamic community).

15. Harbert (2013) argues that in Egypt metal should be considered more an avant-garde musical critique than a popular music, yet his excellent case study reveals a conscientious attention to metal's proliferating subgenres and reverence for an international metal music canon among Egyptian metalheads. These scenic features are highly characteristic of popular music subcultures, not avant-gardes that reject both genre and canon in the service of radical critique.

16. These categories are always contested, of course, in a never-ending dance of inclusion and exclusion. The literature on metal culture, identity and difference is extensive; key texts include Clifford-Napoleone 2015; Dawes 2012; Fellezs 2015; Riches, Lashua and Spracklen 2014; Varas-Díaz et al. 2014a; 2014b; and numerous others.

17. This project benefitted from hanging out with a bunch of people over many years. The authors wish to thank: Kara Attrep, Bryan Bardine, Harry Berger, Andy Brown, Laina Dawes, Matt Donahue, Kevin Ebert, Kevin Fellezs, Paul Greene, Brian Hickam, Keith Kahn-Harris, Lauren Kolenko, Michael Lohr, Brent Luvaas, Kathy Meizel, Sarah Morelli, Wendi Putranto, Niall Scott, Ricky Siahaan, Dan Shoemaker, Arian Tigabelas, Nelson Varas-Díaz, Rob Wallace, and especially Deena Weinstein. We also warmly thank Donna Gaines for reading and commenting on an earlier draft of this essay.

REFERENCES

Anderson, Benedict. 1983. *Imagined Communities: Reflections on the Origin and Spread of Nationalism*. London: Verso.

Baka, Anna. 2015. "The Forming of a Metalhead: Constructing a Subcultural Identity." In *Modern Heavy Metal: Markets, Practices and Cultures*, edited by Toni-Matti Karjalainen and Kimi Kärki, 55–63. Helsinki: Aalto University School of Business.

Barley, Tasa Nugraza. 2009. "How 'Nongkrong' Is Part of Our Culture." *The Jakarta Post*, January 20, www.thejakartapost.com/news/2009/01/20/view-point-how-%E2%80%98nongkrong%E2%80%99-part-our-culture.html#sthashBHRgnZRS.dpuf.

Baulch, Emma. 2007. *Making Scenes: Reggae, Punk, and Death Metal in 1990s Bali*. Durham: Duke University Press.

Berg, Arild, Tore Gulden, Viktor Hiort af Ornäs, Nenad Pavel, and Vibeke Sjøvoll. 2015. "The Metal T-Shirt: Transmedia Storytelling in Products." In *Modern Heavy Metal: Markets, Practices and Cultures*, edited by Toni-Matti Karjalainen and Kimi Kärki, 174–184. Helsinki: Aalto University School of Business.

Berger, Harris M. 1997. "The Practice of Perception: Multi-Functionality and Time in the Musical Experiences of a Heavy Metal Drummer." *Ethnomusicology* 41(3): 464–88.

———. 1999a. *Metal, Rock, and Jazz: Perception and the Phenomenology of Musical Experience*. Middletown, CT: Wesleyan University Press.

———. 1999b. "Death Metal Tonality and the Act of Listening." *Popular Music* 18(2): 161–78.

———. 2004. "Horizons of Melody and the Problem of the Self." In *Identity and Everyday Life: Essays in the Study of Folklore, Music, and Popular Culture*, by Harris M. Berger and Giovanna P. Del Negro, 43–88. Middletown, CT: Wesleyan University Press.

———. 2009. *Stance: Ideas About Emotion, Style, and Meaning for the Study of Expressive Culture*. Middletown, CT: Wesleyan University Press.

Berger, Harris M., and Cornelia Fales. 2005. "'Heaviness' in the Perception of Heavy Metal Guitar Timbres: The Match of Perceptual and Acoustic Features over Time." In *Wired for Sound: Engineering and Technologies in Sonic Cultures*, edited by Paul D. Greene and Thomas Porcello, 181–97. Middletown, CT: Wesleyan University Press.

Byl, Julia. 2014. *Antiphonal Histories: Resonant Pasts in the Toba Batak Musical Present.* Middletown, CT: Wesleyan University Press.

Carr, David. 1994. "Alfred Schutz and the Project of Phenomenological Social Theory." In *Phenomenology of the Cultural Disciplines*, edited by Mano Daniel and Lester Embree, 319–332. Boston: Kluwer Academic Publishers.

Clifford-Napoleone, Amber R. 2015. *Queerness in Heavy Metal: Metal Bent*. New York: Routledge.

Dawes, Laina. 2012. *What Are You Doing Here? A Black Woman's Life and Liberation in Heavy Metal*. New York: Bazillion Points Press.

Donahue, Matthew A. 2011. "The Heavy Metal T-Shirt in Popular Culture and Beyond." Paper presented at the *International Association for the Study of Popular Music—US Branch Annual Conference*, Cincinnati, Ohio, March 11, 2011.

Durkheim, Émile. [1912] 1995. *The Elementary Forms of the Religious Life*. New York: Free Press.

Elliott, Caitlin and Paul Barron, 2015. "Escape To Mayhem? Toward an Understanding of Attendees' Motivations at a Heavy Metal Festival." In *Modern Heavy Metal: Markets, Practices and Cultures*, edited by Toni-Matti Karjalainen and Kimi Kärki, 38– 45. Helsinki: Aalto University School of Business.

Feld, Steven. 1982. *Sound and Sentiment: Birds, Weeping, Poetics, and Song in Kaluli Expression*. Philadelphia: University of Pennsylvania Press.

———. 2012. *Jazz Cosmopolitanism in Accra: Five Musical Years in Ghana*. Durham: Duke University Press.

Fellezs, Kevin. 2015. "Talk Shit, Get Shot: Body Count, Black Masculinity, and Metal Music Culture." In *Modern Heavy Metal: Markets, Practices and Cultures*, edited by Toni-Matti Karjalainen and Kimi Kärki, 283–90. Helsinki: Aalto University School of Business.

Ferrarese, Marco. 2015. "Eastern Desekratorz and Nuclear Metal Lust: Performing 'Authentic' Black Metal in Malaysian Borneo." *Metal Music Studies* 2(1): 211–32.

Fox, Aaron. 2004. *Real Country: Music and Language in Working-Class Culture*. Durham: Duke University Press.

Gaines, Donna. 1998 *Teenage Wasteland: Suburbia's Dead End Kids*. 1991. 2nd ed. Chicago: University of Chicago Press.

———. [2003] 2007. *A Misfit's Manifesto: The Sociological Memoir of a Rock & Roll Heart*. New Brunswick: Rutgers University Press.

Geertz, Clifford. 1973. *The Interpretation of Cultures*. New York: Basic Books.

Harbert, Benjamin J. 2013. "Noise and Its Formless Shadows: Egypt's Extreme Metal as Avant-Garde *Nafas Dawsha*." In *The Arab Avant-Garde: Music, Politics, Modernity*, edited by Thomas Burkhalter, Kay Dickinson, and Benjamin J. Harbert, 229–72. Middletown, CT: Wesleyan University Press.

Hecker, Pierre. 2012. *Turkish Metal: Music, Meaning, and Morality in a Muslim Society*. Farnham, UK: Ashgate.

Hellyar-Caldwell, Tom. 2015. "Battle Jackets, Craft and Folk Culture: Research Through Creative Practice." In *Modern Heavy Metal: Markets, Practices and Cultures*, edited by Toni-Matti Karjalainen and Kimi Kärki, 138–49. Helsinki: Aalto University School of Business.

Hickam, Brian. 2014. "Amalgated Anecdotes: Perspectives on the History of Metal Music and Culture Studies." *Metal Music Studies* 1 (1), 5–23.

Hufford, David. 1982. *The Terror That Comes in the Night: An Experience-Centered Study of Supernatural Assault Traditions*. Philadelphia: University of Pennsylvania Press.

Hutabarat, Felencia, and Iman Rahman Anggawiria Kusumah. 2015. "Market Development Using Community Shared Values: The Story of Burgerkill." In *Modern Heavy Metal: Markets, Practices and Cultures*, edited by Toni-Matti Karjalainen and Kimi Kärki, 532–43. Helsinki: Aalto University School of Business.

James, Kieran, and Rex Walsh. 2015. "Bandung Rocks, Cibinong Shakes: Economics and Applied Ethics within the Indonesian Death-metal Community." *Musicology Australia* 37(1): 28–46.

Kahn-Harris, Keith. 2007. *Extreme Metal: Music and Culture on the Edge*. Oxford: Berg.

LeVine, Mark. 2008. *Heavy Metal Islam: Rock, Resistance, and the Struggle for the Soul of Islam*. New York: Three Rivers Press.

Luvaas, Brent. 2012. *DIY Style: Fashion, Music and Global Digital Cultures*. New York: Berg.

Meintjes, Louise. 2003. *Sound of Africa! Making Music Zulu in a South African Studio*. Durham: Duke University Press.

Olson, Benjamin Hedge. 2013. *This Isn't Paradise, This Is Hell: Discourse, Performance and Identity in the Hawai`i Metal Scene*. PhD Dissertation, University of Hawai'i–Manoa.

Overell, Rosemary. 2014. *Affective Intensities in Extreme Music Scenes: Cases from Australia and Japan*. New York: Palgrave Macmillan.

Porcello, Thomas. 1998. "'Tails Out': Social Phenomenology and the Ethnographic Representation of Technology in Music-Making." *Ethnomusicology* 42(3): 485–510.

Resborn, Lena, and John Resborn. 2012. *Labour of Love and Hate: An Underground Musical Journey through Southeast Asia*. Malmö, Sweden: Bullseye.

Riches, Gabrielle, Brett Lashua, and Karl Spracklen. 2014. "Female, Mosher, Transgressor: "A 'Moshography' of Transgressive Practices within the Leeds Extreme Metal Scene." *Journal of the International Association for the Study of Popular Music* 4(1): 87–100.

Samuels, David. 2004. *Putting a Song on Top of It: Expression and Identity on the San Carlos Apache Reservation*. Tucson: University of Arizona Press.

Schutz, Alfred. 1962. *Collected Papers I: The Problem of Social Reality*. Edited by Maurice Natanson. Boston: Martinus Nijhoff Publishers.

Schutz, Alfred. 1970. *Alfred Schutz on Phenomenology and Social Relations*. Edited by Helmut Wagner. Chicago: University of Chicago Press.

Schutz, Alfred. [1951] 2004. "Making Music Together." In *Popular Music: Critical Concepts in Media and Cultural Studies*, Vol. 1: *Music and Society*, edited by Simon Frith, 197–212. New York: Routledge.

Scott, Niall W. R. 2012. "'Politics?! Nah, Fuck Politics Man!' What Can We Expect from Metal Gods?" In *Reflections in the Metal Void*, edited by Niall W. R. Scott, 215–21. Oxford, UK: Inter-Disciplinary Press.

Siahaan, Ricky (musician), discussion with authors, New York City, October 9, 2014.

Varas-Díaz, Nelson. 2014. "Heavy Metal Music and the Communal Experience." In *Heavy Metal Music and the Communal Experience Academic Conference*, University of Puerto Rico–Rio Piedras, San Juan, March 5.

Varas-Díaz, Nelson, Osvaldo González, Eliut Rivera-Segarra, and Sigrid Mendoza. 2015. *The Distorted Island: Heavy Metal Music and Community in Puerto Rico*. DIY Documentary Film.

Varas-Díaz, Nelson and Eliut Rivera-Segarra. 2014. "Heavy Metal Music in the Caribbean Setting: Politics and Language at the Periphery." In *Hardcore, Punk, and Other Junk: Aggressive Sounds in Contemporary Music*, edited by Eric James Abbey and Colin Helb, 73–90. Lanham, MD: Lexington Books.

Varas-Díaz, Nelson, Eliut Rivera-Segarra, Carmen L. Rivera Medina, Sigrid Mendoza, and Osvaldo González-Sepúlveda. 2014a. "Predictors of Communal Formation in a Small Heavy Metal Scene: Puerto Rico as a Case Study." *Metal Music Studies* 1 (1): 87–103.

Wagner, Helmut. 1970. "Introduction." In *Alfred Schutz on Phenomenology and Social Relations*, edited by Helmut Wagner, 1–50. Chicago: University of Chicago Press.

Wallach, Jeremy. 2008. *Modern Noise, Fluid Genres: Popular Music in Indonesia, 1997–2001*. Madison, WI: University of Wisconsin Press.

Wallach, Jeremy, Harris M. Berger, and Paul D. Greene. 2011. "Affective Overdrive, Scene Dynamics, and Identity in the Global Metal Scene." In *Metal Rules the Globe: Heavy Metal Music Around the World*, edited by Jeremy Wallach, Harris M. Berger, and Paul D. Greene, 3–33. Durham, NC: Duke University Press.

Wallach, Jeremy and Alexandra Levine. 2011. "'I Want *You* to Support Local Metal': A Theory of Metal Scene Formation." *Popular Music History* 6(1/2): 119–39.

Weber, Max. 1930. *The Protestant Ethic and the Spirit of Capitalism*. New York: Routledge.

Part 2

Strengthening Community

FOUR

Ride Between Hell and Paradise

Imaginaerum as Mental Anchoring Place for the Global Nightwish Fan Community

Toni-Matti Karjalainen

Music becomes meaningful through personal experience. The consumption of music however entails strong social characteristics and practices. If strong enough, they may lead to formation of particular communities around and within certain popular music genres. For instance, the heavy metal genre has often been reported to involve strong sense of community among the fans in different parts of the world (e.g., Wallach, Berger, and Greene 2011; Karjalainen and Kärki 2015). Metal communities however are not coherent or similar. Metal is divided into numerous subgenres (such as thrash, death, black, power, doom, industrial, folk, progressive, and symphonic metal), and specific communities occur around them (e.g., Venkatesh et al. 2015). There are also local communities being formed, in particular geographical spots (e.g., Varas-Díaz et al. 2014), as well as transnational communities that are active particularly through different social media outlets (e.g., Urbaniak 2014). Such transnational and global communities are also constructed based on fandom around a particular band. Transnational communities exist both for the big names of global metal, such as *Metallica* and *Iron Maiden*, but also for a smaller and more marginal bands.

The serious—"diehard" or "hardcore"—fans of a band form a community that can even be described as a subculture of its own, inasmuch as that community provides its members with particular meanings and practices that further structure their identities, actions and relationships.

Or, instead of a subculture, it may be more accurate to describe these communities as symbolic tribes. When subcultures are more rigid and prevalent, tribes may occur as more flexible communities—global fan communities typically are not consistently definable; are very varied in terms of demographics and are not tied to certain places. I resort to the notion of Cova and Cova (2002, 598): "Tribes exist in no other form but the symbolically and ritually manifest commitment of their members." Hence, individuals can represent very different subcultures, but together form a rather coherent tribe. However, there needs to be something that keeps the commitment of the tribe members alive, like fans of a band in our case, and glues them together to form a community. As Cova and Cova (2002, 598) further note, "(re)construction or (re)possession of meanings through shared experiences and their enactment through rituals is the most potent form of maintaining tribal identity in our postmodern societies." Tribes may be held together essentially through shared emotion and passion; they are inherently unstable, small-scale, and affectual (Maffesoli 1996).

As suggested in the beginning, music consumption is also an individual experience, perhaps even predominantly, as it is often dictated by personal motives. The personal dimension suggestively is emphasized within the context of hardcore fandom, as it follows from a strong personal commitment in the music and its presenters. Then questions arise: what are then the shared experiences and rituals that extend personal fandom into a larger communal phenomenon? Furthermore, are these experiences mainly grounded on the discourse of individual interpretations, or are there some "universal" meanings the fans derive from music, lyrics, and other artifacts—a collectively experienced narrative, in other words? How is the experiential core of fan tribe, the sense of belonging to a larger narrative, then formed? How and where is this narrative enacted? And can the producers and performers of the music write this narrative upfront and hence generate some affordances to tribal experiences?

To address these questions, in this chapter I will explore the global fan community of the Finnish symphonic metal/rock band *Nightwish*. I explore the personal experience and construction of *Nightwish* fandom, as well as the shared experiences and rituals that build up the global fan tribe of the same band. The focus is on hardcore fans that, as will be shown, indeed form a community that incorporates characteristics of a global tribe that is symbolically manifest even though it consists of heterogeneous members with rather different backgrounds. In a broad sense, first of all, I review *Nightwish*-related experiences, personal and shared. Secondly, some tribal rituals at *Nightwish* concerts and, in particular, within the narrative of the *Imaginaerum* album of *Nightwish* are discussed. As it turns out, the *Imaginaerum* narrative and its connections to the larger *Nightwish* "universe" seem to have key role in creating shared communal experience among the band's fans.

Nightwish is a Finnish symphonic metal band formed in 1996 in Kitee, Finland. The band has sold millions of records worldwide and regularly plays for audiences of several thousands. In addition to Finland, *Nightwish* has gained most of its international success in mainland Europe and in some South American countries, but the recent world tours have reached all the continents. It has a truly global fanbase that is also actively engaged in band-related discussions in various forums, for instance on their Facebook site that has over 4.3 million likes at the time of writing this piece.

RESEARCH FOCUS AND DATA

My specific focus is on the *Imaginaerum* concept of *Nightwish* that was realized through the music album (2011), feature film (2012), and the *Imaginaerum* World Tour (2012–2013). *Imaginaerum* was first concretized by a concept album telling a story of an old composer who goes through his youth on his deathbed. The songs of the album, and different acts of the film, articulate different parts and emotions of the story.

My core data consists of the stories and comments collected from hardcore *Nightwish* fans, primarily by email. The fans wrote about their personal experiences and interpretations concerning *Nightwish*, in general, and the *Imaginaerum* music album and film, in particular. The stories also comprised experiences from the live concerts of the *Imaginaerum* World Tour, and additional notes on *Nightwish*-related issues. The fans were recruited through an announcement on the official Facebook page of Tuomas Holopainen, the keyboardist, mastermind and main songwriter of the band.

Eventually, I received written narratives from over seventy fans representing twenty-nine nationalities. They varied from brief comments to lengthy reviews and analyses. In addition, I interviewed, and chatted with, a number of other fans in connection to the live concerts that I attended (in total twelve shows in Finland, Holland, Germany, Belgium, France, and Japan) or met in other instances in different countries.

Of the fans included in the (email) study, 75 percent were females and 25 percent men. The age of the informants varied between 15 and 55, the average being 27 years. The length of their *Nightwish* fandom was in average 6.7 years, spread from one to thirteen years. I also asked them to rate on a scale from 1 to 10, how serious *Nightwish* fans they consider they are. Answers ranged between 6 and 10; the average was 8.5. As this was well above the average (over 5), it is rather safe to consider this group as hardcore fans of the band.

I asked the fans to write about their connection to the band. Specifically, 1) When and how did they discover it?, 2) How did their fandom
evolve?, 3) Why do they like *Nightwish* and what do they particularly like
about in the band?, 4) What does *Nightwish* mean to them?, and 5) What
are their favorite albums and songs? In terms of the *Imaginaerum* concept,
I asked them to describe, in concrete or abstract terms: 1) What kind of
place is *Imaginaerum* in their eyes?, 2) What is its mood and feeling?, 3)
What is the story about?, 4) What kind of associations does it bring to
their mind?, and 5) What are the songs, lyrics, sounds, and details that
they find the most captivating and important? Furthermore, I also asked
how does the story work in the context of their own culture or country,
and whether they see the story as connected to a particular culture or
country, or as a mere universal theme.

Texts were analyzed using various elemental methods (Saldaña 2009):
structural coding to identify segments of data relating to the specific
research questions above, descriptive coding to identify other emerging
topics in the data, and in vivo (literal) coding to explore terms and expressions used by the respondents themselves. In this chapter, I discuss
four categories that resulted from this initial analysis and were related to
the main topics of community formation. These include: 1) *Nightwish* as
personal experience, 2) *Nightwish* as universal experience, 3) *Nightwish*
concerts as communal meetings, and 4) *Imaginaerum* as an anchoring
place for the global *Nightwish* tribe. Selected quotes from the fan interviews are included in this article to highlight the main categories and
themes of discussion.

NIGHTWISH AS PERSONAL EXPERIENCE

> Nightwish have a very unique place in my heart, they somehow em-
> body what music is for me. (British fan, 19 years, female)

First of all, the data clearly shows that *Nightwish* fandom is constructed
around particularly strong personal experiences. Every interviewee expressed the importance of the band and their music in their everyday life,
particularly in terms of emotional reward it brings along. The stories of
the hardcore fans included numerous examples of experiences that go far
beyond solely the music listening pleasure.

> They're the corner stone of my life. I don't know where I'd be without
> getting addicted to them, but it would certainly be worse than right
> here, right now. (Finnish fan, 19 years, male)

Such strong experiences were often connected to the temporary strong
feelings and moods brought by the music. Both positive and negative
feelings were included. This tension of low and high feelings, desperation

Figure 4.1. Tuomas Holopainen and his Imaginaerum keyboard covered in smoke. Forest National Arena in Brussels, Belgium, on April 16, 2012. Photo by Toni-Matti Karjalainen.

and joy, darkness and light, hell and paradise, was constantly present in many fan descriptions:

> I can find a Nightwish song, no matter in what mood I am. If I'm sad, happy or whatever, there is always a song that feels right in this moment. In hard times, music gives me the power to keep on and with Nightwish, especially *Imaginaerum*, I can close my eyes and go to another world. There is so much cruelty in this world and the music lets me dream about a better place. (German fan, 24 years, female)

The latter aspect of the quote above highlights another dominant feature, or mental consequence, of *Nightwish* music: it provides an outlet for escaping from the real world to the world of dreaming and fantasies. One Italian fan actually wrote her own poem to describe her feelings about the *Imaginaerum* experience and commented on it: "these words are dictated

by my heart . . . my soul cried when I listened to the album, I don't want
to stop dreaming, never ever." The musical and lyrical focus of *Nightwish*
on the fantasy, rich visual imagery, imagination, and, in overall, escapism, is also the primary intention of the songwriter Tuomas Holopainen,
as discussed in many of my interviews with him. And indeed, this emotional escapism seems to be one of the main mental motivations of the
hardcore *Nightwish* fandom.

> The music allows me to escape. (US fan, 55 years, female)

Nightwish seems to provide a kind of a personal sanctuary for the fans;
they describe the music taking them to a place that is in terms of feelings,
somehow familiar and friendly, almost home-like, despite the recognized
scary environments and gloomy moods that are also felt being part of the
Nightwish narrative.

> Somehow this band is the only one who can give me the feeling that
> I'm home and safe while I'm listening to them. I maybe sounds weird,
> but it's true. (Hungarian fan, 22 years, female)

This feeling of familiarity is increased by the particular repeated features
and signature environments that Holopainen has crafted to the *Nightwish*
lyrics and sound. He encodes particular narrative references to the songs
that the hardcore fans, based on their *Nightwish* experience and knowledge, can then decode from the stories and associate themselves with the
storyline more effectively.

Overall, the fans describe their *Nightwish* relationship as a very fundamental and holistic experience. The music and the stories trigger a large
arsenal of diverse feelings for many, and bring forth a range of personal
memories connected to either their earlier *Nightwish* encounters or even
many experiences of the fans' personal histories that are seemingly disconnected from the band and its music.

> For me it [Nightwish] means memories, feelings, message, fantasy,
> wishes, magic, loneliness, desire, love, stories, sorrow, hope, power,
> beauty, anger, joy. (Slovakian fan, 28 years, female)

Indeed, more than momentary pleasure and repeated emotional experiences tied to listening to the music, *Nightwish* seemed to have a far larger
impact on most of the fans. The band and their music were often described as a central aspect of the fans' everyday life. The *Nightwish* fandom has become a way of life for them; an aspect that, in their experience,
has shaped their personality and attitude toward life, even becoming the
core contents of their everyday life.

> A life without Nightwish is thinkable, but useless! (German fan, 41
> years, female)

There also appears to be a specific "transformative" power in the experience of the *Nightwish* music. The data included stories from many long-

term fans who had "lived with" the band for several years, along with their personal upswings and downturns. Fandom had provided them some meaningful contexts, especially in difficult moments, even worked as a media for processing severe emotional issues and for self-development.

> For me personally, Nightwish isn't just a band, neither just a word. Nightwish is the way of living . . . it's a sentence of life. Tuomas Holopainen is my hero. . . . I also consider him as a supernatural being. . . . Nightwish is my life. It has saved me and also changed for better. I don't know where I would be now if not Nightwish. (Polish fan, 20 years, male)

The *Nightwish* fandom was reported to be closely connected with the fans' personal histories. This is not any particular *Nightwish*-related aspect as such, as music in general tends to connect with important personal moments, even life periods, of the fans, thus creating a particular soundtrack of their lives. However, for the hardcore fans, it was particularly the *Nightwish* songs that this soundtrack was compiled from.

> Nightwish to me means . . . the soundtrack of a lifetime. (Colombian fan, 22 years, female)

Although the age range of the fans in the study was wide, many have lived with the band during their teenage years and twenties, which is typically the period of active self-development and strong emotional changes. The rich descriptive stories and soundscape of *Nightwish* music seems to match particularly well with certain moments and moods, as reported by the fans, enabling strong reconstruction and experience of those memories.

> Nightwish is my favourite band because for some reason I have always been able to connect to the songs . . . all of the songs have been connected to certain memories . . . if you took Nightwish out from my brain, you would probably end up taking away my memories as well. (Australian fan, 19 years, female)

Overall, the *Nightwish* experience is extremely personal and intimate for the fans. In the stories this personal dimension was undoubtedly stronger than the felt communal feeling coming along with the fandom. More than to their fellow *Nightwish* fans, they often felt a stronger connection to the band itself, especially the assumed ideology and worldview of the songwriter Tuomas Holopainen.

Nonetheless, *Nightwish* seems to function also as a gateway to other worlds, and form connections to other people. The fans simply want to share and discuss their experiences with other fans. Moreover, in many instances the *Nightwish* narrative seems to create a universal feeling of belonging that the songs are not speaking to me only, but instead to a larger group of like-minded individuals. *Nightwish* music was typically experienced as giving comfort especially to the feelings of loneliness.

> Most of the time I was feeling all alone with my inner misery and bad emotional experiences. And then there comes a band where you find your inner landscapes reflected in the music and lyrics. It's somehow comforting to know that you're not the only one feeling like this every now and then. (German fan, 30 years, female)

Such global sense of connectedness that was inherent in many fans' personal experience forms the basis for the fan tribe, as it may increase their affinity to seek for actual contacts. There appeared a clear need to share and discuss the strong feeling of escapism and the personal trans- formative effects that fans generally reported on being the core of their *Nightwish* experience.

NIGHTWISH AS UNIVERSAL EXPERIENCE

The *Nightwish* fan experience, although being a very personal voyage, hence seems to involve a sense of belonging to a larger narrative, mem- bership of a particular universal tribe. It turned out that the tribal mem- bership is strongly triggered and maintained by certain characteristics of the larger *Nightwish* narrative, represented in the storylines and sounds of individual songs and albums. This global narrative provides the fans both a symbolic and concrete ground to share their personal experiences.

First and mostly, *Nightwish* songs are typically nurturing universal stories that can be related to regardless of the cultural or demographical background of the fan. Despite the nuances and richness of details in the songs, the backbone of the stories often deal with basic universal themes and emotional polarities.

> Imaginaerum is a universal story that reaches around the world . . . does not belong to a particular country or culture. (Spanish fan, 46 years, female)

The interview data revealed quite consistent interpretations by the fans, particularly concerning the *Imaginaerum* album and narrative that was in the focus of my interview study. The bigger idea and characteristics of the *Imaginaerum* story, and the individual songs of the album, seemed to unfold very consistently for the fans. The meanings can be similarly de- coded by people with different cultural or religious background.

> I think one of the tricks in Tuomas' lyrics is that what he's really writ- ing it's very universal . . . if you are a Christian or Buddhist or any- thing, you can find meanings and interpretations because it's the same if you go to see Lord of the Rings or Hobbit . . . you can sort of interpret it as religious one but you can also look at it as a very pagan one. (Estonian fan, 28 years, female)

One obvious reason for such consistent interpretations was the numerous interviews in which the songwriter Tuomas Holopainen explained his ideas and background to the album and its concept (e.g., Ling 2011; Dare 2011; Scharf 2011; and my interviews with Tuomas). He, however, also left many aspects unexplained as he usually does in order to give fans room for their own interpretations. In terms of the universal nature of the *Imaginaerum* narrative, Tuomas also had made it clear in interviews that there were, for example, not any religious meanings intentionally written to the story. The narrative is supposed to be very secular, as all his stories typically are. However, there were some religious meanings attached to it by some of the fans.

When asking the fans to describe the world of *Imaginaerum*, there were again very strong emotions connected to it. Several fans became very poetic and used rich expressions to describe the feelings evoked by the album and its story. *Imaginaerum* was generally seen as some sort of a theme park from another world, a fantasy land, which unfolds as dreamy but concrete at the same time, scary but hopeful, happy and sad, the place of strong contradictions in general: "Imaginaerum reflects the soul, the mind, the consciousness. This is the place where reality meets fantasy. Where everything is possible and where the memory lies," observed a thirty-six-year-old female German fan.

In *Imaginaerum*, in addition to the strong symbolic layer, the lyrics in general are rather literal and descriptive. But even though the stories are attached to certain places and concrete sceneries and there are specific characters within them, many of them (like the roller coaster or the jazz club) can be considered to be very conceptual. The details of the narrative allow diverse interpretations; the general storylines appear quite universal, especially within the Western cultural context, but they are modifiable to the fans' personal experiences and culturally bound interpretations.

> I feel that the Imaginaerum story is very broad culture-wise, however still closely connected to the Western part of the world. . . . The Imaginaerum story quite simply deals with the needs quite high on the Maslow's hierarchy, which makes it irrelevant for many people on the earth. (Danish fan, 19 years, male)

Yet there appeared to be differences in interpretation between different countries. Whether they are due to particular cultural characteristics and discourses of different countries, different media contents or profiles of the band in different countries, or something else, remains to be investigated. Fans in some countries may relate more closely to the "original" idea behind the stories and capture details in more concrete terms, for example, the Finnish fans who can naturally find more endogenous references to their cultural contexts while sharing similar lines of thought with their countrymen who have created and performed the narrative.

> The feelings and moods created by the Imaginaerum songs and their
> parts evoke associations to my childhood summers and winters, to my
> "landscapes of soul," to Finnish woods and lakes. (Finnish fan, 40
> years, male)

Nightwish lyrics and imagery involves many concrete features taken from
Tuomas' personal life and history, his familiar landscapes and stories, but
he has intentionally tried to write the narratives to be as universal as
possible. However, due to the band's Finnish origin, many fans tend to
regard several parts of the narrative as "typically" Finnish, reflecting
their own knowledge or assumptions of the country and its culture. This
in turn, is of course reinforced by the interviews and other messages from
the band.

The Finnish origins of the band have also acted as an "endogenous"
aspect of differentiation (Karjalainen 2014) that suggestively adds some
extra flavor to the image of the band in the eyes of the foreign fans. And
for several fans, the *Nightwish* narrative, and the fandom in general, has
functioned as a particular gateway to Finnish culture, leading them to dig
out more information about Finland, visiting the country, and even moving here.

> Thanks to Nightwish I discovered Finland. I went there last year. . . .
> It's now in my projects to spend a few years studying in Finland and
> maybe work there later. I totally fell in love with the country. (French
> fan, 18 years, female)

But as I mentioned earlier, the strength of the *Imaginaerum* narrative is its
flexibility and adaptability vis-à-vis different cultures—it allows personal
interpretations also in terms of the experienced place. Indeed, many fans
reported on strong connections of the narrative to their own local surroundings.

> As a whole [the album] reminds me of Luna Park in Sydney at night
> when it is completely lit up. I see Imaginaerum as your memories made
> into a theme park. (Australian fan, 19 years, female)

Furthermore, as the universality and flexibility of the narrative is based
on the basic tensions, emotions, and aspects of human life, it cannot only
be shared between different nations and parts of the world but also between different generations. The consistency of fan experiences in my
data was a clear evidence of this. Overall, interpretations and experiences
are rather consistent when thinking about the demographics of the
Nightwish global fan community in general. It is very diverse; for instance
in terms of occupation and education, but the essence of the story seems
to be captured regardless of the background. Moreover, the *Nightwish*
tribe is not a "typical" metal community, as there are not only metal fans
involved. In fact, even the majority of the fans don't consider themselves
metalheads. I asked about the musical preferences and favorite bands of

the fans, and it became clear that they typically had a very diverse taste in music. The most mentioned bands—like *Within Temptation* and *Apocalyptica*—did not come as surprise considering the musical profile and background of *Nightwish*, but the diversity of bands and styles was really notable.

> I consider Nightwish to be such a diverse band, beyond metal. I am not a metalhead and I try not to label this band or others into a single category. (Romanian fan, 31 years, female)

In effect, *Nightwish* being not only metal was often seen as a positive thing; like as a counter aspect to some negative aspects of metal, like certain narrow-minded conservativeness and idealization of aggressiveness, that some fans had experienced. The seemingly friendly and all-inclusive narrative of the band has naturally increased the adoptability of the narrative across different types of people and brought the band merely toward the popular music mainstream than to certain metal subgenre margin.

> They are a metal band, but the band members are not into the very negative aspects of the scene. . . . They are open-minded and tolerant. No racism, no Satanism, no rude ideologies. I think all of them have a lot of respect not only for each other but also toward people and the world. They don't behave like drunken and primitive idiots all the time. Just (ab-)using metal to scream out hate and rage. I really like that in metal music there is a wide range of emotions. Feelings like sadness, melancholy, anger, regret . . . I don't like if it gets too aggressive and discriminating. I think Nightwish would never do. (German fan, 41 years, female)

Despite the varied musical profile and not very strict categorization within heavy metal, *Nightwish* music has also worked as a gateway to metal for some fans.

> Nightwish has expanded my horizons into exploring other metal bands and other types of music. (US fan, 55 years, female)

And as a matter of fact, thanks to the multitude of references in Tuomas Holopainen's songwriting, *Nightwish* songs and albums have functioned as a gateway to many other things as illustrated by the concrete examples of the fans. These rich external references are also key aspects binding some of the members of the *Nightwish* fan tribe together; the references are discussed and shared by the fans, which adds another layer of interest and commitment to the *Nightwish* experience.

> I've learned a lot from Nightwish, which is something I can't say about a lot of bands. The Columbine tragedy really struck a chord in me when I listened to The Kinslayer; Creek Mary's Blood had me reading Native American history for the first time, at least voluntarily; Seven Days to the Wolves has a lot of references to literature that were sort of

lost on me, and the whole Dark Passion Play album made me get a
bunch of books, particularly Whitman's. From Imaginaerum I learned
who Mary Costa is, what Covington Woods is. (Mexican fan, 26 years,
female)

The same phenomenon was visible also with regard to *Imaginaerum* and
the references that Tuomas Holopainen had used in building the story
and its individual pieces. In accordance, a thirty-two-year-old female Brazilian mentioned: "I didn't like poetry until I listened to *Imaginaerum*.
Tuomas taught me to love Walt Whitman and read poetry, it's fascinating!"

   Hence, the universal *Nightwish* narrative, evoking personal yet consistent experiences, provides basis for the existence of the global community, in the first place. It enables the (re)construction and (re)possession of
specific meanings that are first and foremost personal experiences but
become shared—and thus form the tribe—when discussed with other
fans. There are lively *Nightwish*-related discussions in various social media sites and Internet forums, but they are not looked at in this study.
Instead, the focus is on the concerts that function as the ultimate meeting
place and occasion for the fans. It is the place to share, live and co-create
the *Nightwish* experience with fellow fans and the band itself.

COMMUNAL MEETINGS AT CONCERTS

I finally touched this imaginary world and jumped into it. The show
didn't add anything to the story but it showed how bright, inspiring
and sincere it is. It brought the same feelings (as the album) but much
stronger. After the gig I and the people I came with were exhausted but
really happy, calm and inspired, like you see something kind and pure.
For me it wasn't just a gig of a band, it's one of the best memories.
(Russian fan, 19 years, female)

Along with the lines of my study, I looked at the manifestation of shared
experiences in the context of the *Imaginaerum* World Tour concerts. The
tribe is constructed by the shared experiences of the fans and the enactment of these experiences through "rituals" such as the concert. In this
line of thought, the gig is one manifestation of the narrative, concretized
and laid out for the community by the band itself. For the fan, the gig
enables stepping out from the personal world of *Nightwish* experiences
and interpretations to the wider community of like-minded people, people who at least share some of the insights and decode similar meanings
from the narrative.

I've been to many Nightwish shows and hundreds of metal shows in
general and I think there's something unique always in a Nightwish
show. . . . In most of the metal shows you have this strong feeling of

community but I think there is something specific. I don't know what it
is but it's something different. (US fan, age n.a., female)

Of course the gig experience is also strongly personal, but the feel of the
crowd makes it different from the individual moments of music listening.
Many interviewees described the unique atmosphere and the mood of
the audience apparent in the gigs, not just telling their own personal
moods and observations. The feeling of community was also actively
sought after. Most fans were attending the gigs with friends, family
members, or other people. Only a minority of them came to see the show
alone.

The gigs of the *Imaginaerum* World Tour converted the narrative—of
the *Imaginaerum* album and earlier *Nightwish* songs and landscapes—into
flesh and concretized the experience.

> For me the concert was a rollercoaster of feelings and emotions, a show
> full of action, in which I was transported in an accelerator travelling to
> remote sides of my own existence, traveling in time. It was like I was in
> another world, suddenly in a club, then a music hall in an amusement
> park or circus evil decadent. (Spanish fan, 46 years, female)

The experiences of many fans, like the one in the above quote, seemed to
be at the same time personal and communal. She felt to be absorbed into
different public places, laid out by the concretized narrative, concretely
with other people present, however interpreting the narrative through
her own personal experiences. Many other fans shared quite similar stories.

The concert made the album experience also more interactive. Fans
became part of the particular "rituals" carried by the songs and their
moods, accompanied by varying stage decorations. The show enabled a
specific connection between the fans, the narrative, and the band. On
tour, a Polish fan commented, "the story isn't only on the album, fans can
also take part in it." And importantly, the concert strengthens the connection between the band and the fan tribe, by making the band concrete.

> This (concert) is the only point in time where Nightwish actually feels
> like a normal music experience. This is probably because you can phys-
> ically see them as humans. Living in the US, you only see these God-
> like pictures of Nightwish and these prophetic songs and they just
> don't even seem human. And then you see them there in the flesh.
> Sweating, panting, and working their magic on stage right in front of
> you . . . It shows that they are still just good hearted people from Kitee
> playing their hearts out for your enjoyment. (US fan, 21 years, male)

I personally felt the strong communal vibe and excitement in the various
shows of the *Imaginaerum* World Tour. Particularly, when the shows
ended, with the *Imaginaerum* symphonic medley playing as the back tape,
lots of people still staying at the front of the venue seemingly moved,

some in tears, taking pictures, or just staring at the stage, chatting with each other, the communal feeling was very tangible. After seeing over one thousand gigs in my life, I have to admit that the ones of *Nightwish* truly involve a unique atmosphere, magic that resonates with the symbolism and narrative of the band. And more than in many other concerts, the presence of many generations and people with very different backgrounds, coming with the suggestively very inclusive atmosphere, makes the concert special too.

> This band has brought me a lot, for my personal life. Like new friends, great discussions about it with my dad, awesome feelings during the show . . . (French fan, 18 years, female)

The *Nightwish* tribe thus becomes manifest through the particular rituals that take place as communal meeting in concerts, fan occasions, and on social media platforms. The concerts and other occasions seem to function as specific "anchoring places" (Aubert-Gamet and Cova 1999) that provide a "momentary home" for the tribe.

The gigs are the physical meeting place for the fans and the band, and crucial for the formation of strong tribal identity. It is also the occasion where the *Imaginaerum* narrative, as well as the large *Nightwish* "universe" can be lived through in more concrete terms, which fortifies and re-created the fans' personal experience. However, most fans reported that the concerts did not add any new meanings to the narrative per se. The fans had already been strongly immersed to the *Imaginaerum* narrative—the storyline, characters, and places—by listening to the album and reading the lyrics. Interestingly, in addition to the gigs as physical manifestations of the *Imaginaerum* narrative, the imaginary amusement park and other surroundings of the narrative—and the "Nightwish universe" in general—seem to provide the hardcore fans with another common ground for communal encounters. The narrative thus works as a mental anchoring place that enables shared experiences. And as discussed above, it is predominantly transcultural and universal.

IMAGINAERUM AS AN ANCHORING PLACE FOR THE NIGHTWISH TRIBE

> For me Imaginaerum is a one hell of a ride somewhere between hell and paradise. For me it's a place. (Russian fan, 25 years, female)

As proposed, whereas gigs are seen as the physical anchoring places for the tribe, the *Imaginaerum* narrative as such functions as a strong mental anchoring place for the hardcore fans, precisely while it evokes rather consistent interpretations and imagery among the fans. *Imaginaerum* was reported to be a place of magic, fantasy and twisted reality, the store of imagination, stories and personal histories, as the name also suggests.

The narrative is embodied in different surroundings—like the theme park—and through various characters of the story, all of which seemed to evoke extremely concrete and rich descriptions from the fans.

> Made me feel like I was wandering around in a forest belonged to Elves. It stopped every contact to me from outside, and even after the song had finished, I felt that I was still glowing inside because of that feeling. (Turkish fan, 18 years, female)

In fans' images, *Imaginaerum* is a highly visual and lively place, of an absorbing nature. It is a place that is closed from the world outside and allows the fans to escape there, feel the sense of belonging, gather experiences that can be shared with other like-minded fans—thus enabling the construction and reconstructions of meanings as well as their enactment, and further maintaining the tribal identity of the fans.

> It is a very luminous album, that brings me into a fantasy world, like a comforting yet scary bedtime story. I can identify to most if not all of the songs, and they remind me of novels I used to read when I was younger . . . semi-nightmarish tales as Alice in Wonderland, brother Grimm's writings, Russian novels and such. To me, the whole album is very visual, it brings clear images in my mind. (Canadian fan, 27 years, female)

Imaginaerum is like the concretization of the *Nightwish* ideology, the *Nightwish* universe in tangible shape, as experienced by the fans. It allows imagination to wander but entangles the experiences into concrete metaphors.

> I see Imaginaerum as your memories made into a theme park where there are many rides. . . . The story is a journey through the mind, reliving memories through your imagination, and looking in awe at what your imagination can truly be capable of and what a big part it actually plays in your life even though you don't realize it. (Czech fan, 19 years, female)

The function of the album and its narrative as an anchoring place is also enabled by the intentional references to the earlier *Nightwish* albums that Tuomas Holopainen has written into the songs. *Imaginaerum* also comprises lots of such references, contributing to the recreation of the *Nightwish* universe, the imagination land and specific mythology. *Imaginaerum* is not any random place, but a logical one in the larger *Nightwish* narrative that has emerged throughout the history. Familiar characteristics, even characters, are exactly the attributes that anchor the interpretations of the fans and construct the place as a shared *Nightwish* experience.

This repetitive use of central themes and characters builds up, if using semiotic terminology, the paradigmatic coherence of the narrative (De Saussure 1996). Tuomas Holopainen has coded paradigmatic meanings to lyrical, visual, and musical representations of *Nightwish*, with the intention that the fans then are able to decode them from the narrative. They create syntagmatic constructions (De Saussure 1996) that support the narrative and its distinctive character. Such references are used by Holopainen both intentionally and unintentionally.

In comparison to earlier *Nightwish* albums, *Imaginaerum* is perhaps a more concrete and consistent in terms of its narrative, really providing a sense of place for the listener. It is crafted not only around fantasy characters and landscapes but realistic surroundings and artifacts.

> The characters of this album are alive like in no other albums, the atmosphere comes all around you and when you listen it's like you are inside the story. . . . I think this album is more connected to real world, our everyday life, than the others, because besides characters from cartoons, stories and Nightwish world (like "Dead" Boy or bride from "Scaretale") there are things that you can meet in our everyday life . . . like a model poster on the city wall. (Russian fan, 19 years, female)

Again, these surroundings and characters seem to function as an anchoring place for the global *Nightwish* tribe because of their flexible nature. The most central scenes to the narrative are touching traditional universal themes and basic emotions, yet leaving space for personal interpretations.

> [Imaginaerum] has a universal theme, a place to escape in times of stress or illness or sadness, I feel that all people could relate to this. (New Zealand fan, 48 years, female)

Despite the fundamental personal basis of the *Imaginaerum* storyline, the themes and details of the story are written for the global audience. Fans can identify with the story, find it personal and touching, without having more precise understanding of the writers cultural background.

> I'm not sure that Imaginaerum speaks directly to Mexican people, or Latin-American people either. It's more of a universal theme, in my opinion, although some parts of it do seem more related to Eastern Europe of the Middle-East: the mermaids, the Arabesque, rollercoasters, all that seems to be a bit detached from my culture. But the circus is universal, even if tends to be different from one country to another. (Mexican fan, 26 years, female)

Obviously, the strong sense of authenticity was another central attribute enabling the high and continuous commitment, to which many respondents also referred to, directly or indirectly. The felt authenticity of the *Imaginaerum* and *Nightwish* narratives follows from the explicitly present personal touch of Tuomas Holopainen in his songwriting as well as his modest appearance in interviews.

> Tuomas gave his heart and soul to the songs, and that is really the main strength for the band. (French fan, 18 years, female)

This authenticity and experienced honesty makes the *Imaginaerum* a place that is easy for the fans to enter and absorb, and is presumably an important characteristics of an anchoring place that really captures the attention of the fans.

> The music comes from a pure place and that I think is extremely important for the listener to connect and appreciate. (Trinidad & Tobago fan, 28 years, female)

CONCLUDING REMARKS

As shown by the data, the fan experiences of *Imaginaerum* and *Nightwish* are very personal in the first place; almost every fan story included very personal stories and interpretations of the *Imaginaerum* script, events, and characters. And those experiences generally appeared to be extremely strong and meaningful in terms of the fans' identity and personal history. In addition to colorful and personal descriptions, there were fans who sent pictures of their *Nightwish* tattoos, their own *Nightwish*-inspired poems, life-changing experiences with *Nightwish* music, and so forth.

For the fans, the *Imaginaerum* narrative has been a highly immersive experience. The album—through the cinematic sound landscape, rich imagery in lyrics, and mythical visuals—laid the basis for personal interpretations and identification, and the live concerts added the social aspect to the holistic experience. It also seems clear that the fans, the readers of the narrative, have their own distinct ways of interpreting the story based on their personal background and depth of fandom, as well as their cultural surroundings. But still, the experiences and interpretations seem to be consistent and widely shared, and the *Imaginaerum* narrative functioned as the mental anchoring place for the fans.

Nightwish and the songwriter Tuomas Holopainen has succeeded in engaging fans in the narrative. Using two metaphors, transportation and performance, from the literature and film studies as a reference (Gerrig 1993) the listeners, firstly, have been "transported" into the world of the narrative using universal referencing and personalization. Secondly, they are "performing" the narrative within this world; they are called upon to the narrative, using their own experiences and skills, facts and emotions, to give substance to characters and stories. Resonating with the idea of fan tribes introduced in the beginning of this article, transportation enables the (re)construction and (re)possession of meanings, and further shared experiences. Performing the narrative in social context like the concert or social media enables the enactment of these experiences and strengthens the tribal identity of the *Nightwish* community.

This chapter laid down some rather precursory thoughts that need to be further explored and validated with more data. It seems that the

Nightwish fan community offers an extremely fruitful outlet for explorations into the characteristic of music fandom and communities, thanks to the strong emotional content brought along with the band's music and narrative. But it is only one example, and possibly quite a unique case in terms of its peculiar narrative and origins. Therefore, investigations of other bands and fan tribes would presumably provide rather different views. One compelling idea would also be to compare the music fan communities with the customer communities of commercial brands. If considered from the commercial point of view, which is probably quite relevant for many economically successful metal bands too, a fan tribe may indeed resemble a brand community—if we for instance adhere to the definition of brand community as "a specialized, non-geographically-bound community, based on a structured set of social relations among admirers of a brand" (Muniz and O'Guinn 2001, 412). However, brand communities are explicitly commercial, fan tribes maybe less so, at least if considering the basic motivations of the community members. As the *Nightwish* case highlights, fan communities are specific as they are held together essentially through shared emotion and passion of the members.

REFERENCES

Aubert-Gamet, Véronique and Cova, Bernard. 1999. "Servicescapes: From Modern Non-Places to Postmodern Commonplaces." *Journal of Business Research* 44(1): 37–45.

Cova, Bernard and Cova, Véronique. 2002. "Tribal Marketing: The Tribalisation of Society and Its Impact on the Conduct of Marketing." *European Journal of Marketing* 36 (5/6): 595–620.

Dare, Tom. 2011. "Bless the Child." *Terrorizer*, (December) no. 217: 26–29.

De Saussure, Ferdinand. 1996. "Course in General Linguistics." Edited by C. Bally and A. Sechehaye. New York: McGraw-Hill.

Gerrig, Richard J. 1993. *Experiencing Narrative Worlds*. New Haven: Westview Press.

Karjalainen, Toni-Matti. 2014. "The Dead Boy's Narrative Transmediated." In *Transmedia Practice: A Collective Approach*, edited by Deb Polson, Ann-Marie Cook, JT Velikovsky and Adam Brackin, 119–129. Oxford, UK: Inter-Disciplinary Press.

Karjalainen, Toni-Matti and Kärki, Kimi, eds. 2015. *Modern Heavy Metal: Markets, Practices and Cultures. Conference Proceedings*. Helsinki: Aalto University School of Business.

Ling, Dave. 2011. "Nightwish, the Making of Imaginaerum." *Metal Hammer*, December.

Maffesoli, Michel. 1996. *The Time of the Tribes: The Decline of Individualism in Mass Society*. London: Sage.

Muniz, Albert M., and O'Guinn, Thomas C. 2001. "Brand Community." *Journal of Consumer Research*. 27: 412–32.

Nightwish. 2011. *Imaginaerum* [CD]. Donzdorf: Nuclear Blast.

Nightwish. 2012. *Imaginaerum* [Film–DVD]. Directed by Stobe Harju. Helsinki: Solar Films.

Saldaña, Johnny. 2009. *The Coding Manual for Qualitative Researchers*. London: Sage.

Scharf, Natasha. 2011. "Phantasmagoria!" *Prog*, no. 21: 48–50.

Urbaniak, Kathryn. 2014. "Perception of Identity and Expertise in Heavy Metal Fans within One Online Community of Practice." In *Educational, Psychological, and Behav-*

ioral Considerations in Niche Online Communities, edited by V. Venkatesh, J. Wallin, J.C. Castro and Jason Edward Lewis, 395–401. Hershey, PA: IGI Global.

Varas-Díaz, Nelson, Eliut Rivera-Segarra, Carmen L. Rivera Medina, Sigrid Mendoza, and Osvaldo González-Sepúlveda. 2014. "Predictors of Communal Formation in a Small Heavy Metal Scene: Puerto Rico as a Case Study." *Metal Music Studies* 1 (1): 87–103.

Venkatesh, Vivek, Jeffrey S. Podoshen, Kathryn Urbaniak, and Jason J. Wallin. 2015. "Eschewing Community: Black Metal." *Journal of Community & Applied Social Psychology* 25: 66–81.

Wallach, Jeremy, Harris M. Berger, and P. D. Greene. 2011. *Metal Rules the Globe: Heavy Metal Music Around the World*. Durham: Duke University Press.

FIVE

"We're in This Together and We Take Care of Our Own"

Narrative Constructions of Metal Community
Told by Metal Youth

Paula Rowe

The importance of metal communities is commonly referred to in research data, in metal media, and anecdotally between metalheads in passionate terms, but this is most often information about, or provided by, well-established metalheads. The question raised in this chapter is whether *young* metalheads would report that metal communities play any kind of role during the *early* formation of metal identities.

To explore this question, this chapter draws on narrative research with young metal fans living in South Australia. The research was designed in response to the ways that metal youth have routinely been portrayed in academic literature as apathetic, sexually aggressive, having poor educational commitment, forming delinquent peer groups, at risk of poor mental health and developmental issues, and anticipating or even envisioning bleak futures (for examples see Arnett 1996; Roe 1992; Schwartz and Fouts 2003; Tanner, Asbridge, and Wortley 2008). Indeed, for more than two decades, the research space investigating metal youth has seemingly been devoted to reporting on the "problem of metal" (Brown 2011) rather than the ordinary lives of young metalheads. Despite this academic preoccupation with finding a correlation between young people's metal listening habits and risky behaviors and/or poor life outcomes, no *meaningful* evidence to support these hypotheses has been found. Rather, studies of this type have developed their argumentation by textually reemphasizing the long-standing stereotypes and assumptions about metal youth.

One example of this (among many) was Leung and Kier's (2010) research article on music preferences and young people's attitudes toward spending and saving money. In the introduction to their paper, Leung and Kier (2010, 2) drew on various authors to describe fans of deviant music (including heavy metal in this category) as being high-sensation seekers who were more likely to obtain sex-oriented materials over the Internet, more likely to have committed aggressive, delinquent, arrestable, or illegal acts, and more likely to use drugs and/or alcohol. Having painted a troublesome picture of young metal fans in the introduction, the findings that followed were far more benign and generated no meaningful insights around metal youth as they transitioned toward financial independence, or not. But the point here is that the introduction to Leung and Kier's paper carried more weight in terms of reinforcing long-held stereotypes and perhaps misleading non-metal people into thinking that, based on the descriptors above, participation in metal community life might occur in dangerous and undesirable spaces where young metalheads are at risk of all sorts of negative behaviors and poor outcomes. It was clear from reviewing research literature of this type that metal youth needed to be directly consulted to learn more *precisely* what the allure of metal community life is for them, and what *actually* occurs in this space.

THE RESEARCH

To address the issues outlined above, I set out to undertake longitudinal qualitative research with young metalheads in order to speak with them directly and hear *their own* narrative constructions of metal identities and metal communities, and to contextualize this in their everyday lives.[1] Participants were recruited through various "metal" sites across Adelaide, South Australia, including rehearsal rooms, retail music outlets, live music venues, and via metal radio programs and other metal media. There was much diversity within the sample of five females and twenty-three males aged eighteen to twenty-four in terms of socioeconomic circumstances, family dynamics, and also the range of metal subgenres (and therefore communities) they aligned with.

The sample was capped at twenty-eight participants because, early into data collection, the young people's enthusiasm for participating in the project began generating much more narrative data than I had anticipated having to manage by myself. I concluded data collection with a total of forty-four in-depth interviews that were audio-recorded (with consent), some of which were three hours or longer in duration. The following provides an overview of data collection:

- In year one, twenty-eight stage one interviews utilized memory-work interviewing methods to explore participants' reflections on the circumstances and motivations behind their early metal identity formation—captured as *becoming metal.*
- In years two through five, stage two data collection included sixteen repeat in-depth interviews, plus thirty-three sets of telephone and field communications (also audio-recorded with participant consent).
- Stage two interviewing methods explored present realities and future aspiration biographies. This allowed me to trace the ways that participants mapped out their futures and transitioned into the adult world as metalheads—captured as *being metal.*

I personally transcribed all of the interviews and field communications so that I could "stay close" to the narratives and begin thematically coding the data immediately. Transcriptions were analyzed using Riessman's (2008) matrix of narrative analysis methods, with an exclusive focus on thematically analyzing *what* was told, rather than how it was told, or for what purpose.

Combining stage one memory-work methods with stage two present and future imaginings revealed that metal community life took on different meanings, and was important in different ways, at various transition points in the youth phase, from early teen years to young adulthood. The focus of this chapter, however, is informed by stage one data that highlight early narrative constructions of metal community during high school years.

METAL IDENTITY FORMATION ON THE MARGINS OF HIGH SCHOOL CULTURE

The broad research questions driving stage one of the study investigated the interviewees' first metal memories and, once exposed to heavy metal music and culture, what they found so alluring about it. The question then was what motivated them to "ramp up" their relationship to metal by creating a public metal persona. Without exception, these questions transported all participants back to their high school days. Further, their memory-work revealed that the following set of three broad themes was evident (in some form) in all the stories that captured the importance of metal in their young lives:

1. *The listening experience*: the importance of listening to metal for getting in touch with feelings, alleviating frustrations, and difficult emotions, and feeling solidarity with others (enhancing emotional well-being).

2. *A sense of belonging and acceptance*: feelings of being accepted by, and belonging to, a global community of like-minded people with shared tastes and experiences (keeping the "right" people in).

3. *A sense of social protection:* feeling able to withstand rejection by popular peer groups, and creating social space or barriers to keep social threats like bullies away (keeping the "wrong" people away or out).

It was not surprising that the young people would report tremendous enjoyment from listening to metal music, however, the binary of keeping the "right" people in and keeping the "wrong" people out generated fascinating insights into the ways that young people were constructing metal community and what they perceived to gain from metal community membership, as Jake[2] first hints at in the following quote:

> Other people think "Oh that metal dude's evil, don't talk to him," but if you're in the community you think "That's guy's awesome, I wanna know him" . . . You have to be in the community to understand it. (Jake)

The stories of becoming metal were also linked by a fourth theme:

4. That all participants experienced some form of exclusion at school by dominant peer groups.

It became apparent that this complex (and often contradictory) set of themes required a conceptual frame that could accommodate the experiences of metal youth who, on one hand, claimed a deep sense of belonging to community, but who also reported experiences of exclusion and not having strong peer networks. This was particularly evident through the stage one data when participants were consistently describing how important it was to belong to the metal community long before most had ever met another metalhead in person. To better understand these complexities, I will raise ideas throughout this chapter that are framed by notions of imagined collective identity work and the concomitant individualization of metal community membership.

POWER RELATIONS AND THE STRUCTURING OF MARGINAL SCHOOL-BASED IDENTITIES

The experiences of exclusion that participants described ranged from overt bullying, to rejection by certain groups, to feelings of just not fitting in, or even an awareness (or perception) that one simply did not measure up to more popular peers at school, and most likely never would. The idea of being an "outsider" that the young people reported is not new information for anyone associated with metal—the marginal positioning of metalheads more broadly is often expressed anecdotally by metalheads themselves; it has been written about by metal scholars (see Clifford-Napoleone 2015); and it has been reinforced and celebrated by iconic metal musicians—for example, Rob Zombie once defined metal as "outsider music" and described himself an outsider and a loner growing up because his interests were different to his peers. He also remarked that although nobody wants to be the "weird kid," somehow "you just end up being the weird kid," and "metal is like that, except all of the weird kids are in one place" (Dunn, McFadyen, and Joy 2005). The metal youth I interviewed have now been able to shed some light on how being the "weird kid" Zombie spoke of can *actually* play out for some in school settings.

As stated, the feelings of being an "outsider" were reported on a range from having been outright bullied to simply knowing one "just didn't fit in," and reviewing some general research literature on bullying and exclusion in high school settings gave some context for what the young people were saying. For example, Walton and Niblett (2012, 5) found that students were consistently able to articulate two different dimensions of power in bullying relationships. First, students identified individual differences of power between peers and described potential "victims" in these power relations as shy, lacking confidence, or generally being viewed as somewhat defenseless. The second dimension of power that students identified was based on social differences whereby bullies put people down due to certain characteristics which were perceived as different or out of the norm—and students referred to those in this category as unwelcome "outsiders" within school cultural norms (Walton and Niblett 2012, 7). In each case, Walton and Niblett's participants showed a clear understanding of the characteristics of someone who *could* be bullied, or who is an "outsider." This suggests to me that young people *in general* will know precisely where they fit in the social order at school (whether this is enacted in any way), so they need to be continually assessing their social options regardless of current behaviors toward them by others.

Whether there are clear patterns of overt bullying, or whether young people simply *feel* excluded from the social order and work around that, power relations in schools are obviously a major issue sparking intense emotional reactions for the young people engaged in them, much as they have been since schools first opened for business. However, youth cultures, methods of technology and communication, and broader social dynamics are perpetually evolving so we need to keep step with how it feels to be on the margins of school culture, and how young people devise their own strategies for managing this amid changing social conditions. Indeed, there must be many emerging strategies for evading or reducing bullying and exclusion that we are yet to learn from young people. But here, heavy metal provides a compelling case study for investigating how *some* young people deal with exclusion (and its variants) as they navigate high school life in a changing modernity.

To explore this in more detail, I will now share some of the stories the young people told during the interviews. First we will hear *from them* about the importance of belonging to metal communities, before looking at the strong role metal played in their ability to withstand the pressures of high school life.

BELONGING TO A COMMUNITY THAT
KEEPS THE "RIGHT" PEOPLE IN

When I first met Joey he was eighteen years old and had been out of a home and "couch-surfing" (he had no fixed address) for eighteen months. He had lost touch with his father who was leading a transient lifestyle and it wasn't possible for Joey to live with his mother, who he described as "making bad choice after bad choice" in terms of her romantic partners.

Throughout his young life, Joey had tried to protect his mother on numerous occasions when family violence erupted until he was finally "kicked out by her latest boyfriend" for the last time at age sixteen. As a result of moving around so much, and moving back and forth between parents, Joey estimated that he had been enrolled in thirteen different schools over eleven years of schooling in various locations across the state and had found it extremely difficult to make friends "coming in as the new kid all the time":

> The other kids were dickheads man, they're fucking assholes, just cos you're wearing black and stuff, even though it's just band shirts it's like "Oh, you're an emo go cut yourself" and all this dumb shit, those pathetic little school yard kids. They were usually the typical dumb surfie kids who'd listen to crap like Kesha and Lil Wayne, yeah, just dumb music. It's just pathetic, the music has no intellect in it at all, if you listen to the lyrics, it's all about going out, getting laid, and talking about how easy you are. (Joey)

When I asked Joey what music *he* was listening to back then, he smiled at the memory of how important *System of a Down's* music was to him at age twelve because he finally discovered "important lyrics and meaning" and "the music was insanely good." At age thirteen he bought a *Slipknot* album that "blew him away" and, at the time of the interviews, he still rated the *Slipknot* concert he went to as a fifteen year old as the best concert experience of his life:

> I always get goose bumps when I think about that concert, it was defi-nitely the best concert I've ever seen. There's nothing better than metal concerts when you're in the mosh pit, like you've got the few at the front who are just headbanging, then you've got the death pit in the

middle, or circle, where everyone just runs around and goes crazy in there, but everyone looks after each other. That's what metalheads do . . . if you're at a metal concert and someone gets knocked down, everyone who's closest to them instantly tries to help them get up. . . . I remember at the Slipknot concert there was a girl in a wheelchair and there were easily ten people who didn't even know her just making a barricade around her so she could be at the front to see Slipknot. Yeah it's definitely like family, as soon as you're at a concert. I guess some people think kids are just gonna get hurt and stuff, you might get crushed a bit just from how many people are there, but other than that if you fall down you're gonna get helped straight back up for sure. (Joey)

Joey didn't know any other metalheads (at that time); his only face-to-face metal experience was at the Slipknot concert where he conflated the idea of being in a mosh pit with being in a community. He was not alone in thinking this way either; other participants also described how safe it was "in a pit" because "everyone looks after each other" and "community is about looking after each other."

Respondents consistently told me (in various ways) about the feelings of acceptance and belonging that they derived from ideas of metal community life, and one way that acceptance and belonging manifested for these young people was through this deep sense of caring for one another. For some participants, their first experience of feeling "cared" for by peers occurred in metal mosh pits—either witnessed firsthand or viewed on the Internet (which I will discuss later). For Joey, the experience of being in a metal mosh pit with everyone "caring for one another" stood in stark contrast to his experiences of being humiliated and degraded by popular students in the school yard.

Luke had never been to a concert like Joey had, and he did not personally know any other metalheads, but he was also very clear about the importance of metal community life, the closeness of metalheads, and their commitment to taking care of one another:

The metal community, we band together, like fuck what everyone else thinks, we know what we think . . . that sense of tight-knit community is just great . . . we're in this together and we take care of our own. (Luke)

Joey and Luke both had difficult circumstances to manage at home as well as at school, but for most participants, home life was not a major source of tension like school life was. Despite differences in family dynamics, all interviewees described in various ways how "looking after each other" and a sense of "family" were valued aspects of metal community life, as Alex captured in this quote:

I think a lot of the other genres are kind of like, yeah, we listen to this, where I think with metal there is a family associated with that. I think

> Dio said that once you're into metal you're in the family . . . yeah, in the group. (Alex)

Alex described how sharing tastes and beliefs with like-minded others is the essence of metal community life, but he also told me that metal "brings something extra to what community means" because metalheads are visible to each other "all over the world." He elaborated by telling me that some people might really like gardening, and they might be in a community of gardeners, but they would have a hard time recognizing each other on the street if they didn't already know each other. Alex described how he personally grew in confidence once he started wearing metal shirts:

> It [school life] was definitely better when I got into metal, cos I've never been the most confident person, I've always been quite nervous, I always hold back from things, and I think metal just gave me that extra confidence. I guess I was always an outsider, like at parties and stuff during school, but I definitely felt a lot more confident in metal shirts, definitely . . . as soon as I was metal I thought "I don't have to prove anything to anyone, sick!" (Alex)

Alex uses the word "sick" here to mean extremely good. He described how wearing metal shirts relieved the burden of needing to "prove anything" to non-metal peers at school, however the metal shirt *was* critical for proving he had "joined up" with like-minded others, in spirit at least, before he had actually become friends with other metalheads. Jake also heralded the metal shirt as being vitally important for experiencing communion with others:

> If I see someone with a Slayer shirt on, I'm like "That dude looks chilled, I wouldn't mind hanging out with that dude." But yeah, metal's a great community and it's really diverse, it's so individual but so universal, it kind of contradicts itself, in a good way. . . . For me personally, community is a variety of different things . . . but it's more about a feeling . . . if you're on the bus and you see a dude with a Cannibal Corpse shirt on, you kind of know them without even knowing them, you just understand where they're coming from. (Jake)

I question whether or not Jake could *actually* know for sure "where they're coming from"; perhaps a stranger's choice of metal shirt could really only tell Jake what music the person in the shirt likes (if it is even their shirt). But facts did not get in the way of symbolic significance here; facts (or lack thereof) had no impact on the sense of solidarity and inclusion that these young people took comfort in. In short, there was no need to over think it, just feel it and enjoy it. Jake was bullied and excluded by peer groups at school; he did not have any metal friends outside of school either and was quite socially isolated, however he was still able to garner a sense of acceptance and inclusion simply by being in proximity to someone else wearing a metal shirt. From the mouths of teens we get tremendous insight here into the blurring of the lines between community and identity, and further, we can see how open this is to individual interpretation.

BUYING INTO METAL COMMUNITY MEMBERSHIP

Despite repeated claims of how important it was to feel part of the metal community during high school years, it was an *imagined* sense of belonging that participants were actually reconstructing for me during the interviews—none of them had their sense of belonging affirmed by direct involvement with metal community life while they were still at school. Essentially, the metal community membership they were imagining was being underscored by notions of collective identity; understood here as:

> An individual's cognitive, moral and emotional connection with a broader community, category, practice or institution. It is a perception of shared status and relation, which may be imagined rather than experienced directly, and it is distinct from personal identities, although it may form part of a personal identity. (Polletta and Jasper 2001, 285)

What stands out in Polletta and Jasper's (2001, 285) definition is the signaling that collective identity "may be imagined rather than experienced directly," the authors further arguing that collective identity work can increasingly be carried out alone. The metal shirt was the introductory passport to community (via collective identity) for all of these young people well before they had any metal peers to unpack these ideas with, so it was of interest to explore what fostered this sense of belonging to community and to see where they got these ideas from.

Danielle also felt an attachment to people she had never met; she told me "I kind of felt part of the metal community before I even knew anyone." When making this statement, Danielle was referring to knowing that like-minded people existed through watching metal concerts, videos, and interviews online while home alone in her bedroom. Like Danielle, all participants were consuming metal through the Internet and other forms of media during high school years. Most had watched the documentary *Metal: A Headbanger's Journey* (2005) and felt validated by Rob Zombie's comments that a metal concert is a coming together of all the "weird kids." Zombie had signaled that it was okay to be the "weird kid," and that one's metal kin were out there awaiting one's arrival. Each live performance that participants watched online reinforced this message. Whether YouTube clips of Dez Fafara[3] initiating circle pits,[4] or Randy Blythe[5] instructing walls of death,[6] the core message was the same—"we're in this together and we take care of our own" (Luke).[7]

The fact that participants were able to construct a sense of metal community from watching metal media is unsurprising given that symbolic expressions of subcultural identity and the associated practices are more accessible than ever before. Before the rise of digital technologies, individuals would have to physically seek out symbols and actions within a distinct "scene" space to build and claim a subcultural identity: nowadays, the tools and knowledge required for building a subcultural identity are readily available with a "click of the mouse" (Gardner 2010, 73–74). The changing methods of access and availability means that the scope of subcultures has become far more global and diffuse, "popping up in previously unfamiliar spaces and places and thus stretching the boundaries, values, and practices that make up these groups" (Gardner 2010, 73–74).

Metal is a prime illustration of these changes and is being hugely impacted them. One no longer needs to physically attend metal concerts or engage face-to-face with metal peers to construct a metal identity or achieve a sense of metal community membership. This can be done at home, on the Internet, and to a lesser extent, by watching free to air music video shows—although the latter option limits people to engaging with more mainstream bands, whereas underground knowledge and collateral is more accessible via the Internet (Spracklen 2015, 157). Indeed, Brown (2010, 106) suggests that the minimum requirement for participating in contemporary metal youth culture is "the purchase of commodities and an understanding of their symbolic significance and uses." He argues that metal media can provide this understanding by "offering 'clues' as to how to 'live' metal as a youth identity" (Brown 2010, 105). In sum, the increased accessibility of globalized metal and its cultural commodities through the Internet now means that one can forge a metal identity without ever having to leave one's home, whether by choice or circumstance. Young people can watch, consume, and engage with metal from their bedrooms if need be, or if they choose.

McRobbie and Garber first raised the idea of youth bedroom culture in 1976 when writing about the tendency for scholars to omit girls from studies of subculture. McRobbie and Garber (1976) argued that girls might be less visible to subcultural researchers because parents were more protective of daughters than sons, meaning that boys had more social freedom to undertake identity work in common public spaces. The authors argued that, consequently, girls had to manage the social restrictions on their identity work by decorating their bedroom spaces and participating in teenybopper culture that could be accommodated into their leisure time at home (McRobbie and Garber 1976).

More recently, Lincoln's (2012) investigation of the private spaces in young people's lives revealed that bedrooms have grown in significance for boys as well as girls, and that bedrooms function as important sites of identity work and resistance and meaning making through media. I am mindful that having a bedroom at all, let alone of one's own, is not a privilege that all young people have access to, but for those who do, bedrooms can be vitally important identity spaces where young people can be themselves away from the pressures of daily life. Further, they can decorate these spaces to reflect their cultural interests (at least to the extent permitted by their domestic circumstances) whereby the bedroom can become a canvas of "who they are and what they like" (Lincoln 2012, 8). Lincoln (2012, 8) further suggests that increasing online participation means that young people can now be together with others even while alone in their rooms because "in an age of digital media, bedrooms are integral, interconnected hubs of communication," as well as personal identity spaces "marked out as such through the objects, items and things collected within it." What became highly interesting to me was that the idea of metal community could also be marked out in the private space of bedrooms—even if only via the conduit of collective identity—and this was not dependent on active two-way communication with others (as Lincoln alluded to above); rather, this was achievable via the research and consumption of metal media, self-assigning community membership, and marking out one's bedroom as a micro-community space.

In the time I knew Jake, I spent roughly six hours in his bedroom interviewing him. Each time I visited his home he led me straight to his bedroom which, upon entering, told me (as a seasoned metalhead myself) exactly "who he was" and which metal communities he aligned with by the choice of posters that adorned the walls. Jake had only recently completed school several weeks before our first interview so I was privileged to get "a feel" for the space that had been so important to him during his high school years. He would sit on a chair next to his amp and I would sit cross-legged on his bed as we alternated back and forth between general metal conversations and research conversations, and he would self-initiate regular breaks in between all the hours of talk by playing guitar for me. He would play me songs he had written himself, and then he would play riffs from "old-school" death metal guitarists and have me try and guess the songs and sing along. Jake was an extremely talented metal guitarist, but he had never played guitar outside of that room and had never played for another metalhead—yet he spoke of having such a strong connection to the metal community and had no doubts about his purpose and worth as a member of the community. I previously questioned Jake's comments about "just knowing where other metalheads are coming from" because of the metal shirt they might be wearing, however I cannot deny that Jake and I formed an instant connection by virtue of our shared metal identity. There was a thirty-year age difference (and considerable life experience difference) between us; but sitting there together in his bedroom, I *absolutely* felt (as he did) that we belonged to the same community.

Over time, I came to think of Jake and other participants with similar stories as "bedroom metallers." They had created their own metal microcosms complete with guitars, drums, and recording equipment; one par-

ticipant who identified with black metal culture would often wear corpse
paint[8] at home in his room along with the black metal gauntlets his
mother had made for him to wear while practicing guitar in his room.
Even though the young people did not engage directly with other metalheads (during high school years), this had no obvious impact on how
much they knew about metal music and culture, or the extent to which
they could "authentically" embody a metal identity as a result. All participants really "knew their stuff" in terms of metal's various histories, cultures and styles—knowledge that had been available to them via Internet
searches as Stevo described:

> I started looking for heavier stuff online and that's when I started really
> properly being metal so I would've been thirteen or fourteen years
> old. . . . When I was researching metal to find out more about it I read it
> was good to have long hair so you can headbang so I started growing it
> then, yeah, pretty much almost from the start I guess you'd say I
> looked metal . . . I sort of had the impression that no one really listened
> to this thing, like it was something I did on my own, I wasn't really
> looking for other metalheads . . . but at the same time I felt really
> connected to it, I don't know, it was weird, just like I belonged to it.
> (Stevo)

Initially, I thought that participants might have been engaged in online
metal communities in lieu of face-to-face communities during high
school years, but it surprised me that this was not the case. Engagement
with online communities did occur post-school for some as they became
more actively involved in metal community life in general; however, online engagement (during high school years) was more confined to researching metal facts and music and purchasing metal commodities as
Stevo had done. Or as Brown (2010) said, they were looking for clues
online about how to "live" metal.

What they also learned from their online research was the public perception of metal as dangerous and undesirable through reading about the
moral panics that have followed the genre for more than forty years. In
short, they also found clues as to how to "live" metal in non-metal contexts, like the school environment, as the following stories will reveal.

BELONGING TO A COMMUNITY THAT
KEEPS THE "WRONG" PEOPLE OUT

Despite growing up in a poor neighborhood, Luke remembered having a
happy home life with his parents and his older sister prior to his father
passing away when Luke was six years old. He felt that his mother never
got over the shock and her own health suffered as a result; she was
diagnosed with cancer when Luke was twelve and he and his sister cared
for their mother in the family home until she passed away when Luke

was fourteen. Having missed so much schooling through caring for his mother, Luke was quite socially isolated and did not have strong peer networks. He relied heavily on listening to metal at home to manage the pain of losing both of his parents, he also remembered being particularly angry with his mother for dying and felt that he "could get it all out and deal with it" when listening to metal.

Luke's eventual return to high school was a highly traumatic experience for him. He was picked on and bullied for his tall stature, for being overweight, for his unruly hair and his prescription eyeglasses; and there were also cruel rumors circulating around the school about why he and his sister had missed so much school. The bullies were relentless and, even after telling someone, the situation continued to worsen until Luke said he was "at breaking point" and "needed some way to deal with it." Around that time, Luke started getting facial piercings and began exclusively wearing metal shirts to school. He vividly recalled how much differently people started treating him:

> It was going back around five years ago when I was about fourteen. . . . I ramped it right up and that's when it was like nah, let's go, and everyone gave me a wide berth, like pretty much don't fuck with him, and it was good. Like for me, these were the kids that used to tease me and bully me, now that they were giving me this much wider berth, I could breathe just a little bit. . . . To this day I could walk down this main street and everyone will avoid me and I like it that way. It's comforting to have that much personal space. (Luke)

Luke had never engaged in face-to-face metal community life, but nonetheless he gave a very strong commentary on how important it was for him throughout the interviews. He told of how "the sense of tight-knit community is just great," but it seemed more useful to him in practice to use his metal aesthetic to insulate himself against the bullies at school by intimidating them and driving them away.

As stated, participants had become acutely aware of the moral panics that have followed metal throughout its history, and they were able to use metal's negative image to their advantage at school in varying ways. For some this meant outright intimidating and repelling people who were actively harming their mental health (as Luke and others did), but for some it served as more of an insurance policy for avoiding bad things happening. For example, Tim wasn't overtly bullied, but he did not fit in with the dominant order of "jocks" at his all-boy Christian college because he was not athletically gifted (or inclined). For Tim, publicly signaling a collective metal identity served as a warning to the larger framed and more popular boys that they should leave him alone:

> I guess I tried to make people aware that I listened to metal so people wouldn't really pick on you that much . . . it was kind of like saying "I'm into metal, fuck off." There's that toughness element in metal,

where people view it and think "Oh I'm not gonna fuck with that guy cos he listens to metal." Their general idea of it is a lot different to what it really is, and that works in your favour at school, definitely. The idea that we're violent is just an image, compared to people who go out dressed in Everlast gear just to start fights. It's crazy what other people think of us when we're really harmless. (Tim)

Tim makes several references in the quote above to *listening to metal*, but it was his *identification with metal* that served as a deterrent to others and helped put a "safe" distance between him and the popular students. Further, this was an innovative disruption to dominant school norms because Tim said he knew he "wouldn't have to punch on with them," all he had to do was play on metal's negative image to keep the "wrong" people away from him. Jake describes his own experience of this in the following quote:

I told once [about the bullying] and it got worse after that so I thought fuck it, I need some way to deal with it, and being the mama's boy I am, I didn't wanna go out and find drugs or start drinking myself stupid or picking fights, cos I know I'll get bashed, so I needed something. . . . I started growing my hair as long as I could and on casual day I'd wear metal shirts which didn't go down well in a Christian school, but I didn't care. I used to draw band logos on everything, I'd write Slayer on my arm, you should see my school bag, it's got all Pantera and Slayer all over it, you get instant respect. . . . For three years I barely spoke a word, I just sat there with my iPod. . . . I would've been voted most likely to come back with a gun and shoot everyone . . . if you can just intimidate them and get them to pull back then you've won, you've got 'em. . . . It was just a way to shield myself. . . . I mean being metal is intimidating for some people, come on, you've got a dead corpse on your shirt! Yeah in a way it's reflecting "Don't talk to me," not that you'll do any harm, but they don't know that. You've had enough bad experiences, you just don't wanna deal with it anymore, this is a way to kind of keep people at bay, just a way to deal with the shit at school. (Jake)

In the quote above, Jake mentions "keeping people at bay" and earlier Luke talked about "being given a wide berth"; indeed many descriptors and metaphors were used by participants to signify the "breathing space" they created for themselves in hostile school environments by embodying a metal persona. Options for managing social challenges at school are severely limited by the fact that young people are trapped in their school environments and cannot avoid being drawn in to power relations unless they feign illness or truant which is only a temporary reprieve and does nothing to address the balance of power (Macklem 2003, 61). Young people do not have choices over which students they are placed with, and if victimized by bullies, cannot easily get to a safe place (Macklem 2003, 61). But here, these young people deployed metal identities to create their own space at school and put a safe distance between themselves and those they perceived as posing threats to their well-being. These were highly creative strategies for disrupting power relations and reducing or evading bullying, and crucially, these transformative strategies were able to be researched, devised, and enacted alone.

Despite the fact that social change was only being created at the level of the individual, there was still a strong sense that others were out there fighting the same fight as Jake captures below:

> If you've got that happening [being bullied] you kinda got nothing to look up to, you just say "What's the point?" . . . but you get into metal and you see other people going through shit and you know it's not just my cause. If all these guys got through it and are singing about it, I'm gonna get through it and sing about it, and I don't have to go and stab someone and go to jail to get even. It's true, metal gives people hope, it gives you power when you're powerless. (Jake)

Perhaps for Jake and others, the role of metal as a political change agent in the school environment did not get much more important than its perceived capacity for redistributing power in favor of the powerless—but as Jake highlighted, even though the construction and deployment of metal identities was highly individualized, there was also a deep sense of communion with others who might be facing similar struggles.

COLLECTIVE IDENTITY WORK IN A CHANGING MODERNITY

To this point we have seen that the idea of metal community was able to provide a sense of self-worth and acceptance for these young people through the conduit of imagined identification with like-minded metal peers, captured as keeping the "right" people in. We have also seen that collective metal identity formation was a good fit for keeping the "wrong" people out by playing on negative stereotypes of metal to intimidate and repel people at school who posed a threat to one's well-being. The anchor point for successfully achieving both of these outcomes hinged on the ways that metal, as an identity choice, could be drawn on as an individualized solution for fulfilling both requirements.

Indeed, it has become widely accepted that the burden of choosing, trialing, and revising identity options, and responsibility for failing at the task, has become an entrenched feature of modern living. Many have argued that the "individualization boost" to late modernity has arisen from profound global changes within the social, economic, and policy milieus that have rendered social structures and institutions less stable and less predictable than in previous generations—and with this, normative markers of identity have become less visible, if not completely unrecognizable in Western democracies (Bauman 2001b; Beck and Beck-Gernsheim 2001; Furlong and Cartmel 2007; Giddens 1991; Touraine

2007). As a consequence modern identities are chosen and built out of many diverse pieces, however the choices on offer are shaped and constrained by the identity resources one has access to at different points throughout one's life (Bauman 2001b; Shildrick, Blackman and MacDonald 2009). The youth phase can be like a weathervane for these changes because transitions to adulthood are especially complicated for young people *in general* by a growing range of life choices and concomitant uncertainty about how to choose—but here we are privy to the experiences of a particular group of young people who exemplify the need to access individualized solutions to challenging social circumstances, namely those who are marginally positioned as loners or outsiders in the school environment.

Through these young people's stories, we can see that their metal identity work was in a complex relationship with the micro-politics of exclusion at school and the broader social dynamics of individualization, and one place this was observable (among others) was in the ways that participants were individualizing their experiences of metal community life. For instance, metal *seemed* able to somewhat paradoxically resolve the contradictions between individualism and community[9] because the young people were able to access *what* they needed *when* they needed it without any external negotiations taking place—whether this was fulfilling a need to feel accepted and validated by a global community of like-minded peers at a time when they were otherwise feeling very alone, or whether it was meeting a need to repel people who posed a threat to their mental health and well-being. In both cases, a temporal sense of collective metal identity was sufficient for helping to mediate exclusion and survive school life.

When contemplating the blurring of identity and community in late modernity, Bauman (2001a, 16) proposed that shared vulnerabilities might prompt identity builders to "seek pegs on which they can together hang their individually experienced fears and anxieties, and having done that, perform the exorcism rites in the company of other similarly afraid and anxious individuals." He further wrote that:

> Whether such peg communities provide what it is hoped they offer—collective insurance against individually confronted uncertainties—is a moot question; but no doubt marching shoulder to shoulder along a street or two, mounting a barricade in the company of others or rubbing elbows in crowded trenches may supply a momentary respite from the loneliness. With good, bad, or no results, something at least has been done; one can derive some comfort from having refused to offer a sitting target and from having raised one's hands against the blows. (Bauman 2001a, 16)

At the micro-level of the individual who was hurt by social rejection, it seems that participants could indeed, as Bauman (2001a, 16) suggested, "derive some comfort from having refused to offer a sitting target and from having raised one's hands against the blows"—for these young people, embodying a metal identity was the move that metaphorically depicted raising one's hands against the blows of exclusion by popular peers, whether one had experienced this directly, or simply felt vulnerable to it occurring in future. Signaling metal community membership (to non-metal peers) was an individually orchestrated solution to emancipating oneself from social injustice. Reclaiming marginal "outsider" status as something to be celebrated (and even aspired to), self-insulating against social threats, and disrupting dominant social norms all amounted to a sense of "something at least having been done."

CONCLUSION

As Luke mentioned, being "in this together and taking care of our own" was largely the imagined experience of participants who had never met another metalhead in person during high school years—yet they had a definite sense of belonging to the metal community and seemed proud to take their place as the "weird kid" in their school (as Zombie put it) who refused to conform or comply with the dominant social order, spiritually marching shoulder to shoulder with the "weird kid" in the next school, and the next school, and the next.

When they reflected on what metal meant to them during high school years, it was common to hear statements such as "metal saved my life," "metal was always there for me," and "metal was the only thing that got me through school." It was clear that metal played a vital role in their biographies of survival, and crucially, the protective factors metal was able to elucidate were transferable between private and public spaces. At home participants worked on self-assigning metal community membership, and through this they developed a sense of belonging and acceptance and purpose; in public, they could create a safe space "on the run" by embodying a collective metal identity and deploying it in hostile environments, like school, to keep negative events at bay. So on one hand this was about self-protection and avoiding bad outcomes (a good outcome in itself), but it was also about gaining other positive outcomes that were reported as feelings of increased confidence, attaining respect, developing self-esteem and self-worth, and establishing a sense of self-empowerment—collectively amounting to an overall increase in personal resilience for dealing with adversity in their young lives.

As I wrote in the introduction, most of the existing information we have about the positive benefits of metal community life is provided by well-established metalheads, but in this chapter we have seen the importance of investigating *early* metal community formation and the *ways* metal youth feel connected to the metal community, often before they have met another metalhead in person. The communal bonds that the young people imagined during high school years were critical for protecting mental health, fostering well-being, and assisting positive developmental outcomes, a fact which challenges long-held assumptions that metal youth are "at-risk" *because* of the music they listen to and the subculture they align with. Hence the importance of investigating early metal community formation is two-fold: to unpack negative assumptions about metal communities and youth "at-risk," and to better understand how young people use metal music and culture as a positive coping strategy that generates protective factors for mental health and well-being. The results from this pilot study indicate that more research is needed in this area.

In closing, I acknowledge that metal community life must surely have its problems and tensions as all communities do, and that the stories told here do not represent all metal youth, however, none of the "problems" that have been attributed to young metalheads in previous studies (without direct or contextualized evidence) were reported or observed *in this research sample* (such as delinquent acts, substance (mis)use, aggressive behaviors, criminal histories). As it turned out, these were quite "ordinary kids" trying to find their own way of surviving high school and getting on with life. The more remarkable feature of their stories was the complex role that metal played in their ability to achieve this—a journey that began with powerful early imaginings of belonging to the global metal community.

NOTES

1. The research was approved by the University of South Australia's Human Research Ethics Committee. Participants provided written consent to the publishing of their transcripts.

2. Participant names used here are pseudonyms.

3. Dez Fafara is the vocalist for US band *Devil Driver*.

4. A "circle pit" is a moshing practice in which participants run in a circular motion creating a whirlpool effect, usually conducted in the middle of the crowd area behind the front rows of headbangers at concerts.

5. Randy Blythe is the vocalist for US band *Lamb of God*.

6. A "wall of death" is a moshing practice at concerts whereby participants are directed by the lead singer to line up in two rows at either side of the stage and are then instructed to run straight at each other in a style akin to foot soldiers on a battlefield.

7. Fafara and Blythe are renowned for instigating and choreographing extreme mosh pit participation by young people. Participants made repeated references to watching media clips of both bands and described what it was like to be in circle pits and walls of death, most without having actually participated in person.

8. Corpse paint is a style of make-up worn on the face, largely within black metal culture. The style of make-up is generally used to depict a corpse-like appearance.

9. Here I am talking about broader social dynamics of individualism, however Varas-Díaz et al. (2015, 90) have previously noted that contradictions also exist between the importance placed on individualism in metal lyrics, and the consistent

referencing of the concept of community in heavy metal. It is beyond the scope of this chapter to engage in a discussion around narratives of individualism in contemporary metal lyrics, but this does pose questions for future research as to whether metal youth feel obliged to take personal responsibility for their circumstances from messages they receive through metal lyrics, or whether metal lyrics validate and support the individualized solutions they are already undertaking in a changing modernity.

REFERENCES

Arnett, Jeffrey. 1996. *Metalheads: Heavy Metal Music and Adolescent Alienation.* Colorado: Westview Press.

Bauman, Zygmunt. 2001(a). *Community: Seeking Safety in an Insecure World.* Cambridge, UK: Polity Press.

———. 2001(b). *The Individualized Society.* Cambridge, UK: Polity Press.

Beck, Ulrich, and E. Beck-Gernsheim. 2001. *Individualization.* London: Sage Publications.

Brown, Andy R. 2010. "The Importance of Being Metal: The Metal Music Tabloid and Youth Identity Construction." In *The Metal Void: First Gatherings*, edited by N. W. R. Scott and I. V. Helden, 105–37. Oxford: Inter-Disciplinary Press.

———. 2011. "Heavy Genealogy: Mapping the Currents, Contraflows and Conflicts of the Emergent Field of Metal Studies, 1978–2010." *Journal for Cultural Research.* 15(3): 213–42.

Clifford-Napoleone, Amber. R. 2015. "Living in the Margins: Metal's Self-in-Reflection." *Metal Music Studies.* 1(3): 379–84.

Dunn, Sam, Scott McFadyen, and Jessica Joy Wise. 2005. *Metal: A Headbanger's Journey.* DVD. California: Banger Productions, Warner Home Video.

Furlong, Andy, and Fred Cartmel. 2007. *Young People and Social Change: New Perspectives.* 2nd edition. Berkshire: Open University Press.

Gardner, Robert. 2010. "Introduction — Spaces of Musical Interaction: Scenes, Subcultures and Communities." *Studies in Symbolic Interaction* 35: 71–77.

Giddens, Anthony. 1991. *Modernity and Self-identity.* United Kingdom: Polity Press.

Leung, Ambrose, and Cheryl Kier. 2010. "Music Preferences and Young People's Attitudes Towards Spending and Saving." *Journal of Youth Studies* 13, 681–98.

Lincoln, Siân. 2012. *Youth Culture and Private Space.* United Kingdom: Palgrave Mac-Millan.

Macklem, Gayle. 2003. *Bullying and Teasing: Social Power in Children's Groups.* New York: Kluwer Academic/Plenum Publishers.

McRobbie, Angela, and Jenny Garber. 2006. "Girls and Subcultures." In *Resistance Through Ritual*, edited by Stuart Hall and Tony Jefferson. 2nd edition. London: Routledge.

Polletta, Francesca, and James M. Jasper. 2001. "Collective Identity and Social Movements." *Annual Review of Sociology* 27: 283–305.

Riessman, Catherine Kohler. 2008. *Narrative Methods for the Human Sciences.* Thousand Oaks, CA: Sage Publications.

Roe, Keith. 1992. "Different Destinies, Different Melodies: School Achievement, Anticipated Status and Adolescents' Tastes in Music." *European Journal of Communication* 7(3): 335–58.

Schwartz, Kelly D., and Gregory Fouts. 2003. "Music Preferences, Personality Style, and Developmental Issues of Adolescents." *Journal of Youth and Adolescence* 32(3): 205–13.

Shildrick, Tracy, Shane Blackman, and Robert MacDonald. 2009. "Young People, Class and Place." *Journal of Youth Studies* 12(5): 457–65.

Spracklen, Karl. 2015. *Digital Leisure, the Internet, and Popular Culture: Communities and Identities in a Digital Age.* United Kingdom: Palgrave MacMillan.

Tanner, Julian, Mark Asbridge, and Scot Wortley. 2008. "Our Favourite Melodies: Musical Consumption and Teenage Lifestyles." *British Journal of Sociology* 59(1): 117–44.

Touraine, Alain. 2007. *Thinking Differently*. Cambridge, UK: Polity Press.

Varas-Díaz, Nelson, Eliut Rivera-Segarra, Carmen L. Rivera Medina, Sigrid Mendoza, and Osvaldo González-Sepúlveda. 2015. "Predictors of Communal Formation in a Small Heavy Metal Scene: Puerto Rico as a Case Study." *Metal Music Studies*. 1(1): 87–103.

Walton, Gerald, and Blair Niblett. 2012. "Investigating the Problem of Bullying Through Photo Elicitation." *Journal of Youth Studies 16*: 646–62.

Part 3

Communities in Contextual Interaction

SIX

Porous Communities

Critical Interactions Between Metal Music and Local Culture in the Caribbean Context

Nelson Varas-Díaz, Sigrid Mendoza, and Eric Morales

The scholarly examination of metal music has continued to grow in the past years and researchers involved in the field have further contributed to strengthening an interdisciplinary area of study which addresses a musical genre that was until recently almost systematically ignored in the social sciences (Hickam 2015). This expanding interest in metal continues to yield a plethora of new directions in which scholars have focused their interests and attention. Some of these include metal's relation to ethnicity (Wallach, Berger, and Greene 2012), race (Dawes 2013), religiosity (Moberg 2012; 2015), gender (Mendoza and Varas-Díaz 2013; Riches, Lashua, and Spracklen 2014), and sexuality (Clifford-Napoleone 2015), to name a few areas of inquiry.

One area of study that has also garnered attention has been the process of community building via metal. Although this might seem surprising to outsiders due to existing social prejudices, references to the communal experience are readily apparent in this musical genre. Shared experiences through music, geographical spaces, dress codes (e.g., shirts, battle jackets), dancing styles (e.g., moshing) and common symbols (e.g., hand gestures) are just some of the examples that point toward the importance of a common or shared experience in the process of creating or consuming metal (Snell and Hodgetts 2007).

Published literature on the formation of metal scenes has addressed how these groups are formed and sustained in light of metal (Wallach and Levine 2012). The existence of work on the subject evidences the importance of community building (frequently under the concept of scenes), while simultaneously recognizing that this is a complex process that warrants detailed scholarly attention. One reason why this area of study needs to be discussed in detail has to do with apparent tensions in the process of community formation, many of which are discussed in this edited volume. One area of particular importance for the formation of communities in metal has to do with the borders established between groups. The process through which communities define themselves and establish criteria for membership relies upon the closure of borders. This is a necessary process to establish group narratives and cohesion. Still, this process is sometimes simultaneously accompanied by aperture to the cultural context of a specific community. In this chapter we aim to document this interaction between communal closure and its contextual interaction using the Caribbean region as an example. We focus on how metal communities in Puerto Rico and Cuba interact with their cultural context, and highlight this process via three examples: 1) the critical examination of local folk tales via lyrical content, 2) the use of artwork to link local culture to metal's dark undercurrent, and 3) the challenging of communal borders via the integration of local instrumentation into metal. These three examples will help us highlight how the porous nature of metal communities in the region are part of a critical agenda that aims to use metal music as a way to challenge social norms and expectations.

COMMUNITY AS CLOSURE

To outsiders, metal communities might seem to be composed of groups of individuals that are difficult to access for newcomers. There is a plethora of symbolic practices that need to be understood in order to access these communal spaces. This is not necessarily a problematic situation, as communities tend to guard their borders, particularly when they have been socially labeled and persecuted. This process of policing communal borders is evidenced in theoretical perspectives on community. These multiple theoretical propositions have almost uniformly, albeit sometimes tacitly or indirectly, fostered the idea that communal formation is dependent on closure of borders. This entails a process through which members of the community identify each other and subsequently differentiate themselves from outsiders.

The idea of group closure or limits is ubiquitously present in many theoretical contributions to the subject of community. For example, community psychologists have written extensively about the role of geographical proximity in the creation of communal consciousness (Sánchez

2000; Rappaport and Seidman 2006). In these approaches, physical proximity and face-to-face interaction are prerequisites for communal formation. Psychologists have also focused on the functional aspects of the community addressing concepts like "social support" and "in-group vs. out-group dynamics" (Montero 2002; 2009). These endeavors have aimed to examine the purpose of communities, specifically, what people gain from entering communal practices (Wenger 1998). In these psychology-based approaches those that are physically proximal and have a supportive purpose in the collective are labeled as insiders, and those who do not are conversely outsiders.

Sociological approaches have focused on how communities are "imagined" when face-to-face interaction is scarce (Anderson 2006). This approach places importance on how communities develop a historical perspective that strengthens their existence. Sociology has also focused on the emotional connectedness of the communal experience in late modernity through the concept of "neo-tribes" (Maffesoli 1996). The central idea here is that modern institutions based on metanarratives of progress and rationality have run their course and a return to more primitive-style groupings is taking place focusing on emotional connectedness. From these perspectives, group closure is intimately related to shared imagined historical events in the communal past and emotional linkages between its members. People who do not share these narratives of emergence and the subsequent emotional connection these bring forth may not be considered part of the community.

Although these theoretical perspectives on community are not necessarily complimentary to each other and emerge from different areas of knowledge, they have served to understand how individuals come together and the reasons they have to do so. These theoretical propositions on communal formation have also served to delineate a process through which outsiders are identified and labeled as foreign members to the community. That is, while research focuses on establishing the mechanisms through which a community is formed it simultaneously describes a process through which outsiders are identified. For example, these theoretical perspectives have focused on the importance of place, function, emotional connectedness, and shared history as important aspects of the communal experience. Therefore, those who *do not* share a place, function, historical connection, or emotional attachment to the group may be labeled as outsiders to the community. This is important for communal formation, as it gives members specific criteria to identify as a group.

The process of analyzing community formation has been extremely valuable since it helps understand how groups are formed and sustained. In the case of metal, it has provided evidence of the complex processes that communities put in place to grant membership. This has been particularly present in small metal scenes where face-to-face contact is frequent and almost inevitable. For example, our team's previous research on community formation in the Caribbean, specifically Puerto Rico's metal scene, evidenced that in order to be considered a member of the local metal scene individuals had to meet multiple criteria related to knowledge, frequency of participation, and sense of belonging. Lower sense of community was documented among participants that did not meet the stringent criteria set by members of the collective (Varas-Díaz et al. 2015). Notable research efforts that explore how communal borders are constructed have been carried out. Nevertheless, they only reveal one side of the story in the process of group formation. Further research needs to also focus on how those communal borders are strategically breached for the benefit of the members of the community.

Our concern is that while describing inclusion criteria for communal membership scholars have neglected to explore the process through which those same members might need to challenge those borders in order to interact with the world outside of their immediate communities. For the purpose of advancing research on metal communities throughout the world, we understand that the following questions must be addressed: What happens when metal communities decide to explore beyond their borders? How do we document such border transgressions and ruptures with the process of closure? For what purposes is communal border transgression enacted? We discuss some of these issues in the following sections.

POROUS COMMUNITIES

As stated before, scholarly work on the communal experience has placed an important focus on how communities are formed via inclusion criteria that yield collective identity narratives and experiences through the establishment of borders. Some of these efforts have simultaneously taken into consideration how those groups are embedded in particular cultural contexts that help shape their communal experience. This has become an important line of research as metal continues to spread to evermore-varied geographies.

Wallach, Berger, and Greene's work on metal and globalization has challenged and motivated scholars to understand this musical genre as an ever-expanding global phenomenon that is present in diverse cultural settings (Wallach, Berger, and Greene 2012). This invitation to explore metal from a pluralistic perspective has been echoed by many researchers engaged in efforts to understand how metal scenes are formed throughout the world. This has been an ongoing agenda that has yielded research in diverse settings like Nepal (Green 2012), Israel (Kahn-Harris 2012), Japan (Kawano and Hosokawa 2012), Malta (Bell 2012), Turkey (Hecker 2012), South Africa (Hoad 2014), Puerto Rico (Varas-Díaz et al. 2014) and

Egypt (LeVine 2008), just to name a selection. These studies have been crucial to further understand how metal has been received in these settings and how consumers, when possible, have constituted communal experiences centered on the musical genre throughout the world. More importantly, they have shed light on how the local cultural context in which these groups are embedded can influence communal formation, both in a positive or negative manner.

One particular way in which we can examine the influence of local culture on metal is through the music and accompanying practices being created in a specific community. Metal has its particular cannons and rules for sounds, images, and performances that allow individuals to identify it as distinct from other musical genres. Still, this does not mean that these practices and the communities that are created around it are isolated from their context (Varas-Díaz and Mendoza 2015). This is particularly true for bands that have integrated elements of their cultural context into their sound and aesthetic practices (Varas-Díaz et al. 2014). We are using the concept of cultural context to reflect a wide variety of constructs that are characteristic of the setting in which a musical community is embedded. This can include references to national origin or ethnic composition of the community under examination. This integration of the local into metal is clearly evident in bands that embrace elements of their cultural setting into their music, including but not limited to: instrumentation, visual images, and lyrical content.

Latin America is a great example to evidence how metal communities have relaxed their borders in order to interact with the local cultural context. The region is rich in a vast diversity of languages, ethnic groups, nationalities and cultural practices that are sometimes not discussed or outright overlooked at the epicenters of metal production or academic scholarship. As a quick example for the uninitiated in Latin American metal, Table 6.1 provides a summary of bands from multiple countries in the region that integrate local cultural elements into metal and successfully establish a dialogue between traditional metal sounds and regional cultural elements. A glance at the table will immediately evidence to readers that the integration of local culture into metal has been present in this region for a long time and has been manifested by bands in varied subgenres of metal. This integration encompasses, in varied combinations, the use of native instruments in music, lyrical content and overall imagery in their artwork.

The ongoing integration of local culture into metal in Latin America serves as an example of how these communities are not built on isolation. Their borders are porous and in constant interaction with the cultural context in which they are embedded. This integration of the local cultural context into metal could be explained in many ways. For example, it could be argued that the decision is commercially motivated in order to stand out in a saturated international market. If this were the main rea-

Table 6.1.   Example of bands from Latin America that integrate local culture into their music.

Country	Band	Type of cultural integration (instruments, lyrical content, visual imagery)
Argentina	Yanaconas	Instruments, lyrical content, and imagery.
Bolivia	Alcoholika	Instruments and lyrical content.
Brazil	Arandu Arakuaas	Instruments, lyrical content, and imagery.
Chile	Huinca	Instruments, lyrical content, and imagery.
Colombia	Eware	Instruments, lyrical content, and imagery.
Costa Rica	Mantra	Lyrical content.
Cuba	Tendencia	Instruments, lyrical content, and imagery.
Dominican Republic	Toque Profundo (hard rock)	Lyrical content and imagery.
Ecuador	Aztra	Instruments, lyrical content, and imagery.
El Salvador	Kabala	Lyrical content and imagery.
Guatemala	Magma	Lyrical content.
Honduras	Delirium	Lyrical content and imagery.
México	Cemican	Instruments, lyrical content, and imagery.
Nicaragua	Vortex	Lyrical content and imagery.
Panama	Spirit of the Deep Waters	Instruments, lyrical content, and imagery.
Paraguay	Acrux	Lyrical content and imagery.
Peru	Chaska	Instruments, lyrical content, and imagery.
Puerto Rico	Dantesco	Lyrical content and imagery.
Uruguay	Pecho e' Fierro	Instruments, lyrical content, and imagery.
Venezuela	Gillman	Lyrical content and imagery.

son, it would still be valid in light of the great number of metal bands throughout the world and the need for new ones to stand out as different. Although this might be an acceptable commercially laden point to explain such a decision, we understand that this process is more complex.

As we will show with specific examples in this chapter, a more detailed examination of how local culture is integrated into metal points to a more critical agenda that aims to engage in three simultaneous processes: 1) to differentiate local metal communities from the homogenization fostered by an international metal scene, 2) to critically discuss how metal communal identities are interrelated to other group identities (e.g., race, religion) in these contexts, and 3) to critically examine the messages being proposed by local cultures with regard to the socialization of individuals via culture.

In order to understand this critical agenda in the integration of local culture into metal music, it would be useful to examine how communal agency has been addressed in the academic literature in the region. For example, Venezuelan community psychologist Maritza Montero has addressed the subject of communal involvement and critical consciousness in Latin America. One of her many concerns with the issue of community is related to how minority communities, who frequently have little access to power circles in the region, have been rarely understood in light of their capacity for resistance and challenging the status quo in which they are embedded. Instead, most accounts focus on how they are a site of oppression and its manifestations. She has stated the following:

> The capacity for resistance of minorities (understood in a social sense as powerless or submitted groups) have been frequently underestimated, which can be a consequence of the need to highlight the effects of oppression. This can lead to a lessening of the image of these groups who, when observed in detail, can show an amazing amount of resources that can allow them to keep their beliefs, customs and identity alive, developing and conserving them in adverse situations. (Montero 2006, 127) [our translation]

Therefore, she calls for a different perspective in understanding communities in which we examine how they can be a source of critical reflection regarding their context, and even resistance to oppressive power dynamics.

> We should add that in the case of communities that act like active minorities (not all do), when they evaluate their needs and available resources, the community engages in a different power balance and can situate conflict in a different perspective, looking to even out forces. (Montero 2006, 134)

Montero's positions on communal resistance to power dynamics of oppression echo proposals on critical consciousness of other more widely recognized authors in the region like Brazilian educator Paulo Freire's proposals on critical pedagogy (1970) and Colombian sociologist Orlando Fals Borda's position on participatory research (1991), just to name two examples. All of them share the notion that communities engage in critical explorations of their context in order to react to it in varied manners. Active communities can be critical regarding their positions and situations in specific geographical, historical and cultural contexts. Could the same, or at least something similar, be expected of communities constructed around metal music?

CARIBBEAN HEAVY METAL AS A POROUS COMMUNITY

Our team has engaged in research with the local metal scenes in Puerto Rico, the Dominican Republic, and Cuba with the overall goals of: 1) documenting the development of these local scenes from a historical perspective, and 2) exploring how local cultures interact with metal music and vice versa (Varas-Díaz and Rivera 2014). The study has incorporated multiple techniques for data gathering including extensive ethnographic observations, in-depth interviews, quantitative surveys with local fans and musicians, and documentary filmmaking. The methodological approach of the study has integrated elements of Community Based Participatory Research (CBPR) (Jason 2004; Whyte 1991) through which local scene members have become part of our team and engaged in the process of data gathering and interpretation (McIntyre 2008). In general, we have carried out more than eighty interviews in the three countries and engaged in more than five hundred hours of observation. Since our team is based in Puerto Rico, this has entailed multiple ethnographic visits to the Dominican Republic and Cuba throughout 2014 and 2015.

As mentioned before, in this chapter we discuss three examples that evidence the interaction between metal communities and their cultural context. These include the following: 1) the critical examination of local folk tales via lyrical content (Puerto Rico), 2) the use of artwork to link local culture to metal's dark undercurrent (Puerto Rico) and 3) the challenging of communal borders via the integration of local instrumentation into metal (Cuba).

Example #1: Critically Examining Local Folk Tales via Lyrics

The approximation of metal to local culture in Puerto Rico can be exemplified with the interplay between bands and local folk tales or narratives. One particular band that has participated in this practice is *Dantesco*. They are a doom/epic metal band from the rural town of Cayey. They have released five full length albums including the self-titled *Dantesco* (Dantesco 2004), *De la Mano de la Muerte* (Dantesco 2005), *Pagano* (Dantesco 2008), *The Ten Commandments of Metal* (Dantesco 2010), *Seven Years of Battle* (Dantesco 2011), and *We Don't Fear Your God* (Dantesco 2013). *Dantesco* has been signed to international labels such as Cruz del Sur (Italy) and Inframundo Records (Mexico). They have played shows in Panamá (2004), Costa Rica (2004), Colombia (2005), Germany (2006), and the United States (2008, 2009, 2011, 2013).

Dantesco has stood apart from other local bands due to their consecutive release of albums, having more than any other band in the history of the local scene. Their lyrics address philosophical issues related to death, violence, and religion. Vocalist Eric Morales, a trained tenor singer, has made the ensemble stand apart from others through his skills in lyrical compositions, which are heavily influenced by his master's degree in philosophy. *Dantesco* has garnered underground followers across Latin America and Europe.

For the purpose of this chapter their importance lies in the content of their lyrics. Throughout their catalogue, *Dantesco*'s singer has made a conscious decision to integrate narrative aspects of Puerto Rico's history into their music. For example, they have addressed issues of colonial resistance in descriptions of battles between native indigenous populations and Spanish conquistadors (e.g., *Morir de Pie*). This constant interaction between metal music and discussions over local culture could be considered somewhat minor when compared to the rest of their lyrical content. Still, it came to full realization as part of an EP they released in 2015 entitled *Venancio* (Dantesco 2015) (see figure 6.1). The EP has as its title the name of the main character of a Puerto Rican folk tale that is well known in the countryside of the island.

The folk tale describes the life of a fisherman who lived in the rural and mountainous town of Orocovis. He depended on the river to feed his family. Venancio was a humble and religious man described as devout and obedient to god. He carried with him a wooden cross that his father had made for him as an amulet of protection against evil. One night, as Venancio was fishing, he lost track of time and night closed in on him. Lost in the countryside and with no light to guide him, he decided to set his cross on fire to light his way home. Although that action would allow him to find his way back home, he had inadvertently condemned his soul forever. He died shortly after that day and god doomed him to roam the countryside until he could gather all the ashes from the burnt cross. Of course, this was an impossible endeavor and Venancio's soul roamed forever in penance and darkness. The folk tale ends with a cautionary warning to the unbelieving listener. All of those who would call out to Venancio and offer him the sought after ashes, would bear witness to the fisherman and die alongside the river (table 6.2 shows the song's lyrics).

Like all folk tales, the story of Venancio has a sociocultural role to play in local communities. Its main objective is to ensure that transgressions against religion and god are curtailed by fear of its negative consequences, in this case physical and spiritual death. In the countryside the folk tale is used to educate locals, particularly the uneducated and the young, about the consequences of religious transgression. Even today, the elderly can attest to the effects of the tale in their development as

Figure 6.1.   Artwork for Dantesco's album *Venancio*. Image used with permission from artist Kadriel Betsen.

young Puerto Ricans living on the island. *Dantesco* skillfully uses the folk tale for a completely opposite effect. Specifically, the band aims to pose a critical analysis of the role of religion in Puerto Rican life. Eric Morales explained his intent when writing the lyrics for *Dantesco*:[1]

> I have always been fascinated with the legends and folk tales of our Island. Some of them are very colorful and mix superstition with reality. Venancio's story is very particular as a good man is turned into a ghost that haunts people in the countryside who dare make fun of his spiritual conundrum. Venancio is forced to roam the earth looking for the ashes of the cross his father gave him, and which he had to use to keep warm and find his way back home. Here we can see how superstition and the illness we call "faith" strips him from all his good qualities and denies his salvation for a mere piece of wood, in this case shaped as a cross. It is culturally important as it shows local respect for religious figures and family dynamics, as it was his father who gave him the cross as a gift. . . . In the end, god denies salvation for this good man who has made only one mistake in his life. Venancio's story is about

Table 6.2. Lyrics for the song *Venancio* from Puerto Rican band *Dantesco*.

Lyrics: Eric Morales
Translation: Kayra Fuster

English translation	Original version in Spanish
Days of hunger and despair Venancio the fisherman endured. Fishes he lured to feed his brood from the bowels of the island of disenchantment.	Los tiempos del hambre y desesperación los vivió Venancio el pescador. Y del río en el centro de la tierra del espanto, el buen hombre a su familia alimentó.
Darkness, always on his side, soulmate to his plight. Always true to the river, but tonight, his moon will die.	La oscuridad siempre fue su gran amiga. Hermana de su realidad. Él siempre fiel a las aguas del río, hoy su luna se apagará.
Venanio, diligent and just. Venancio, you never imagined what death could entrust.	Venancio, hombre justo y de bien. Venancio, no te imagines lo que la muerte te traerá.
Faithful man, cross in hand, a gift from the Father. Never he imagined it would seal his fate one stormy night.	Hombre de gran fe con su sagrada cruz. Bendición que de su padre heredó. Jamás imaginó que lo cubriera el negro manto, solo un una noche de lluvia sin final.
Bitter cold took over, and he, stricken and lonely turned his cross into a torch, and for all eternity forsook his soul.	Y el frío cruel lo arropó en esa noche. Y este hombre enfermo en soledad prendió la cruz y con ella hizo un jacho. Maldijo su eternidad.
Piscator Venancio soon died; his soul lost the fight. He was denied eternal rest, forced to wander every night the ashes of the cross to find.	Poco después Venancio falleció y su alma no encontró salvación. Descanso eterno te fue negado. Vagarás en pena Venancio. ¡Busca las cenizas de tu cruz!
At dawn you can hear him cry like a wounded creature. Watch the fire in the sky! If you think it can't be, if you want yourself to see, go ahead, offer him the ashes he seeks.	Y de madrugada se le escucha llorando como animal herido y el fuego se fue volando. ¡Y si tú no lo crees! ¡Y si lo quieres ver! Solo ve y ofrécele las cenizas de su cruz.

Lyrics: Eric Morales
Translation: Kayra Fuster

English translation	Original version in Spanish
Venancio,	¡Venancio,
have your ashes!	aquí están tus cenizas!
Fire takes over the forest	Y un fuego se enciende en el medio del
and you he watches.	bosque
Run, before he catches you	Y sus ojos te ven
and drags you with him!	¡Corre! ¡Corre que te agarra!
You'll burn alive	Y tu alma se lleva a vagar con él.
and next to the river, you'll die,	Amanecerás en el río,
and no one will know why.	quemado tu cuerpo
Venacio,	y nadie sabrá por qué.
have your ashes!	¡Venancio,
	Aquí están tus cenizas!

how faith is used to instill fear and how this is transmitted in our local customs.

The importance of *Dantesco's* take on the Venancio folk tale is dual. First, it evidences how the interaction between metal and local culture in this setting is done from a critical perspective. That is, the folk tale is reframed to expose the injustices carried out under the Christian faith and warns listeners about the negative consequences of religiosity. Second, it is one among many examples of how local metal bands have made efforts to integrate local culture into their music, in this case their lyrical content. The reception to the song among Puerto Rican metal fans has been extremely positive, as it has been interpreted as a strategic effort to link the local metal scene with the wider cultural content in which it is embedded. Eric Morales explained this as part of our interviews on the subject:

> Venancio was a historical character. He existed in Puerto Rico and died alone and sick, before being integrated into this folk story. Using his story is my way of linking Dantesco and myself to Puerto Rico's cultural landscape and our folklore. It is a way to delve into the people's past, fears and beliefs. It was a natural progression for Dantesco who had written about other heroes and legends. Why not do it with someone from my country? We have written about other legends and heroes like Anibal, Viriatus, Vlad Tepes, Beowulf, Ricardo and Saladino, Rasputin, Odin, and Lucifer, among others. It was Venancio's time . . . and in the future we will continue with others local figures.

Finally, members of the local metal scene have interpreted *Dantesco's* incursion into local folklore as a strategy to inform the rest of the world of Puerto Rico's culture. In this case, metal is interpreted as a vehicle for cultural dissemination. Rafael Bracero, a local leader in the metal scene and president of the Puerto Rico Metal Alliance, interpreted *Dantesco's* resignification of Venancio in the following manner:

Puerto Rico has a rich culture due to its fusion of different ethnicities and customs from indigenous, African and European populations. However, it is not visible enough so that other people and the rest of the world know about it. Dantesco is the ideal instrument to make this happen because of Eric's talent as a storyteller through his lyrics, as shown in songs like Venancio. It's time to let the world know our folklore through a different musical perspective.

Example #2: Finding Brutality in the Local via Artwork

Another approximation of metal and local culture in Puerto Rico can be found in the artwork developed for the promotion of concerts throughout the island. Usually this artwork is developed by local musicians and reflects very traditional images now intimately related to metal music throughout the world (e.g., skulls, death, musical instruments, dark landscapes). Therefore, it is not unusual to see obscure imagery being part of most promotional artwork for local shows. Still, more recently the use of images has become more refined and complex, as we will show in the following example.

During 2015 a series of events took place in Puerto Rico celebrating the presence of a small yet burgeoning black metal scene on the island. These events were developed by Adversary Productions under the title "Blackened: An Insular Black Metal Orgy." The concerts were promoted under the leadership of local musician and graphic artist Kadriel Betsen. One immediate difference between these events and other concerts in the history of the local metal scene was the use of alternative artwork for promotional purposes. Gone were the black metal images traditionally used to associate an event with the genre, as they were substituted by reinterpretations of local traditional Puerto Rican art.

Our team interviewed artist Kadriel Betsen on several occasions and there we explored his decision to use traditional Puerto Rican artwork as part of the promotion of the event. It quickly became evident that the decision was not taken lightly and that there was a deep underlying reflection on the role of local culture in black metal. Specifically, the need to merge the music with local elements as a reflection of the differences between the lived experiences of black metal musicians on the island as compared to the genre's region of origin. Betsen explained the following:

> Heavy Metal in all its forms and expressions is an affirmation of individualism and rebellion. It is a ground where everything from the divine to the profane is discussed ruthlessly and openly. This individualistic perspective is also influenced by culture, which shapes how we see and understand the world. Metal in Puerto Rico is not exempt from local culture, but instead of examining that culture . . . we sometimes limit ourselves to emulating cultural manifestations of other bands that have no relation to us. There is nothing wrong with admiring and adopting the qualities of other cultures, but when you are searching for

honesty in your musical expression I find it difficult to focus on those. As a black metal musician I can say it is attractive to emulate and reproduce what Nordic bands have done, which pays tribute to their culture. Do they influence us? Of course they do! They infuse their music with their experiences. Still, what I feel and live is different; my culture is different. Therefore, if I am going to be honest with my music and myself I can't limit myself to the Nordic vision in the genre.

In order to reflect local culture's potential interaction with black metal music, Kadriel focused on the artwork that would be used to promote the event. This artwork, disseminated via electronic media to the local metal community, would reach a vast number of music fans throughout Puerto Rico.[2] Ironically, even those who were not present for the concerts themselves were at some point exposed to the artistic imagery developed for the event, which was disseminated via Facebook and discussed in a long running college radio show. The artists used this strategy to reflect on the dark imagery of Puerto Rican origin, which was ubiquitous to locals. He mentioned the following:

> Just like in other genres, visual art is an important part of music. Black metal artists use frozen landscapes and Viking symbols in their art. Some in Puerto Rico might think that using indigenous symbols or "jíbaro"[3] imagery could compromise the genre's aesthetics. I think our culture is much more than "casabe"[4] and indigenous representations of the sun. Our culture is also rich in darkness and morbidity. We have representations of demons (e.g., vejigantes[5]), myths and legends of wandering spirits like the fisherman Venancio.

One of the most salient promotional images used for the shows was based on the work of local artist Francisco Oller (1833–1917). Oller is one of Puerto Rico's most important painters. During his lifetime he had the opportunity to live and train in Madrid and Paris, where he co-existed and was influenced by European Impressionism. In 1868 he founded the Free Academy of Drawing and Painting in Puerto Rico and is therefore considered one of the forefathers of local painting (Temin 2006, 167). One of his most important painting is entitled *El Velorio* (The Wake) (see figure 6.2). The painting captures a traditional scene from the Puerto Rican countryside (also present in other Latin American countries) where local communities would carry out a celebration when faced with the death and burial of a minor (i.e., Baquiné). This practice was based on the Christian influenced idea that a small and baptized child who died suddenly had instant access to heaven in the afterlife. The community would then celebrate while facing the difficult situation and in turn expect blessing from the departed from beyond. Authors have argued that Oller, while aiming to depict an image of Puerto Rican life, also posed a more elevated critique on death as a freeing event (Erazo 2008). After all, those left behind would need to face the difficulties of life while the departed waited in heavenly ecstasy. The University of Puerto Rico houses the original painting to this day. Kadriel Betsen mentioned the following as a rationale for the use of the painting:

> I personally look for manifestations in our culture that focus on darkness, primary instinct, and hedonism. Some of these elements can be found in the work of one of our greatest artists, Francisco Oller. His piece "Baquiné," a word of African descent, shows the wake of a child. We can see in this painting our customs, but it also shows excess, religious indifference, and a cult of death. That piece of work has all the requisites of the black metal aesthetic.

One of the most important aspects explained by Betsen for his selection of the piece is his direct relation with black metal aesthetics. In our conversations he would describe the original piece as "brutal" and "morbid." Ironically, most people in Puerto Rico would link traditional pastoral and countryside imagery to an idyllic past. Still, Betsen's reinterpretation had a different agenda (see figure 6.3). The image is used in black and white to provide it with an even more dreary composition. The final image focuses on the dead child in the middle of the room and the dead animal hanging from the house rafters. In this reinterpretation several issues stand out: 1) the central aspect of death as an unspoken issue in Puerto Rican culture (this is shared with Oller's original intent, but now reinvented for local metal fans), 2) the correlation between the death of a human child and that of an animal as equivalents and therefore diminish-

Figure 6.2. "El Velorio" (The Wake) by Francisco Oller (1893). Oil on Canvas, 8' x 10'. Collection, University of Puerto Rico's History, Anthropology and Art Museum.

ing the supremacy of the former (human) over the latter (animal), and 3) the ironical celebration of death by religious individuals who seem to be more concentrated on the afterlife than the present human condition. In summary, Betsen successfully shows that local culture can also be inherently dark and concentrate on the less talked about issues in contemporary local society that are deemed too dark. Most importantly, his intent to position local culture as a source of inspiration for black metal music served as a conversation piece for the local community who would then look for dark roots of inspiration in their cultural backyard, far away from the Nordic origins of the genre. He clearly achieves his goal of highlighting how the narratives of the local metal community in Puerto Rico are slowly becoming intertwined with other contextual narratives regarding religion and ethnicity.

Figure 6.3.   Reinterpretation of Francisco Oller's "El Velorio" for a local black metal concert. Image used with permission from artist Kadriel Betsen.

Example #3: Challenging Borders via Local Instrumentation

A third example of how metal communities interact with their cultural context is the integration of local musical instrumentation into their music. In the Caribbean this is perfectly reflected by the Cuban band *Tendencia*. The band is one of the longest running bands in Cuba having released their first demo in 1995. They have released three full-length albums throughout their career entitled *Re-evolución (2001), Rebeldes (2004)* and *Confidencial (2009)*. Their sound can be described as thrash metal with the integration of Afro Caribbean instrumentation. Specifically, they prominently use *congas* and *timbales* as part of their rhythm section. The band identifies itself as mestizo metal. Mestizo is the local word to reference individuals who are of mixed racial and ethnic heritage. This entails that the band has assumed a musical identity based on the integration of different races into their sound. More importantly, their choice of instrumentation seems to highlight the centrality of their African identity.

During our ethnographic work done in the Caribbean metal scenes, specifically in Cuba during 2015, multiple conversations were held with *Tendencia's* guitarist Sergio Ernesto. He discussed how the band integrated racial and ethnic elements from their immediate cultural context into their music. He described their use of the label mestizo metal:

> Mestizo metal is a term we used because we did not want to be pushed into a box. Since we were always asked how we labeled ourselves . . . we decided upon mestizo metal in light of Cuba's mestizo heritage. Also, our music is a hybrid . . . a "culinary stew" of many things. Respect for the human race is important for us, and therefore we claim respect for the Latin race, our customs, music, ideas and ways of living. That is what we sing about in our lyrics.

The use of the mestizo metal label as part of their musical identity is an important issue to consider when understanding the band's proposal for metal in their setting. It reflects the interaction between traditional metal practices with local cultural instrumentation. This is best exemplified in their integration of local instruments into their rhythm section, specifically the *Batá* drum (See figure 6.4). The drum is mainly used as part of practices in the Yoruba religion and Santería, which have deep roots in the influx of communities of African origin brought to Cuba as part of the slave trade. The set is composed of three drums with distinct names and sounds. *Iyá* is the largest of the drums and referred to as "mother drum." *Itótele* is the mid-sixed drum and is referred to as the "father." Finally, *Okónkolo* is the "baby" drum. The drums are played in specific rhythmic patters as part of religious practices in Cuba. Furthermore, a Santero usually prepares the drum set in a religious ceremony before being given to a particular musician. *Tendencia* have managed to integrate this local rhythmic instrument to their metal sound in a seamless manner.

The existence of a metal band that uses the label mestizo metal and incorporates local instruments to their sound is an important example of the interaction between metal communities and their cultural context. Their conscious decision to highlight their Afro-Caribbean roots is particularly important since the discussion of race and religion can be sometimes difficult to openly carry out in the Spanish speaking Caribbean Islands. For example, discussions over race in the Dominican Republic and Puerto Rico have always been tense, and systematic efforts have been carried out by local governments to lessen the importance of the African roots in their population (Varas-Díaz and Mendoza 2015). The same has happened with local religious traditions that are interpreted as deviations from traditional Catholicism. Although Cuba has made strides in discussing the role of racism in the Caribbean, particularly after the 1959 revolution, racial tensions are still an issue. *Tendencia* highlights how critical discussions over race and religion are being carried out via metal music in the context of Cuba via direct interaction with their cultural context. They evidence how metal is richly embedded within local identities that require critical discussions over issues of race, religion, and the colonial histories of these islands.

Figure 6.4.   Member of the Cuban band Tendencia playing the Batá drum.

MOVING FORWARD WITH COMMUNITY RESEARCH
IN HEAVY METAL

As stated at the onset of this chapter, metal studies is a young burgeoning interdisciplinary area of study. Therefore, we will inevitably continue to see research efforts being carried out in diverse settings and addressing a plethora of issues that are of interest to scholars, musicians, and fans. Judging by the published scholarly work in the past decade, research aiming to understand small metal scenes throughout the world will continue to thrive as it allows readers and music fans insight on how metal is consumed and created in places of the world where they would otherwise have little access. The emergence of small scenes throughout the world, and their subsequent self-identification as communities will surely be an important part of this larger research endeavor in the future.

As this research agenda on communal formation and metal moves forward, it is important to understand how its members describe the communal experience. This includes providing rich descriptions of the criteria they use to identify long-standing members in their groups, and how these same criteria are used to assess and include/exclude new members into the fold. Just as important, we need to understand how these communities, once formed and self-aware of their collective status, decide to interact with their context in different ways. As evidenced in the examples provided in this chapter, this interaction can reflect particularities of their cultural contexts while simultaneously being critical of their underlying socializing agenda. This closure/porous dynamic process will provide scholars with a better understanding of how communities are formed and sustained, and more importantly, what purpose does this process serve beyond musical enjoyment.

The porous nature of metal communities will continue to be an important issue to address in the near future for metal scholars. As metal continues to spread across the world it will interact with an even more diverse audience that will represent local cultures and their relation to this musical genre (and vice versa). Issues related to race, ethnicity, language, religion, politics, and folklore, just to name some axes of analysis, will inevitably continue to inform future perusals on metal throughout the world. The examination of the porous dynamic of metal communities with regard to their cultural context will inevitably find cases where such interaction is used as part of a commercial identity (i.e., gimmick). In a global community where authenticity is highly valued, some in the metal community might interpret this decision as inauthentic or purely commercial; and they might be right. Still, the possibility should not deter researchers from examining other functions ascribed to this interaction with local culture.

The examples provided in this chapter evidence how bands in the Caribbean setting have integrated local culture into their metal related practices. This is possible partly because of their porous constitution that allows interaction with the extremely diverse settings that can be found in the region; mostly generated due to its history of colonization and subsequent cultural clashes between groups and ideas. This interaction allows local metal communities to differentiate themselves from other epicenters of metal production that have little cultural relevance for them (e.g., the United States, Europe). This is itself an interesting challenge to the sometimes-present tendency toward homogenization in the global metal scene (e.g., only one legitimate way of sounding, looking, acting). More importantly, the integration of local culture into metal music becomes a mechanism to critically explore the latter and the messages that are being transmitted through it to younger generations. It seems quite clear that in the provided examples for this chapter that the integration of local culture into metal is strategically used to extend the music's critical perspective toward its immediate surroundings. If metal musicians and fans are going to open their communities to their cultural context, they seem to prefer to do so through a critical lens that challenges the values transmitted through it.

As authors, we are aware that this critical agenda that seems to accompany the porous condition of the metal communities under study will almost inevitably cross over into politics, as subjects related to religion and ethnicity are clearly related to colonization in the Americas. This is interesting since scholars in metal music studies have documented how metal music seems to avoid, to some extent, incursions into the political arena (Scott 2012). Still, it seems to us that any openness to local cultures in the region will lend itself to overlaps with political analysis due to its historical and colonial past. The porous nature of metal communities in the Caribbean, when part of a critical agenda, will almost inevitably intersect with political analysis on identities, ethnicities, and religions.

In the end, scholars will be better equipped to understand small metal communities through the lens of the apparent paradox of closure/porousness. Although closure ensures membership and survival, the porous constitution of the metal community will allow it to critically reflect upon its context and inject the international scene with ever more diverse voices and experiences. The three examples provided in this chapter evidence how the closure/porousness dynamic serves to build the boundaries of the metal community while simultaneously allowing it access to its surroundings. Hopefully more communities throughout the world will be able to use their porous constitution to further metal's utility as a vehicle for a critical examination of their context.[6]

NOTES

1. All verbalizations in this chapter stem from in-depth interviews with research participants. These have not been published elsewhere.

2. Other artwork, in the same thematic line of the one presented in this chapter can be found in Adversary Production's Facebook page: www.facebook.com/viadversaryproductions?fref=ts.

3. Bread made from the yucca plant's edible root. Originally, it was the bread made by Puerto Rico's indigenous peoples: the taínos. After Christopher Columbus arrived, casabe was considered a fundamental meal for the Spanish conquerors (Valdés and Porro 1995).

4. Name attributed to the rural peasant of Puerto Rico during the XIX century. In the twentieth century, the jíbaro imagery was constructed to depict our national identity (Esterrich 2009).

5. Appearing in popular festivities in Puerto Rico, the vejigantes represent North African and Arab Muslim figures. The popular festivals celebrate the victory of Christians over Muslims. In the festivals, the vejigante figures run through the streets tantalizing onlookers with strange shouts and scaring them with the threats of slaps and the suggestion that, with their colorful shawls and long wide sleeves, they might be able to strike out at parade watchers and then just fly away. Vejigantes are double-faced and have a fixed and enchanted sadness. They are portrayed as grotesque figures with prominent noses, jutting teeth, and wide-open lips. The top of their heads protrudes wooden horns (Carrillo 2003, 6).

6. Our team wishes to thank local musician Eric Morales for collaborating in the development of this chapter. As part of our methodological approach he was involved in the development of this chapter, except in those instances where he or his band *Dantesco* are mentioned.

REFERENCES

Anderson, Benedict. 2006. *Imagined Communities: Reflections on the Origin and Spread of Nationalism*. New York: Verso.

Bell, Albert. 2012. "Metal in a Micro Island State: An Insider's Perspective." In *Metal Rules the Globe*, edited by Jeremy Wallach, Harris M. Berger, and Paul Greene, 271–93. Duke University Press.

Carrillo, Karen Juanita. 2003. "PR's Vejigante Festival Annually Puts Loíza on the Map." *The New York Amsterdam News*, August 21–27.

Clifford-Napoleone, Amber. 2015. *Queerness in Heavy Metal Music: Metal Bent*. New York: Routledge.

Dantesco. 2004. *Dantesco*. San Juan, Puerto Rico: Independent. Demo CD-ROM.

———. 2005. *De La Mano de La Muerte*. San Juan, Puerto Rico: Independent. CD-ROM.

———. 2008. *Pagano*. Italy: Cruz del Sur Records. CD-ROM.

———. 2010. *The Ten Commandments of Metal*. San Juan, Puerto Rico: Jurakan. CD-ROM.

———. 2011. *Seven Years of Battle*. California, USA: Stormspell Records. CD-ROM.

———. 2013. *We Don't Fear You God*. México: Inframundo Records. CD-ROM.

———. 2015. *Venancio*. Germany: Barbarian Wrath. CD-ROM.

Dawes, Laina. 2013. *What Are You Doing Here?: A Black Woman's Life and Liberation in Heavy Metal*. Bazillion Points.

Erazo, Marisol. 2008. Expresiones Del Arte Puertorriqueño. *Worcester Polythecniuc Institute*.

Esterrich, Carmelo. 2009. "Edenes Instostenibles: El Campo de la Ciudad en la Intentona Cultural de los Cincuenta." *CENTRO Journal* XXI: 181–99.

Fals-Borda, Orlando, and Mohammad Anisur Rahman. 1991. *Action and Knowledge: Breaking the Monopoly with Participatory Action Research.* New York: Bloomsbury.

Freire, Paulo. 1970. *Pedagodía del Oprimido [Pedagogy of the Oppressed].* México: Siglo Veintiuno Editores.

Green, Paul. 2012. "Electronic and Affective Overdrive: Tropes of Transgression in Nepal's Heavy Metal Scene." In *Metal Rules the Globe,* edited by Jeremy Wallach, Harris M. Berger, and Paul D. Greene, 109–34. Durham, NC: Duke University Press.

Hecker, Pierre. 2012. *Turkish Metal: Music, Meaning, and Morality in a Muslim Society (Ashgate Popular and Folk Music Series).* New York: Ashgate Pub Co.

Hickam, Brian. 2015. "Amalgamated Anecdotes: Perspectives on the History of Metal Music and Culture Studies." *Metal Music Studies* 1 (1): 5–23. doi:10.1386/mms.1.1.5.

Hoad, Catherine. 2014. "'Ons Is Saam'—Afrikaans Metal and Rebuilding Whiteness in the Rainbow Nation." *International Journal of Community Music* 7 (2): 189–204. doi:10.1386/ijcm.7.2.189.

Jason, L. 2004. *Participatory Community Research: Theories and Methods in Action. APA Decade of Behavior Volume.* 1st ed. Washington, DC: American Psychological Association. doi:10.1037/10726-000.

Kahn-Harris, Keith. 2012. "'You Are from Israel and That Is Enough to Hate You Forever': Racism, Globalization, and Play within the Global Extreme Metal Scene." In *Metal Rules the Globe,* edited by Jeremy Wallach, Harris M. Berger, and Paul Greene, 200–26. Durham, NC: Duke University Press.

Kawano, Kei, and Shuhei Hosokawa. 2012. "Thunder in the Far East: The Heavy Metal Industry in 1990s Japan." In *Metal Rules the Globe,* edited by Jeremy Wallach, Harris M. Berger, and Paul Greene, 247–70. Durham, NC: Duke University Press.

LeVine, Mark. 2008. *Heavy Metal Islam: Rock, Resistance, and the Struggle for the Soul of Islam.* 1st ed. New York: Three Rivers Press.

Maffesoli, Michel. 1996. *The Time of the Tribes: The Decline of Individualism in Mass Society.* 1st ed. London: Sage Publications.

Mendoza, Sigrid, and Nelson Varas-Díaz. 2013. "Female Gender Practices in Puerto Rico's Heavy Metal Scene." In *International Congress on Heavy Metal and Popular Culture.* Bowling Green, OH: Bowling Green State University.

McIntyre, Alice. 2008. *Participatory Action Research. Qualitative Research Methods Series.* Los Angeles: Sage Publications.

Moberg, Marcus. 2012. "The 'Double Controversy' of Christian Metal." *Popular Music History* 6 (1): 85–99. doi:10.1558/pomh.v6i1/2.8.

———. 2015. *Christian Metal: History, Ideology, Scene.* New York: Bloomsbury Academics.

Montero, Maritza. 2002. "On the Construction of Reality and Truth. Towards an Epistemology of Community Social Psychology." *American Journal of Community Psychology* 30 (4): 571–84. www.ncbi.nlm.nih.gov/pubmed/12125783.

———. 2009. "Community Action and Research as Citizenship Construction." *American Journal of Community Psychology* 43 (1–2): 149–61. doi:10.1007/s10464-008-9224-6. www.ncbi.nlm.nih.gov/pubmed/19130211.

Montero, Maritza. 2006. "Actividad y Resistencia en la Comunidad." In *Teoría y Práctica de la Psicología Comunitaria: La Tensión entre Comunidad y Sociedad,* 119–42. Argentina: Editorial Paidós.

Rappaport, Juliam, and Edward Seidman. 2006. *Handbook of Community Psychology.* New York: Springer.

Riches, Gabrielle, Brett Lashua, and Karl Spracklen. 2014. "Female, Mosher, Transgressor: A 'Moshography' of Transgressive Practices within the Leeds Extreme Metal Scene." *Journal of the International Association for the Study of Popular Music* 4 (1) (February 18): 87–100. doi:10.5429/2079-3871(2014)v4i1.7en.

Sánchez, Euclides. 2000. "*Todos Con La "Esperanza": Continuidad de La Participación Comunitaria.*" Caracas, Venezuela: Comisión de Estudios de Postgrado, Fac. de Humanidades y Educación, Universidad Central de Venezuela.

Scott, Niall. 2012. "Heavy Metal and the Deafening Threat of the Apolitical." *Popular Music History* 6: 224–39.

Snell, Dave, and Darrin Hodgetts. 2007. "Heavy Metal, Identity and the Social Negotiation of a Community of Practice." *Journal of Community & Applied Social Psychology* 17 (6): 430–45. doi:10.1002/casp.943.

Temin, Christine. 2006. "José Campeche and Francisco Oller: Painting Puerto Rico." *Magazine Antiques* 170 (5): 162–69.

Tendencia. 2001. *Re-Evolución*. Habana, Cuba: System Shock. CD-ROM.

———. 2004. *Rebeldes*. Habana, Cuba: Independent. CD-ROM.

———. 2009. *Confidencial*. Habana, Cuba: Santo Grial Records. CD-ROM.

Valdés, Frand and Felipe Porro. 1995. "El Casabe en la República Dominicana: Una Agroindustria Tradicional." In *Agroindustrial Rural Recursos Técnicos y Alimentación*, edited by François Boucher and José Muchnik, 305–20. Canada: Centro Internacional de Investigaciones para el Desarrollo.

Varas-Díaz, Nelson, and Sigrid Mendoza. 2015. "Ethnicity, Politics and Otherness in Caribbean Heavy Metal Music: Experiences from Puerto Rico, Dominican Republic and Cuba." In *Modern Heavy Metal: Market, Practices and Culture.*, ed. Toni-Matti Karjalainen and Kimi Kärki, 291–99. Helsinki, Finland: Department of Management Studies: Aalto University.

Varas-Díaz, Nelson, and Eliut Rivera. 2014. "Heavy Metal Music in the Caribbean Setting: Politics and Language at the Periphery." In *Hardcore, Punk and Other Junk: Aggressive Sounds in Contemporary Music*, edited by Eric Abbey and Colin Helb, 73–90. Lanham, MD: Lexington Press.

Varas-Díaz, Nelson, Eliut Rivera, Sigrid Mendoza, and Osvaldo González. 2014. "On Your Knees and Pray! The Role of Religion in the Development of a Metal Scene in the Caribbean Island of Puerto Rico." *International Journal of Community Music* 7 (2): 243–57. doi:10.1386/ijcm.7.2.243.

Varas-Díaz, Nelson, Eliut Rivera-Segarra, Carmen L. Rivera Medina, Sigrid Mendoza, and Osvaldo González-Sepúlveda. 2015. "Predictors of Communal Formation in a Small Heavy Metal Scene: Puerto Rico as a Case Study." *Metal Music Studies* 1 (1): 87–103. doi:10.1386/mms.1.1.87.

Wallach, Jeremy, Harris M. Berger, and Paul D. Greene. 2012. *Metal Rules the Globe: Heavy Metal Music Around the World*. Durham, NC: Duke University Press.

Wallach, Jeremy, and Alexandra Levine. 2012. "'I Want You to Support Local Metal': A Theory of Metal Scene Formation." *Popular Music History* 6 (1) (May 14): 116–34. doi:10.1558/pomh.v6i1/2.116. www.equinoxpub.com/PMH/article/view/14440.

Wenger, Etienne. 1998. *Communities of Practice : Learning, Meaning, and Identity*. Cambridge, UK: Cambridge University Press.

Whyte, William Foote. 1991. *Participatory Action Research. Sage Focus Editions*. London: Sage Publications.

Part 4

Tensions Within
the Communal Experience

SEVEN

Exploring the Language and Spectacle of Online Hate Speech in the Black Metal Scene

Developing Theoretical and Methodological Intersections Between the Social Sciences and the Humanities

Vivek Venkatesh, Bradley J. Nelson, Tieja Thomas, Jason J. Wallin, Jeffrey S. Podoshen, Christopher Thompson, Kathryn Jezer-Morton, Jihan Rabah, Kathryn Urbaniak, and Méi-Ra St. Laurent

Instances of racism and hateful comments via online forums and public commentary on online website for media outlets are not a new phenomenon (Hawdon 2012; Hughey and Daniels 2013; van Dijk 2000, 1997, 1992). The broader extreme metal music scene has seen its fair share of online hate speech of the misogynistic, racist, homo/transphobic and religious variety, among many others (Venkatesh et al. 2014). This chapter presents an analysis of several paradigm cases of online incidences of hate speech in the extreme metal community, namely, an antisemitic weblog run by erstwhile Norwegian black metal musician, Varg Vikernes; discussions around an anti-Islam Facebook post made by Norwegian black metal band *God Seed*; as well as several reddit and forum feeds that discuss black metal, racism, and National Socialism. Building on the content analytical and sociology-influenced qualitative methodologies used to analyze hate speech in the extreme metal scene (Podoshen, Venkatesh, and Jin 2014; Venkatesh et al. 2014), this chapter looks at how the combination of novel quantitative methods applied to critical discourse analyses, psychoanalytic approaches, and humanities-based analytical techniques yield a nuanced portrait of hate speech in the online realm of the global black metal scene. The theoretical framework we use is partly couched in the intersection of consumer culture and social psychology; it builds partially on assertions made by Venkatesh, Podoshen, Urbaniak, and Wallin (2015) of the importance attached to promoting individuality over the community in the global black metal scene, as well as the simulational and emotional contagion (Podoshen 2013) that nourish the dark dystopic (Podoshen et al. 2015) and hyperreal (Podoshen, Venkatesh, and Jin 2014) experiences of black metal scene members—consumers and producers alike. Using a mixed methodology, we conduct a linguistic and corpus-assisted critical discourse analysis (Thomas 2015) of the texts present in the abovementioned paradigm cases to illustrate how online hate speech is produced, received, and diffused within the black metal scene. We also incorporate Nelson's (2002, 2004) cognitive cultural-based work, grounded in an analysis of early modern Spanish literary giant, Miguel de Cervantes, thereby addressing issues of transgression and/versus subversion as related to the question of reception, an area we contend black metal scene members are weakest in the understanding and acknowledging the meaning and reach of their own art. Our work questions black metal scene members' claims to counter-culture status and conversely, underlines their complicity with the increasingly hegemonic influence of racist, anti-immigration, antisemitic, and sexist discourses emanating from Western Europe and North America. Additionally, our work, which is partially grounded in Wallin's (2012, 2014) psychoanalytic techniques, sheds light on "misanthropy" as an alibi to maintain fascist thought and perhaps some identification of a turn in extreme metal toward a greater sensitivity toward a more inclusive politics. We discuss our findings in light of the need for interdisciplinary methodologies in the study of the impact of the spread of hate speech within the black metal scene.

HATE SPEECH ON THE INTERNET

Hate speech has been present on the Internet since its earliest days of public use (Oksanen, Rasanen, and Hawdon 2014). With increased adoption of online forums and social media, it has been proliferating at exponentially large rates in online environments (Goldberg 2011; Hughey and Daniels 2013). The Internet is uniquely suited for the broadcasting of hate speech because users can remain anonymous while communicating with a virtually boundless number of people (Oksanen, Rasanen, and Hawdon 2014). Indeed, hate groups have become a permanent element of the online ecosystem and have been thriving in that environment since the mid-1990s (Chau and Xu 2007). Hate groups' online presence is diverse, from clearly marginal zones of radical violent language to sites with a more moderate rhetoric that, at first glance, can appear mainstream in design and tone (Meddaugh and Kay 2009), especially when sublimated and disguised as free speech.

Stormfront, founded in 1990, is widely considered the first hate website. It serves as a nexus of online hate because it connects disparate arms of the white supremacist movement internationally (Meddaugh and Kay 2009). It calls itself a "community of racial realists and idealists" that argues in favor of "*true* diversity and a homeland for *all* peoples" (Stormfront.org, emphasis theirs). Indeed, the rhetoric on the landing pages of the site are not overtly hateful and for the uninitiated, it may not seem like a hate website at first. Meddaugh and Kay (2009) note that Stormfront.org acts as a gateway to online hate for many users, attracting them with arguments based on scientific study and gradually normalizing racist arguments.

Once racist or otherwise prejudiced Internet users encounter hate speech online, what compels them to want to add their voice to the chorus? Understanding the social utility of anonymity is important for understanding how individuals are drawn to spread hate online. Internet users who may not express any prejudice in their offline lives may subscribe to "two sets of values," as Delgado and Stefancic (2014, 333) write. A second, private set of values is only expressed in privacy among peers that an individual considers like-minded. Anonymous online platforms provide users a place to express prejudices they may keep private in their offline social lives, and for this reason, hate speech has proliferated online in a way that has not been seen offline.

Another reason hate speech tends to be more visible online is that state and federal censorship laws are often successfully bypassed in virtual environments (Oksanen et al. 2014). Where comment moderation is present, such as on Facebook and YouTube, it is often the responsibility of fellow users to report criminal or harassing messages. Because of the massive volume of data generated by these sites daily, hate speech can remain visible for long periods of time before being detected (Oksanen et al. 2014).

Despite the distinctions made above, the social dynamics that govern online communities based on hate can be understood as analogs to those present in offline communities. Anonymity on the Internet can serve to reinforce rather than erode group norms. This dynamic is explained by the "social identity model of deindividuation effects" (SIDE) (Postmes, Spears, and Lea 1998). This theory posits that when an individual communicates with a group anonymously, a shift from an individual to a group identity is experienced, and conformity to group norms increases. Group norm reinforcement is particularly noticeable among new members of a group, or non-members who are hoping to gain acceptance. SIDE states in anonymous environments, familiarity with and adherence to norms becomes shorthand for establishing credibility (Postmes, Spears, and Lea 1998). When the norms in question are composed of antipathy toward an identifiable outgroup, a heightened motivation is seen for spreading hateful messages.

But while SIDE helps researchers understand how otherwise civil individuals are compelled to participate in hate speech on online forums, some online hate-mongers appear to be simply bad apples. Buckels, Trapnell and Paulhus (2014, 99) found that users who identified as online trolls had personality traits that fall within social psychology's "Dark Tetrad" of narcissism, sadism, and Machiavellianism (willingness to manipulate others). In other words, while the Internet provides cover for otherwise civil users to engage in hate speech, some users who spread online hate would probably engage in that type of behavior regardless of the medium or the circumstance.

BLACK METAL: A PRIMER

Heavy metal's popularity has been steadily increasing since its inception in the late 1960s. One could also argue that the unidimensional blue-collar ethos that governed the identity of the heavy metal fan through the music's blues-rock and hair-metal phases of the 1970s and 1980s, has given way to a slightly more nuanced and globalized "metalhead"—a discerning fan of an extreme form of music who, more often than not, has bought into a post-colonial, capitalist trend to consume several aspects of heavy metal including the physical and digital forms of its music and visual art, the corporeal elements of fashion including clothing, tattoos, and paraphernalia, as well as live entertainment ranging in size from small, underground venues accommodating a few hundred fans to large festivals which welcome tens of thousands of fans. This movement runs parallel to the emergence of institutions that encouraged and supported modernist art throughout the twentieth century. Academics and film-makers have made cogent arguments about the importance of the notion of community in heavy metal and its role as a concept that helps bind fringe members of an underground subculture (see Dunn and McFadyen 2008; Dunn, McFadyen, and Wise 2005; Snell and Hodgetts 2007; Wallach, Berger, and Greene 2011). Some of us (Venkatesh et al. 2015; Wallin and Venkatesh in press) have proposed a less neoliberally charged characterization of the anti-community in heavy metal, addressing how conceptions of individuality and concomitantly, philosophical as well as psychoanalytic approaches to fandom and cultural consumption shape the development of metal music fandom, especially in subgenres like black metal music, which deviate sharply from communal aspects of other heavy metal subgenres. We also squarely reject the use of subcultures as a descriptor of the heavy metal community, instead adopting and adapting the notion of music scenes (Peterson and Bennett 2004; Straw 1991, 2002, 2004), thereby allowing us to study the interplay between stakeholders such as musicians, journalists, fans, and record label executives both in physically delimited geographical spaces and in the broader online realm. Our present work extends research that we have been conducting in the realm of online hate speech in extreme metal scenes wherein we have explored factors impacting the unreflexive practices of scene members in taking responsibility for racist and hateful utterances (Venkatesh et al. 2014). Specifically, in this chapter, we focus on hate speech in black metal which, in addition to consistently focusing on lyrical, musical and visual depictions of dystopia, desolation, destruction, blasphemy, loneliness, suicide and anti-Christianity, has been long associated with National Socialism, and more recently with anti-Islam and overtly racist rhetoric (Podoshen, Venkatesh, and Jin 2014; Venkatesh et al. 2014).

As a musical genre, we build on Thompson's (2014) contention that black metal is more difficult to define than other genres of extreme metal. Vindsval from the French black metal band *Blut Aus Nord* speaks about "black metal [as] a feeling, not a typical kind of riff, sound or attitude, and this feeling is the essence of our music" (Futado 2011). This esoteric nature of black metal (*Vice Magazine* 2011, 2012) is echoed by some of the progenitors of its genre, including Gylve "Fenriz" Nagell, from Norwegian band *Darkthrone* (Aites and Ewell 2009), and Ørjan 'Hoest' Stedjeberg from *Taake* (Metamorfosis 2011; Sheol-mag 2009). For many of its fans, black metal is guided by a strict adherence to a set of ideological beliefs and is disconnected and separated from the aesthetic quality of the music that is produced and performed. Øystein Aarseth, better known as Euronymous, from the Norwegian black metal band *Mayhem* is probably responsible for the prevalence of this esoteric quality in black metal. Much, if not all, of the Aarseth's preoccupation with Satanism and the occult was begotten from a desire for a musically raw and unadulterated approach to the creation and propagation of the art form of black metal. This crude lens applied to the production of black metal is in direct contrast to the more refined development and production of the Florida death metal sound in the late 1980s at Scott Burns' *Morrisound Studios*. The clash between the Scandinavian and Florida ethea was enshrined in the credo of Aarseth's label *Deathlike Silence Productions*: "no fun, no mosh, no core, no trends." Born from the dissatisfaction Aarseth felt toward the commercialization of thrash and death metal, this attitude became instilled in the fast evolving Norwegian black metal scene of the early 1990s and formed the ideological roots of black metal as a whole. Though Aarseth was less concerned with the musical aspects of the genre, the foundation of the modern black metal sound was established during the same period. Drawing upon *Venom, Celtic Frost, Bathory,* and other bands that can now be considered the first wave of black metal, the bands in the Norwegian scene each had their own interpretation of the sound of black metal. The resulting output from bands such as *Darkthrone*, *Emperor*, and *Immortal* varied greatly for bands that are considered to be a part of the same musical scene. While some variation is to be expected among different bands, the degree of difference between many of the bands in the Norwegian scene can be explained by black metal's focus on individuality and open negation of the boundaries of the genre; this very assertion was confirmed in late 2014 in conversations that one of the researchers had with stalwarts of the Bergen black metal scene. This has resulted in instruments ranging from the typically distorted electric guitars, bass, and drums (which are utilized in other genres of extreme metal) to more unique sounds from mellotrons, banjos, fiddles, and synthesizers being utilized in black metal's musical aesthetic, in large part to promote the individuality so valued by black metal musicians, especially in Norway.

Black metal's emphasis on individuality and open negotiation of meaning has also impacted the ideological boundaries of the genre. Starting as a general devotion to death and opposition toward conformity, black metal's ideology has developed into an elaborate philosophy that celebrates the strength and the will of the individual, all the while shunning community. Spracklen (2010) asserts that black metal is opposed to "the instrumental rationalities that dominate Western society: It is anti-Christianity, anti-State, anti-commercialisation" and exists outside the "commodified world of corporate rock," allowing for a negotiation of the boundaries of black metal (91). As such, the "nationalism and extremism associated with black metal can be seen as an example of the liberal nature of the meaning-setting discourse and action" that ultimately "allows such extremism to prosper without censure" (91). Moreover, an open meaning setting has allowed for the inclusion of Norse inspired mythologies and romanticized interpretations of the past. It is not surprising to see right-leaning populist and fascist sentiments linked to modern black metal because, like Satanism, these are seen to be opposed to Christianity, liberalism, multiculturalism and in addition, they represent a rejection of modernity. This irony worth exploring here is whether black metal scene members recognize that fascism can be seen as the culmination of a modern, imperialistic, and nationalistic ideology: in other words, could fascism promote the ethos that there is nothing more modern that the nation state?

In some sense, Spracklen's analysis mirrors that of Kahn-Harris (2007) in his description of black metal's "reflexive anti-reflexivity" (145) which essentially entails that members of the black metal scene are aware of the potentially problematic symbols in the music, but purposely exclude them from the discourse as links to racism and fascism could have a negative impact on the reception of their music. However, the exclusion of this discourse allows for more racism and fascism to be included than might otherwise be allowed because of black metal's liberalized negotiation of meaning. Therefore, it creates a space in which more mainstream bands may border or even cross the boundaries typically associated with populist and right wing political parties and thereby avoid criticism by striking a non-political posture. As a result, when these bands use certain symbols and discursive elements typically associated with broadly accepted concepts of history and national imagining, cultural and ethnic boundaries are reinforced not only by the bands themselves, but also by those who do not question the validity of their supposed non-political claims.

SOLIPSISM AND FASCISM IN BLACK METAL: A PSYCHOANALYTIC PERSPECTIVE

Wallin (2012, 2014) provides extended analyses of black metal's insular tendencies to reject its anti-reflexive characterizations. In addition, Wallin and Venkatesh (forthcoming) contend that the solipsistic character of black metal is in part born from a resistance to the orthodox demands and injunctions of contemporary social life. As Fenriz articulates, black metal is in its inception a style of living and thinking counter to the doxa of social expectation and conformism to how life ought to go as advanced by the Church, the State, and the advertising and marketing powers of neoliberal capitalism (Aites and Ewell 2009). As Fenriz further states, the aim of black metal is tied to the antithesis of the good life: its goals, projects, and preferences (Fenriz quoted in Aites and Ewell 2009). Implicated herein is black metal's fundamental antagonism toward common sense, or rather, those dominant regimes of social signification to which the body and its desires are submitted that one become "socialized." It is indicative of black metal's antipathy toward common sense and its founding of social conformism that quintessential examples of "true" black metal reflect the denunciation of the social participation by way of misanthropy, solipsism, and both symbolic and literal violence leveled at socializing institutions. Black metal herein turns away from contemporary vectors of social adaptation and conformity in lieu of both a neo-primitivist return to nature and elsewhere, a renewed emphasis on the exceptionalism of the individual unfettered from the domesticating yoke of the social good.

While black metal constitutes a unique fulcrum for framing an ontology seemingly separate from social orthodoxy, the psychology of black metal's escape into solipsism shares in certain instances fidelity with a fascist conceptualization of others as less and never alongside (Theleweit 1989). Such a conceptualization is, of course, evident via the performance of elitism in black metal, wherein there persists a macro struggle to territorialize the genre and hence negate its intrusion by pejoratively dubbed "hipster metal" and further, the tourist-gaze of the fashion industry poised to capitalize on black metal's relatively untapped semiotics. While a relatively moot example of the attempt to preserve its boundaries and authenticity in often bitterly tyrannical and neurotically repressive ways, such black metal "border skirmishes" might be seen as symptomatic of a parallel psychodynamic process equally predicated on the territorialization of the body. That is, where the solipsistic tendencies of black metal eschew invasion by common sense and taste, there is an equal proclivity in solipsism to "steel the body" against its outside and seek in lieu of relationality the distance of insularity and atomism of undeath—the frozen, static, and bounded corpse-body of black metal being an indexical case. This conception of the body as both highly controlled and cut-off from the social sphere marks a fascist repression of desire, or specific to black metal, the delimitation of desire upon new albeit restrictive models of individualism and masculine neo-primitivism. Such models might be dubbed restrictive due to their general inability to call into question the established order of society insofar as solipsistic individualism plays ideally into neoliberal capitalism's vested interest in isolation and hence non-revolution as does the incommensurability of neo-paganism with the now indistinguishable interrelation of nature and culture exemplified in global warming.

This multifaceted theoretical approach to the characterization of black metal enables us to situate the hateful utterances seen in myriad online forums and social media via multiple methodologies. We now present, in turn, a quantitatively-grounded discourse analytical approach to online texts, followed by content analyses of a weblog, and finally a cognitive cultural analysis of the online texts and weblog presented.

CORPUS-ASSISTED CRITICAL DISCOURSE ANALYSIS OF HATE SPEECH IN BLACK METAL-RELATED SOCIAL MEDIA AND FORUMS

In this first analytical section, we explore how racist, nationalist, and to a lesser extent, Islamophobic themes are circulated within online extreme metal communities focused on the genre of black metal. Our discussion is informed by corpus-assisted critical discourse analyses (CACDA) (Thomas 2015) of three electronically-encoded corpora made up of online discussions appearing within three distinct online environments, namely: reddit, Facebook, and online forums dedicated to discussions of black metal. A brief descriptive portrait of each corpus appears in Table 7.1 and the sites from which the data were drawn are listed in Appendix 1.

As an analytic technique, CACDA provides both a quantitative portrait of data in terms of frequency information and associative textual patterns, and a qualitative interpretation of the discursive context sur-

Table 7.1.   Description of corpus analyzed using CACDA.

Corpus	Reddit	Online Forums	Facebook
Documents	14	7	1
Total number of words[1]	30,536	39,099	5,328
Total number of unique words[2]	26,229	33,134	4,578
Sentences	948	1,159	240
Language(s)	English	French, English	English

[1] Refers to the cumulative amount of words within a corpus (i.e., total word count).
[2] Refers only to instances of unique word forms within a corpus.

rounding significant associations. It combines traditional corpus linguistic techniques (*cf.* Hunston 2002) with critical discourse analysis (*cf.* Fairclough 2003). The quantitative techniques associated with corpus linguistics can help to reveal the focus of a given corpus. For example, frequency counts and dispersion analysis (plots, clusters) can reveal the use and dispersion of important concepts within a corpus. Concordance analysis can be used to reveal not only the frequency of particular keywords within a corpus, but can also facilitate detailed analysis of the context surrounding each instance of the terms, which can expose certain discursive constructions. Collocation analysis, which was used extensively in this research, can help to reveal the strength of the relationship between two or more words.

Our collocation analyses were conducted as follows: we entered a series of keywords one at a time into the Word Sketch function within Sketch Engine™. From there, the software identified collocates (terms statistically associated with the keyword at a statistically significant level) from a span of ten words on either side of the keyword. Statistical significance of relational strength was determined by the *logDice* statistic. This statistic was appropriate given the relatively small size of each of our corpora (Rychlý 2008).

Once a series of collocates were identified for each keyword, we used critical discourse analysis in order to examine the discursive context immediately surrounding collocates with a *logDice* value of 9 or greater. This threshold was chosen because *logDice* holds a theoretical minimum of 0 and a maximum of 14 and it is widely accepted that a collocations that carry a *logDice* value of 10 or greater reveal particularly strong discursive relationships (Baker, Gabrielatos, and McEnery 2013; Rychlý 2008). In what follows, we report our critical interpretation of corpora belonging to the three online environments previously identified.

Interpretation of CACDA

The corpus was built from data appearing on reddit centers on discussions of the perceived links between the black metal music genre and nationalism. Frequently used salient terms within this corpus include: racist, nationalism, racism, ideology, National, white, nationalist, racial, race, nation, national, Nationalism, racially, races, nationalistic. The corpus built from data appearing on online forums deals with similar themes and includes similar frequently used geographically contextualized and salient terms: français, culture, nationalism, nationalist, cultures, national, nationalisme, cultural, Français.

Our analysis of keywords belonging to the RACIST|RACE* (e.g., racist, racism, racial, race, racially, races) and NATIONAL* (e.g., nationalism, national, nationalist) lexical sets across both the reddit and online forums revealed several key debates including whether nationalism is synonymous with racism and where the line between the two phenomena is drawn, and whether someone holding and expressing racist views is alone enough for them to be considered a racist. Most notably, however, one of the key debates concerns the degree of authenticity behind the racist views espoused through black metal and the potential impact of these ideals on the black metal and national socialist black metal music fan base. In what follows, we highlight a selection of our analyses relating to this debate.

BLACK METAL:
RACISM, MISANTHROPY, OR SHOCK COMMODITY?

Our analyses revealed many attempts within the discussions appearing on both reddit and online forums to determine the extent to which as a genre, black metal is racist or whether black metal's (and national socialist black metal's) apparent affinity for expressing racist ideology is merely reflective of the genre's aspiration to misanthropy. For example, our collocation analysis of the reddit corpus revealed that when used as an adjective "racist" held a statistically significant and relatively strong discursive relationship with "nationalism" (*logDice* = 9.26). Our examination of the discursive context surrounding this associative relationship revealed attempts to minimize the gravity of the racist ideology circulating within black metal music:

> Even if a band's nationalism does lead to racism, it shouldn't matter too much to the fans, since black metal is generally misanthropic in nature, antihuman, hateful of all people, very nihilistic. Racism seems to be a less severe, more discriminating hatred. It's not friendly or anything, but in all actuality, it's less extreme than hating everyone and everything. (reddit, Thread 2).

Other comments reinforced the distinction between racism and misanthropy and in the process, minimized the significance of racist connotations by driving attention to the quality of music, rather than the message it promotes: "Black metal is about general misanthropy, not racism. It's a non issue [*sic*] though, because there isn't a single good outright nazi [*sic*] band out there that I can find, most likely because the band members are too fucking stupid to have the capacity to create good music" (reddit, Thread 3).

A similar current ran through the corpus assembled from the online forum discussion threads. Here, collocation analysis revealed that when used as a noun "nationalism" held a discursively strong and statistically significant relationship with the word "moderate" (*logDice* = 12.41). Interestingly, instead of being used to describe a tempered version of nationalism, analysis of the discursive context surrounding the associative relationship between "moderate nationalism" revealed a simultaneous implicit justification for, and dismissal of black metal's more hateful themes on the basis that the genre is known for espousing extreme views: "Sure you don't see as much of that moderate nationalism in black metal. But I'd say it's more because you don't see moderate anything in black metal, and not an indication that they're really nazis [*sic*] in many cases" (Online Forums, Thread 1). Likewise, the significance of lyrical themes associated with extreme nationalism and racism was diminished on the grounds that it's merely a device to achieve shock value: "National Socialism is politics. Often, it is politics specific to a particular country. Also, for some bands, it's the new Satan, in a way: it's edgy, it gets people riled up, and it puts people on guard" (reddit, Thread 1).

The corpus derived from Facebook data is built from one discussion thread that deals with pointedly Islamophobic themes. This particular discussion thread resulted from one post on *God Seed's* Facebook page in which they posted an anti-Muslim documentary video originally hosted on YouTube™. Frequently-used salient terms within this corpus include: religion, Islam, hate, religions, religious, Religion, war. Analysis of both the RELIGION* (e.g., religion, religions, religious, Religion) and ISLAM* (e.g., Islam, islam, Islamic) lexical sets revealed debates concerning the potential links between black metal music, and anti-theist and atheist beliefs. For example, comments such as, "You're telling me I can only listen to black metal if I hate religion well that's just a load of crap" called into question the association between the music and religion.

On the other hand, some discussion comments used self-expressed *God Seed* fandom and their video post as a starting point for the expression of widespread hatred toward organized religion, broadly, and Islam, specifically: "This doubled my love for God Seed. Fuck Islam. Fuck religion,"and "Any fucking religion shall be fought. But islam [*sic*] first. Lets [*sic*] start a massive war against all brainwashers and dumb refugees. Kill all gods." Interestingly, however, these views were not unequivocally supported. While echoing much of the anti-theist sentiment, some discussion comments were quick to point out the discriminatory nature of targeting Islam specifically: "There is a big difference between 'fuck religion' as emancipatory politics and 'fuck islam [sic]' or 'fuck Judaism [sic]' as idiotic racism." Regardless of the nuances of the anti-theist expression, the majority of comments appearing in response to *God Seed's* video post contained overtly hateful anti-religious statements.

VARG VIKERNES AND REPACKAGED NAZI PROPAGANDA

We now turn to a brief analysis of Neo-Nazi utterances in a weblog run by Varg Vikernes. From January 2013 to his arrest by French authorities in July of 2013, famed former Norwegian black metal artist Varg (nee Christian) Vikernes ran an extremely popular and pervasive blog that rehashed and slightly reconfigured Nazi-themed propaganda under the moniker "The Thulean Perspective." The blog's advertised theme and intentions were to explore Europe's "pagan past," however, the blog was little more than a thinly veiled display of racist ideology among followers of Vikernes' black metal act, *Burzum*, with additional appeal to Neo-Nazis across both North America and Europe.

Vikernes, elevated by his prominence as one of the forefathers of Norwegian black metal and its association to both murder and arson (the burning of Norwegian churches as seen in Aites and Ewell 2009) utilized a wealth of propaganda techniques borrowed from Nazi Germany, specifically targeting the Jews and what the Nazi's referred to as an international Jewish conspiracy. Vikernes, in his blog notes that there is a plan set forth of those from the Abrahamic religions to control the world—largely at the expense of the pagan or naturalist European who (ancestrally) embraces the "natural world."

> The modern European struggles; he is not allowed any direction, any point of origin, any path of dignity, because he lives in not only an anti-natural world but first and foremost an anti-European world. Our deities (and what they stand for) are actively suppressed by this modern Judeo-Christian-dominated world; they are raped, murdered and spat upon every single day in the media, in the school system, in commercials, in entertainment, in art and everywhere else to. (Vikernes 2013a)

With Vikernes' vilification of Judeo-Christianity (and Islam) firmly intact, he can easily manipulate his willing followers by condemning the origin of anything that comes from the world of "Judeo-Christian psychosis." Thus, if something originates from Jews, Muslims, or Christians, it is automatically bad. Further, Vikernes crafts a narrative whereby the fabricated Abrahamic religious conspiracy declares war on the "environmentalist," "pro-animal rights," "naturalist" Europeans who look to fight for true diversity in nature and European species. Appearing to be "pro animal rights" is another technique borrowed directly from the Nazis. Again, Vikernes uses animal rights and alleged love of nature as his hook-turned-vitriol against "race mixing":

> In a former conservative newspaper, Aftenposten, which is now 100% hard-core anti-European Jew-kneeling traitor newspaper, there was an article about [environmental diversity]. They discuss how foreign plants and animals threaten the native plants and animals in Norway, and destroy the Norwegian flora and fauna in the process, and of course the comment field under is full of comments about the non-European immigration instead. Yes; the ruling socialist "elite" really want to mongrelize Europe. (Vikernes 2013b)

In an effort to enhance and encourage involvement with the blog, Vikernes responded frequently to posts and used a variety of techniques to create greater resonance with his audience. Often referred to as the "similar to me" technique, Vikernes looked to find commonalities with his followers along the lines of interests (such as role playing games, nature study and religion—all paramount themes in black metal) and even developmental issues (such as autism) to act as the hook. As Byrne (1971) and Cialdini (2001) mention, we like people who are similar to us in the areas of opinions, traits, background, or lifestyle. Using similarities with the target audience along these variables will often allow an increase in manipulation and liking—even if the similarities appear to be trivial (Tajfel 1981). Vikernes, of course, also had the trait of being a black metal pioneer preaching to a flock of hungry black metal fans.

While Vikernes' propaganda techniques are not particularly innovative, he is able to use his notoriety as a famed black metal artist and notorious murderer to gain both respect and eyeballs from the online metal community. Appealing to pagan traditions often found in black metal culture, and expounding on growing xenophobic fear in Europe, while turning Judaism, Islam, and Christianity into mental illnesses allow Vikernes to pit his brand of rehashed Nazi junk science and propaganda into an easily accessible and conversant online realm. Vikernes' continued condemnation of the origin of nearly all science and literature from Judeo-Christian sources melds perfectly with his target audience of Neo-Nazi dabblers and paranoid conspiracy theorists on the fringes of society.

A THEATRICAL FRAMEWORK APPLIED TO ONLINE HATE SPEECH IN BLACK METAL

In the final phase of analysis, we turn to a proposal for the role of the humanities in analyzing contemporary hate speech produced in the black metal scene by considering an early modern Spanish author, Miguel de Cervantes, who was renowned for his subtly ironic attacks on the ideologies of blood purity and religious intolerance.[1] The recent exhumation of Cervantes' cadaver from its resting place in a Trinitarian chapel in Madrid and the nationalistic necrophilia that has become attached to the worm-eaten remains of the inventor of modern fiction constitute a productive frame for considering the relationship between online hate speech and black metal music. Indeed, it is rather disturbing when placed alongside Cervantes' aesthetic attacks on mysticism and monumentalization, tropes shared by Counter Reformation ideology and black metal self-characterizations. Reading through the posts in reddit analyzed earlier in this chapter, one is struck by the wide range of interpretive positions held by black metal fans as well as the acute contradictions that occur within singular posts. These range from individuals who question whether their own enjoyment of certain bands' music makes them accomplices and/or ritualistic participants in the more racist, misogynistic, homophobic, and/or related Nationalist Socialist ideologies supposedly communicated through the music; to individuals who attempt to erect barriers between a band's hateful lyrics and their music; to those who define a more or less "pure" black metal uncontaminated by ideology and politics, an aesthetic engine of destruction, as it were, that drives all collectivist ideologies into an abyss, where they are ritualistically dismembered and immolated. To an outsider, black metal's overt and histrionic expressions of racist and sexually violent motifs seemingly constitute a tragically ironic reflection of neoliberalism's ideological unconscious and as such, might be considered a modern or postmodern artistic expression *par excellence*. Nevertheless, a close inspection of the online community produces a number of difficult questions that Cervantes' resuscitated dramatic aesthetic can help untangle, if not solve.

To begin, in addition to the racist, homophobic, and misogynistic motifs or structures mentioned above, it would be important to add a kind of libertarian individualism, what can rightly be called an individualistic will to power, in the Nietzschean sense. This is arguably the most problematic and disturbing ideological element of black metal fandom in that it allows the spectator or enthusiast to perform the aesthetic disassociation of lyrics from melody, artist from ideology, and aesthetic taste from political commitments in ways that are not dissimilar to recent political movements in the West that rhetorically separate the "freedom" to discriminate from homophobia, anti-immigrant political platforms from racism, and welfare "reform" and "fetus protection" laws from institutionalized forms of sexual violence. This is not meant to condemn black metal as an art form, because the second realization that comes from reading the blog posts is that although much digital ink is spilled by fans, as well as artists such as Vikernes, in attempting to define, ideologically frame, and ultimately redeem black metal, the one thing that has become clear is that black metal defies definitive descriptions and identifications. Much like a Lacanian quilting point, it functions as a virtual space into which ideological contradictions and ethical inconsistencies are erased through acts of identification and/or interpellation.

To show how this functions in practice, it will be useful to reflect debates concerning the socio-political roles and functions of black metal off Cervantes' (1990) seventeenth-century metatheatrical interlude *The Screen of Wonders* (*El Retablo de las Maravillas*). Even in aesthetic terms, *The Screen's* dramatic structure, in which a lone and tone-deaf "musician" bangs a tambourine while Chanfalla and Chirinos, the impresarios-con artists, direct the spectators to see-imagine mythological monstrosities (Castillo and Egginton 1994) on a formless and blank sheet, provides a productive frame for considering the culture of spectacle that undergirds all contemporary rock shows, but especially the comparatively sparse and Spartan spectacles that typify the black metal anti-spectacle. The basic premise of the play finds the aforementioned con artists traveling to a rural village to convince the town aldermen to finance and watch their edifying theater. When the Governor asks what makes their play so "wonderful," Chanfalla answers that the *retablo* is structured in such a way that only "old Christians" who are the legitimate children of their parents can perceive them: "it was fabricated and composed by the wise Tontonelo under such parallels, rhumbs, planets and stars, with such points, signs and observations, that no one can see what is shown who has Jewish blood, or who was not procreated by their parents in a legiti- mate marriage; and anyone contaminated (*contagiado*) with these two very common diseases can forget about seeing the things, never before seen nor heard, in my screen" (Cervantes 1990, 220). In essence, what we have is an "Emperor's New Clothes" kind of aesthetic experiment in which the proper point of view hinges on a marriage of desire, obedience, and ideology, which together constitute the intangible but absolute price of admission to the show, a price that greatly overshadows the material arrangement between the dramatists and the aldermen.

The town councilors and their families are of course eager to display their superiority over the "common people" they govern, even though they themselves are excluded from the real centers of aristocratic, i.e., blue blooded, power; so they immediately agree to an exclusive debut in the house of the Governor.[2] After a few comments on the spare nature of the stage props— basically, a curtain and a musician named Rabelín—the "spectacle" begins, which simply means that Chanfalla proceeds to de- scribe fearful and threatening images, while Chirinos expresses her sur- prise and dismay, thus encouraging the spectators to see and react to what is not there. Unlike Hans Christian Anderson's nineteenth-century adaptation, in which individual advisors to the king are isolated and thus placed in an compromised position between the weavers and the king, Cervantes mounts a quasi-public spectacle that slyly and humorously demonstrates how the spectacle, itself, isolates and separates the group into fearful individuals, or stated otherwise, blind fanatics. When

Chanfalla describes a hairless Samson bringing down the columns of the Philistine temple, Capacho asks Castrado "Do you see it, Castrado?" and Castrado answers "Why wouldn't I see it? Don't I have eyes in the back of my head?" (227). One can easily see the doubt in Capacho's opening query, while Castrado's rhetorical questions, and even his strange statement about having eyes in the back of his head, do not answer the question directly. This is left to the aides of the Governor, who repeatedly and fearfully laments his "blindness," which he blames on his suddenly and surprisingly tainted lineage, rather than on the gullible nature of his neighbors: "What a miraculous case! I can't see Samson any better than I can see the Great Turk. And yet I truly take myself for a legitimate and venerable Christian" (228).

The scenario continues, as Chanfalla announces the appearance of a fearsome Bull (ancient Spanish symbol of virility), an infestation of mice that have fled Noah's ark, the source of the river Jordan (renowned for turning men's beards blond, which is considered a feminine trait), fanged bears and lions, and finally, the appearance of Salomé's mother Herodias. Note that Salomé agreed to dance for her father Herod only after the Jewish patriarch gave her St. John the Baptist's head on a platter. All of these images invoke extremely potent and threatening beasts, or Biblical stories featuring Jewish characters. The fact that Jews and their converted descendants were thought to be spiritually blind due to their "inability" to perceive Christ's divine nature, makes this theatrical structure both suggestive and potentially problematic for an intolerant and hierarchical regime, since the protagonists of the spectacle would ostensibly be unable to see the spectacle in which they are featured. What Cervantes does, much like in online forums where users can choose to remain cloaked in relative anonymity, is mount a play within a play that makes the readers/spectators doubt their own superiority to the townspeople and by extension, their ontological stability. Things become even more complicated in the climax of the play. In the middle of Herodias' dance, during which Repollo's nephew leaps up to dance with the Jewish matriarch, an agent for the military arrives on the scene to warn the aldermen that thirty soldiers who will need billeting are on their way to town.[3] The first reaction of Benito Repollo is to consider this interruption part of Tontonelo's wondrous spectacle: "So Tontonelo is still at it? I swear by God, Author of smoke and fraud, you will pay for this!" (234). Castrado agrees and instructs Chanfalla to continue the spectacle. When the king's representative asks what spectacle they are referring to, since he sees nothing but an empty curtain, the townspeople point at him and declare "De *ex illis es*, de *ex illis es*," meaning, "he is one of them!" These are the very words uttered by the servant of Caiaphas when pointing out that the disciple Peter was one of Christ's apostles—Caiaphas being the Jewish high priest who organized the murder plot to kill Jesus.

All of this religious confusion proves useful for analyzing the religious imagery that abounds in black metal, because first, the townspeople end up identifying with and upholding the illusion of their own blood purity and religious identity in the face of the historical materiality of the king's military representative; and second, rather than collapsing in the face of empirical insight, as occurs in Anderson's tale, the spectacle and the ideological blindness of the spectators persists beyond the end of the play.

More to the point, what lessons does Cervantes' brilliant play of mirrors hold for our analysis of the content and prevalence of hate speech in social media groups surrounding black metal? The first lesson is that the unfettered individualism celebrated by some fans is not unrelated to the "enslaving" groupthink lamented by those very same fans. This means that the strident declaration of individualism is in essence an invitation to see the intangible and unfettered "art form" behind the wondrous screen of ideologically compromised lyrics where likeminded individuals can commune and agree on the nothingness into which they see the music flow. A second lesson would be that black metal's use of anti-Christian imagery should be subjected to a more historically-informed analysis, one that can draw analogies between black metal's use of Satanic motifs and say, Protestant representations of the Catholic pope, or Catholic caricatures of Protestants during the Counter Reformation. In every case, meaning is produced dialectically and not iconologically. Third, individuals like Varg Vikernes, who attempt to interpellate their listeners and an entire genre into a racial and/or ethnic identity are not unlike the theatrical con artists in Cervantes' play, who, in turn, fit the description of an Internet troll provided earlier in this chapter. To wit, they exhibit the "dark Tetrad" of narcissism, sadism, and Machiavellianism mentioned earlier in this chapter. It is good to keep in mind that Cervantes' target in all of this hilarious subversion are those playwrights who use their art to seduce Spanish subjects into identifying with an ideological apparatus that has nothing to do with their material needs and everything to do with an imperialistic and xenophobic monarchical regime's will to power. This, of course, is one of the principle points of this chapter: for all of the claims to subversion made by the protagonists of social media groups dedicated to extolling the liberating esotericism of black metal, there are a compelling number of similarities between neoliberal positions on immigration, sexual (in)equality, etc., and the more violent rhetoric of black metal. All of this is not meant to dismiss black metal as a legitimate art form, but rather to point out that black metal, like any other art form, can be yoked to all manner of social or political agendas by artists and spectators alike. Thus the goal of the cultural critic might best be defined as the analysis of how artistic strategies and sociopolitical agendas of more or less progressive ilks become linked and just as importantly, how they manage to interpellate subjects into their wondrous visions.

CONCLUSION AND POSSIBLE FUTURE DIRECTIONS

Our chapter traverses multiple methodologies—from those grounded in a positivist tradition to those that summon psychoanalytic, interpretive and humanist ways of thinking—to shed light on not only how specific types of online hate speech in the black metal scene are interpreted by scene members, but also how such discourses mirror and extend literary narratives grounded in public debates about race, heritage, class, religion and tolerance. Our team members' research programs have also drawn from multiple sources of data—both in the physical and virtual scenes thereby enabling triangulation and some sense of theoretical saturation. Within the reddit threads, our analyses reveal that scene members are discussing a variety of aspects of racism, nationalism, and hate speech. Future research can further delve into the debate about whether black metal is inherently racist or rather black metal's (and national socialist black metal's) apparent affinity for expressing racist ideology is merely reflective of the genre (and for shock value), rather than reflective of any authentically held racist beliefs. Another question worth exploring for future research is whether nationalism is synonymous with racism and where the line between the two phenomena can be drawn. One reddit thread we analyzed related to the distinction between holding racist views and actually be a racist—here, one of the main arguments was that there is a difference between having racist thoughts and actually acting on these beliefs. The public pedagogical and curricular potential of such discussions cannot be understated.

With regard to national socialist ideologies, most comments on the reddit threads rationalized black metal's relationship to Nazi ideology on the basis that it's a function of the genre (e.g., it's just a part of an identity/persona), rather than an authentic expression of racist beliefs. A number of fans commenting on the reddit threads rejected black metal music with openly Nazi ideology (e.g., when the lyrics are racist), rather than the artists being racist (most users are indifferent to this assertion). Interestingly, our analyses also revealed that racism is commonly aligned with such phenomena as xenophobia, homophobia, and Nazi worship, but distinguished from misanthropy—the latter being a central tenet of the black metal scene. Also, comments supported the view that racism is not inherent, as it is something that results from nationalism and homogeneous cultures; therefore, it is something that needs an external cause in order to be actively maintained. Future research could explore these distinctions more deeply.

Our work benefits from the deep immersion as well as the resultant social and political capital that three of our team members—Venkatesh, Podoshen, and Wallin—have developed within extreme metal scenes in North America and Scandinavia. Within this latter geographical context, it is interesting to observe how the ethos of individuality in black metal could be seen as a reaction to the cultural phenomenon known as Janteloven (the law of Jante), which essentially denies members of Scandinavian society the opportunity to stand out and be recognized for individual achievements favoring, instead, communal anonymity (Koldau 2013). In recent conversations with our research team, members of the Oslo and Bergen black metal scenes acknowledge that the criminal indiscretions committed by members of the Norwegian scene in the early 1990s could be read partially as a reaction to Janteloven. In the minds of these scene members, though, multiculturalism has hastened an evolution to the concept of Janteloven, with minority immigrant communities seeking to establish, maintain, and propagate a unique social, political, and cultural identity as they integrate into the broader, multicultural Scandinavian context. In future research, it will be necessary to better integrate the literary and historical bases for the Janteloven phenomenon to frame conversations that speak to anti-Christianity, Islamophobia, atheism, and anti-religious hate speech as integral aspects of black metal fandom. For example, in analyzing the *God Seed* Facebook thread, we observed that most anti-Islamic speech was framed as arguments for atheism and against all religions—not Islam in particular. In fact, there was a marked subset of pro-atheism comments that explicitly took issue with anti-Islamic hate. These comments often appeared to call out people for using atheism as a sort of umbrella for their prejudice against Islam in particular. Another argument posed in this thread was that there is a double-standard in how discourses of atheism are treated. Commenters complained that while black metal bands have long sung about their hatred for Christianity without raising significant hackles "within the scene," when a band sings anti-Islamic lyrics, feathers are ruffled. For example, one commenter states:

> All you muslims whining about [black metal] bands picking on your religion should realise that black metal bands have been hating on christianity [*sic*] and judaism [*sic*] for over 20 years now. That horse has been beaten to death and more. Get over this victim mentality. [Black metal] hates on all the major monotheistic religions. You treat your women like dirt and your unholy book threatens "infidels" with death. Fuck you and fuck all religions.

Therefore, some of the comments that expressed support for *God Seed*'s posting of the anti-Islam video didn't express an antipathy toward Islam per se but seemed to support the anti-Islam message on principle. Basically, these included variations on one of the statements in the Facebook

thread which thanked *God Seed* for having the "courage" to post something of an anti-Islam nature. Whether this sentiment is born of an anti-
Islam stance or umbrella atheism is impossible to determine, however.

It is evident that the negative characteristics of hatred, violence, and
misanthropy constitute the pulsional motors of black metal art and history. However, the reduction of black metal to a genre of music steeped in a
celebration of such hatred in any general sense constitutes an analytic
misstep, for as our analysis demonstrates, the practices of disavowal intimate to black metal and its scenes often seek varied psychodynamic and
social effects. And while ressentiment is intimate to the genetics of black
metal, its analysis and theorization must continue to grapple with the
ways in which such negativity functions and further, what it preserves.
In this manner, black metal is neither condemned to an a priori commitment to racism nor absolved where its negativity preserves a commitment to racialized hate.

NOTES

1. Miguel de Cervantes (1545–1616) lived and wrote during the time of the Counter Reformation, under the Hapsburg monarchy, in early modern Spain. Bradley J.
Nelson makes all Spanish translations of Cervantes' text that appear in this chapter.
2. Cervantes begins the subversion of the artifice by giving his protagonists names
such as Benito Repollo (Ben Cabbage, cabbage being a decidedly vaginal image), Juan
Castrado (John Castrated), Capacho (from the sterile "capon"), and so on. The point
being that the gullible spectators embody the cognitive impotence on which such
ideologically directed spectacles feed.
3. The number "thirty" resonates of course with the religious symbolism, since it
brings to mind the number of silver pieces Judas accepted to give up Christ to the
Roman soldiers. And Judas' kiss is likewise suggested through the nephew's attempts
to embrace the phantasmatic Herodias.

REFERENCES

Aites, Aaron, and Audrey Ewell. 2009. *Until the Light Takes Us*. DVD. Directed by
    Aaron Aites and Audrey Ewell. United States of America: Variance Films.
Baker, Paul, Costas Gabrielatos, and Tony McEnery. 2013. "Sketching Muslims: A
    Corpus Driven Analysis of Representations Around the Word 'Muslim' in the Brit-
    ish Press 1998–2009." *Applied Linguistics* 34(3): 255–78. doi:10.1093/applin/ams048.
Buckels, Erin E., Paul D. Trapnell, and Delroy L. Paulhus. 2014. "Trolls Just Want to
    Have Fun." *Personality and Individual Differences* 67: 97–102.
Byrne, Donn. 1971. *The Attraction Paradigm*. New York: Academic Press.
Castillo, David R., and William Egginton. 1994. "The Rules of Chanfalla's Game."
    Romance Languages Annual 6: 444–49.
Cervantes, Miguel de. 1990. *"Entremeses."* Edited by Nicholas Spadaccini. Madrid:
    Cátedra.
Chau, Michael, and Jennifer Xu. 2007. "Mining Communities and Their Relationships
    in Blogs: A Study of Online Hate Groups." *International Journal of Human-Computer
    Studies* 65(1): 57–70.
Cialdini, Robert. 2001. *Influence: Science and practice*. Boston: Allyn and Bacon.

Delgado, Richard, and Jean Stefancic. 2014. "Hate Speech in Cyberspace." *Wake Forest Law Review* 49: 319–433.

Dunn, Sam, Scot McFadyen, and Jessica, J. Wise. 2005. *Metal: A Headbanger's Journey.* DVD. Directed by Sam Dunn, Scot McFadyen and Jessica Joy Wise. Canada: Banger Films.

Dunn, Sam, and Scot McFadyen 2008. *Global Metal.* Directed by Scot McFadyen and Sam Dunn. Canada: Banger Films.

Fairclough, Norman. 2003. *Analysing Discourse: Textual Snalysis for Social Research.* New York: Routledge.

Furtado, Bob. 2011. "Interview: Blut Aus Nord's Vindsval." *Invisible Oranges.* www.invisibleoranges.com/2011/12/interview-blut-aus-nords-vindsval (accessed August 12, 2013).

Goldberg, Greg. 2011. "Rethinking the Public/Virtual Sphere: The Problem with Participation." *New Media and Society* 13(5): 739–54.

Hawdon, James. 2012. "Applying Differential Association Theory to Online Hate Groups: A Theoretical Statement." *Research on Finnish Society*, no. 5: 39–47.

Hughey, Matthew W., and Jessie Daniels. 2013. "Racist Comments at Online News Sites: A Methodological Dilemma for Discourse Analysis." *Media, Culture and Society* 35(3): 332–47.

Hunston, Susan. 2002. *Corpora in Applied Linguistics.* New York: Cambridge University Press.

Kahn-Harris, Keith. 2007. *Extreme Metal: Music and Culture on the Edge.* New York: Berg.

Koldau, Linda Maria. 2013. *Educational Disaster. The Destruction of Our Universities: The Danish Case.* Hamburg: Tredition.

Meddaugh, Priscilla, M., and Jack Kay. 2009. "Hate Speech or "Reasonable Racism? The Other in Stormfront." *Journal of Mass Media Ethics* 24(4): 251–68.

Metamorfosis. 2011. *Taake en Puebla 2011.* www.youtube.com/watch?v=HSMNY BVwiVE (accessed February 17, 2013).

Nelson, Bradley, J. 2004. "Icons of Honor: Cervantes, Lope, and the Staging of Blind Faith." *Bulletin of the Comediantes* 56(2): 413–41.

Nelson, Bradley, J. 2002. "The Marriage of Art and Honor: Anamorphosis and Control in Calderon's La Dama Duende." *Bulletin of the Comediantes* 54(2): 407–41.

Oksanen, Atte, Pekka Rasanen, and James Hawdon. 2014. "Hate Groups: From Offline to Online Social Identification." In *The Causes and Consequences of Group Violence*, edited by J. Hawdon, J. Ryan, and M. Lucht, 21–33. New York: Lexington Books.

Peterson, Richard A., and Andy Bennett. 2004. "Introducing Music Scenes." In *Music Scenes: Local, Trans-Local and Virtual*, edited by A. Bennett and R. A. Peterson, 1–16. Nashville, TN: University of Vanderbilt Press.

Podoshen, Jeffrey, S. 2013. "Dark Tourism Motivations: Simulation, Emotional Contagion and Topographic Comparison." *Tourism Management*, no. 35: 263–71.

Podoshen, Jeffrey. S., Vivek Venkatesh, and Zheng Jin. 2014. "Theoretical Reflections on Dystopian Consumer Culture: Black Metal." *Marketing Theory* 14(2): 207–27.

Podoshen, Jeffrey. S., Vivek Venkatesh, Jason J. Wallin, Susan A. Andrzejewski, and Zheng Jin. 2015. "Dystopian Dark Tourism: An Exploratory Examination." *Tourism Management.* doi:10.1016/j.tourman.2015.05.002.

Postmes, Tom, Russell Spears, and Martin Lea. 1998. "Breaching or Building Social Boundaries? SIDE-Effects of Computer-Mediated Communication." *Communication Research* 25(6): 689–715.

Rychlý, Pavel. 2008. "A Lexicographer-Friendly Association Score." In *Proceedings of Recent Advances in Slavonic National Language Processing*, edited by Petr. Sojka and A leš Horák, 6–9. Brno: Masaryk University.

Sheol-mag. 2009. "Taake Interview." OOcities.www.oocities.org/de/damned_child_666/Interviews/taake.htm(accessed February 17, 2013).

Snell, Dave, and Darrin Hodgetts. 2007. "Heavy Metal, Identity and the Social Negotiation of a Community of Practice." *Journal of Community and Applied Social Psychology* 17(6): 430–45.

Spracklen, Karl. 2010. "True Aryan Black Metal: The Meaning of Leisure, Belonging, and the Construction of Whiteness in Black Metal Music." In *The Metal Void*, edited by N. W. R. Scott and I. Von Helden, 91. Oxford: Inter-Disciplinary Press.

Straw, Will. 1991. "Systems of Articulation, Logics of Change: Communities and Scenes in Popular Music." *Cultural Studies* 5(3): 368–88.

Straw, Will. 2002. "Scenes and Sensibilities." *Public* 22/23: 245–57.

Straw, Will. 2004. "Cultural Scenes." *Loisir et societe/Society and Leisure* 27(2): 411–22.

Tajfel, Henri. 1981. *Human Groups and Social Categories*. London: Cambridge University Press.

Theweleit, Klaus. 1989. *Male Fantasies Volume 2: Psychoanalyzing the White Terror*. Minneapolis, MN: University of Minneapolis Press.

Thomas, Tieja. 2015. Analyzing Online Discourses of Canadian Citizenship: O Canada! True North, Strong, and Free? PhD dissertation, Concordia University: Montreal, Canada.

Thompson, Chris. 2014. "Blasts from the Past: The Use of History, Romantic Identity, and Norwegian Black Metal." In *Coda: Andra Antologin om Musik och Samhälle*, edited by M. Askander, J. A. Lundin, and J. Söderman, 73. Malmö: Kira Förslag.

Van Dijk, Teun A. 1992. "Discourse and the Denial of Racism." *Discourse and Society* 3(1): 87–118.

Van Dijk, Teun A. 1997. "Political Discourse and Racism: Describing Others in Western Parliaments." In *The Language and Politics of Exclusion: Others in Discourse*, edited by S. H. Riggins, 31–64. Thousand Oaks, CA: Sage.

Van Dijk, Teun A. 2000. "New(s) Racism: A Discourse Analytical Approach." In *Ethnic Minorities and the Media*, edited by S. Cottle, 33–49. Open University Press.

Venkatesh, Vivek, Jeffrey S. Podoshen, Kathryn Urbaniak, and Jason J. Wallin. 2015. "Eschewing Community: Black Metal." *Journal of Community and Applied Social Psychology* 26(1): 66–81. doi:10.1002/casp.2197.

Venkatesh, Vivek, Jeffrey S. Podoshen, David Perri, and Kathryn Urbaniak. 2014. "From Pride to Prejudice to Shame: Multiple Facets of the Black Metal Scene Within and Without Online Environments." In *Educational, Behavioral and Psychological Considerations in Niche Online Communities*, edited by V. Venkatesh, J. Wallin, J. C. Castro, and J. E. Lewis, 364–88. Hershey, PA: IGI Worldwide.

Vice Magazine. 2011. *True Norwegian Black Metal*.www.vice.com/video/true-norwegian-black-metal(accessed February 17, 2013).

Vice Magazine. 2012. *One Man Metal*. noisey.vice.com/noisey-specials/one-man-metal-part-one (accessed February 17, 2013).

Vikernes, Varg. 2013a. *Endangered Species*. thuleanperspective.com/ (accessed May 13, 2013).

Vikernes, Varg. 2013b. *The Sacred Dance*. thuleanperspective.com/2013/02/07/the-sacred-dance/ (accessed April 13, 2015).

Wallach, Jeremy, Harris M. Berger, and Paul D. Greene. 2011. "Affective Overdrive, Scene Dynamics, and Identity in the Global Metal Scene." In *Metal Rules the Globe*, edited by J. Wallach, H. M. Berger, and P. D. Greene, 3–33. Durham, NC: Duke University Press.

Wallin, Jason, J. 2012. "On the Plains of Gorgoroth: Black Metal, Youth Culture, and the Psychoanalytic Question of Evil." *Cultural Formations* 1. Accessed February 17, 2013. culturalformations.org/on-the-plains-of-gorgoroth-black-metal-youth-culture-and-the-psychoanalytic-question-of-evil/.

Wallin, Jason, J. 2014. "The Dark Ecology of Black Metal." In *Educational, Behavioral and Psychological Considerations in Niche Online Communities*, edited by V. Venkatesh, J. Wallin, J. C. Castro, and J. E. Lewis, 389–94. Hershey, PA: IGI Worldwide.

Wallin, Jason, J. and Vivek Venkatesh. Forthcoming. "No Satisfaction, No Fun, No Future: Black Metal and the Occult." In *Dark Accelerationism and the Occult*, edited by E. Keller, T. Matts, and B. Noys. Brooklyn: Punctum Books.

DATA USED FROM ONLINE SOURCES

N.B.: Threads marked with an asterisk (*) are referenced in the chapter

reddit Threads: Titles and URLs

*Black Metal Shows and Racism
 www.reddit.com/r/Metal/comments/1jwt2r/black_metal_shows_and_racism/
*Nationalism and Black Metal
 www.reddit.com/r/Metal/comments/q414i/nationalism_and_black_metal/
*What Are Your Thoughts About NSBM
 www.reddit.com/r/BlackMetal/comments/1aenim/rblackmetal_what_are_your_
 thoughts_on_nsbm/
A Question Concerning
 www.reddit.com/r/Metal/comments/17d5vj/a_question_concerning_burzum_and_
 varg_vikernes/
Anal Blasphemy Sexual Desecration
 www.reddit.com/r/BlackMetal/comments/2nnele/anal_blasphemy_sexual_
 desecration_of_islam_faith/
Anti-Islamic Black Metal
 www.reddit.com/r/BlackMetal/comments/2j4oh2/antiislamic_black_metal/
Heavy Metal Unites Jews, Muslims
 www.reddit.com/r/Metal/comments/tes6v/heavy_metal_unites_jews_muslims_
 across_middle_east/
Janaza-Islamic ties
 www.reddit.com/r/BlackMetal/comments/2jwdzi/janaza_islamic_lies_burning_
 quran_ceremony_female/
Still Don't Understand
 www.reddit.com/r/Metal/comments/2higqb/still_cant_understand/
When Black Metal's Anti-Religious Message Gets Turned
 www.reddit.com/r/BlackMetal/comments/wfj21/when_black_metals_antireligious_
 message_gets/
Who Is the Biggest Asshole in Black Metal
 www.reddit.com/r/BlackMetal/comments/1hutgy/who_do_you_think_is_the_
 biggest_asshole_in_black/
Question Regarding NSBM
 www.reddit.com/r/BlackMetal/comments/1se0qq/question_regarding_nsbm_not_
 if_its_ok_or_not/
Peste Noire Question
 www.reddit.com/r/BlackMetal/comments/2ok99p/peste_noire_question/
A Problem with NSBM
 www.reddit.com/r/BlackMetal/comments/2nk02o/a_problem_with_nsbm/

Facebook Page: Title and URL

*God Seed's Anti-Islam Facebook Thread
 www.facebook.com/GodSeedOfficial/posts/10152245343977407?notif_t=comment_
 mention

Online Forum: Title and URLs

*black metal québécois, français et black metal, nationalist and black metal
  www.capitaledumetal.com/forum_v3/index.php?showtopic=16973
sur black metal québécois
  www.metal-archives.com/board/viewtopic.php?f=1&t=102365
Our Land
  www.cvltnation.com/our-land-a-brief-consideration-of-quebecs-black-metal/
Snow covered ashes
  punbasedname.blogspot.ca/2014/03/the-snow-covered-ashes-of-defeat-metal.html
NSBM2
  www.spirit-of-metal.com/forum/lire_topic-sujet-NSBM_2-id-13312-p-1-l-fr.htm

EIGHT

What Did the Norwegians Ever Do for Us?

Actor-Network Theory, the Second Wave of Black Metal, and the Imaginary Community of Heavy Metal

Karl Spracklen

The so-called "second wave" of black metal, which emerged in Norway in the early 1990s, is now infamous in heavy metal circles, the subject of myth-making and the construction of symbolic boundaries. The bands that emerged in Norway around the *Helvete* record shop—primarily *Mayhem, Darkthrone, Satyricon, Emperor, Enslaved, Burzum,* and possibly *Dimmu Borgir* and *Immortal*—have become bands that are listened to and watched by heavy metal fans around the world, and to a greater or lesser extent they have transferred their underground reputations into mainstream heavy metal success. The Church burnings and murders associated with the second wave—especially the murder of the *Mayhem* guitarist Euronymous by Varg Vikernes of *Burzum*—have even become well-known beyond the imaginary community of heavy metal, in popular culture and the learned academy.

In this chapter, I will use the concept of the imaginary community and Bruno Latour's (1987) Actor-Network Theory to undertake two analyses. The imaginary community of heavy metal is defined by the symbolic boundaries fans make for it in the present through their communicative rationality and their contestations over meaning, but it is also defined as an Andersonian imagined community of traditions and myths. Actor-Network Theory is an attempt to map the social, literary-philosophical,

and natural objects that together combine and act on each other to produce networks of meaning. Latour created Actor-Network Theory to help
understand how science achieved truth and consensus over things. I will
first of all show that the second wave of black metal was the product of
the same kind of network of technologies, assumptions, epistemologies,
hegemonies, and agents as any other form of heavy metal. The second
wave was merely an extension of the communicative rationality already
at work in extreme metal. But the second-wave itself has developed into a
technology and an epistemology that has become a key element of the
network of belonging and identity that defines the imaginary community
of heavy metal today, becoming more mythical with each retelling. Before I turn to my own Actor-Network Theory analysis of the second wave
of black metal, it is necessary to discuss the key theoretical, epistemological and methodological concepts already briefly outlined. As imaginary
community is mentioned first in this introduction without any explanation of what it means, this will be the subject of the next section. After an
account of the imaginary community, I will turn to Actor-Network Theory, before my own attempt to use it to make sense of what—to borrow
and adapt a joke from Monty Python—the Norwegians might have ever
done for us: the metal community and scholars of heavy metal.

IMAGINARY COMMUNITY

I first used the idea of an imaginary community in my PhD research on
rugby league in the north of England (Spracklen 1996). The game of
rugby league is played professionally in Australia, New Zealand,
England, and France, and is a form of football that split from rugby union
in 1895. Rugby league had been a professional team sport popular in
certain small towns and city-districts in northern England in which
white, working-class communities had defined themselves through invented traditions of hegemonic masculinity and northernness (Spracklen
1996, 2007; Spracklen and Spracklen 2008; Spracklen, Timmins, and Long
2010). When the industries were still going in these communities, rugby
league exemplified their parochial pride, their sense of identity and
northernness. To be a rugby league fan was to embrace the white, northern, working-class masculine culture exemplified in Richard Hoggart's
(1957) *The Uses of Literacy*, or in David Storey's novel *This Sporting Life*
(Storey 1960). When I did my PhD, the industries, the mills, and the
mines had been closed down. Rugby-league districts were ravaged by
urban blight and social deprivation, so for the fans of rugby league the
teams and the game itself became the only symbolic places they had for
belonging.

Rugby league itself became what I called an "imaginary community"—to follow rugby league in these towns was to identify with a

shared working-class masculinity, working-class northernness, mythology of separatism and suspicion of the capital, of southerners and the elites who controlled rugby union, from which rugby league had split at the end of the nineteenth century. The imaginary community was a symbolic community (Cohen 1985). I was using anthropological ideas of community being bounded by cultural artifacts, language, and shared mythologies. Rugby-league fans have rivalries between clubs and national teams, but these are transcended by a recognition that they are all rugby-league fans positioned against a world that does not accept rugby league, a world that dismisses it as a parochial, northern English sport, an illegitimate form of rugby union, or a sport that is only really popular among Australians in New South Wales and Queensland. This brings the imaginary community together. All one needs to do to find acceptance in a pub in Featherstone (Yorkshire, England) is to walk in it wearing the colors or jersey of any rugby-league club. If you can then talk with knowledge about the local club, or the highlights of the last twenty years of finals and international matches, then you have penetrated deeper into the imaginary community. The idea of the split from rugby union was an example of an invented tradition (Hobsbawm and Ranger 1983), a story used to create identity within the community through delineating outsiders, a myth that explained to people in rugby league why it was culturally important to continue supporting the game.

There are clear echoes of the imaginary community of rugby league in the imaginary community of heavy metal. Metalheads (people who are serious fans of heavy metal) look out for each other, and use clothing to bond with strangers in unfamiliar places (Lucas, Deeks, and Spracklen 2011). Metalheads find a shared sense of being metal more important than liking one band or one subgenre. Metalheads think other metalheads think like us, and are offended when it turns out a metalhead is an obnoxious racist. Metalheads think metal is about being against the mainstream of pop music, against the mundanity of rock and rap, and being for freedom of expression and individualism (Hill 2014). The imaginary community of heavy metal is defined by the symbolic boundaries fans make for it in the present through their communicative rationality and their contestations over meaning, but it is also defined as a community of traditions and myths (Lucas, Deeks, and Spracklen 2011; Spracklen, Lucas, and Deeks 2014). Anderson (1983) describes a similar community of meanings when he discusses the "imagined community." But although there is a phonetic similarity, Anderson's concept explores how a community in the present is defined by myths of the past it creates. In other words, the community makes a biased reading of the past to justify its values in the present, hence legitimizing itself as a coherent community. One can see that the imagined community is also one that is created and defined by symbols, though these symbols are historically contrived — such as the myths of the Norwegian black metal scene (Spracklen 2014a).

That is, the imagined is one component of the imaginary, but not all of it. The ways in which the imaginary community of heavy metal might be constructed are equally to do with artifacts and language, as they are histories and myths. Being a metalhead, part of the imaginary community of metal, is to be part of a self-sustaining network with different levels of belonging, and different level of exclusion.

ACTOR-NETWORK THEORY AND
METHODOLOGICAL FRAMEWORK

The application of theory to research poses a number of problems. If we can define theory to mean, in a common-sensical way, an idea that attempts to shed some light on a research phenomenon, then we can (ideally) describe data as either the phenomenon itself (data = reality), or an interpretation of that phenomenon (Craib 1992). Generally, theory is seen as the brainwork and the data that is related to that theory comes from the research. In the sociological case, such data is presented in the form of interviews, observations, and statistics. Yet the relationship between theory and data is not as simple as it first appears.

One argument is that theory must be explanatory (Friedman 1974; Lipton 1991). A theory must be able to explain the facts, not just describe them. It is not enough to present the data, one must also say why the results are, and why they explain. What this entails is the traditional scientific approach, which suggests hypotheses taken from theory are tested by the field (Hempel 1966). In essence, the field becomes a site for proving or disproving (Popper 1968) theories. This approach has a number of flaws, especially when applied to sociology (Winch 1958). It assumes a scientific method actually exists, though a definition of what that is has proved elusive to philosophers and sociologists of science (Feyerabend 1975; Latour 1987; Lipton 1991). It ignores problems of objectivity, representation, and truth correspondence (Hesse 1980), such as the problem that any one set of data can be explained by a number of opposing hypotheses, with no way of deciding between them without recourse to inductive logic (Chalmers 1982).

Another approach suggests that the researcher enters the field without any preconceptions, and listens to the field without prejudice. From the data collected, the researcher sees patterns that form ideas, which are supported by further fieldwork (Ely 1991). This method forms the basis of naturalistic paradigms, and this position of theoretical production is known as Grounded Theory (Glaser and Strauss 1967). However, the assumption that anyone can enter the field without any preconceptions is untenable. We have all gone through a system that has enculturated us with mental tools of reckoning, language, and perceptions that are all laden with theory (Latour 1987). This chapter has used already a wealth of theoretical language with no apology or qualification, as it belongs to the tacit knowledge shared by scholars (Bloor 1976; Collins 1985; Fuller 1992; Wittgenstein 1968). In addition, it can be argued that all data is theory laden (Chalmers 1982; Kuhn 1977).

Actor-Network Theory is an attempt to map the social, literary-philosophical and natural objects that together combine and act on each other to produce networks of meaning. Bruno Latour has been an influential and controversial figure in science and technology studies, moving from sociology of science's critiques of science, to technological critiques of sociology (Latour 1987, 1988, 1990, 1993, 2007, 2011; Latour and Woolgar 1979). Latour (1987) created Actor-Network Theory to help understand how science achieved truth and consensus over things. He was dissatisfied with epistemologies that reified the natural, but he was also dissatisfied with social scientists who argued everything was fundamentally social. Latour argues that to fully analyze and explain anything, it is necessary to look at all the relationships without necessarily privileging one over another: how ideas are passed around, how technologies and objects move, how people act and are constrained, and how objects might themselves have agency. That, we must assume that all parts of a network—social, material, human, and non-human—have the agency and power to move around the network. Does that mean that we should believe that non-human objects have agency? Some non-human living creatures clearly do have agency. But what about rocks and pens? While such a claim is obviously meant to be understood ontologically as a metaphor, the assumption helps us make sense of the complexities that shape our world (Latour 2011).

I will take as my starting point in the analysis a methodological and theoretical stance based on the work of Bruno Latour, but this stance will not be uncritical. In particular, I will use Latour's third rule of method, which famously argues for a sociology of science that understands that "since the settlement of a controversy is the cause of Nature's representation, not its consequence, we can never use this consequence, Nature, to explain how and why a controversy has been settled" (Latour 1987, 99). I follow Latour cautiously, and interpret that rule as being one about how epistemological arguments can be used to define ontological representations—how representations of nature are contested, and how the actors in controversies try to define nature by trying to make a definitive representation.[1] The Latourian approach to the sociology of science has been criticized, not least by other sociologists of science such as Collins and Yearley (1992)[2] and scientific realists questioning the validity of anything that may undermine such epistemological realism (Bird 1992).

But if Latour faces criticism for his portrayal of science, his sociology provides a number of ways into discourses about science. Following Hacking (2000), I want to use Latour's concern with representations of nature[3] to examine the way in which sociological debates about technologies, histories, and scenes are defined and shaped by reference to assumptions about the epistemology of popular music, community, and the alternative. In doing so, my approach to sociological theory will be guided by pragmatic analytical concerns, adopting concepts of hegemony (Gramsci 1971), myth (Barthes 1957) and the imaginary community (Cohen 1985). In recent years, Latour has become more critical of his earlier arguments, or rather, more critical toward those who have misused his work (Latour 2007, 2011). He believes that the methodological concern to deprivilege the material over the social or linguistic has led others to abandon the material altogether, which he now says was never his intention. With that in mind, let us now begin to follow the actors in the networks around the second wave of black metal, bearing in mind this later Latourian rule that we should privilege the material and the social and linguistic at the same time.

THE *HELVETE* NETWORK

Black metal is a form of extreme metal typified by "dark" lyrical themes, elitism, blastbeats, screeched vocals and "evil"-sounding riffs (Spracklen, 2006). The second wave of Norwegian black metal in the 1990s is undoubtedly responsible for the growth in black metal, its key ideologies, musical themes, and symbols. The first wave of black metal emerged in the 1980s as a form of extreme metal, inspired by *Venom*, the British band that coined the term "black metal." The first wave constructed the ideologies of black metal, and some of the sonic template. The second wave of black metal started as an attempt to define and distinguish black metal, or an attempt to purify black metal of its roots in extreme metal and death metal. It is clearly the source of black metal as that subgenre is constructed and consumed today. There is, however, nothing essential about Norway or Scandinavia that made it the place from where black metal's second-wave had to emerge from. Assuming this essential, causal link is an epistemological error (*post hoc ergo procter hoc*), though such essentialism and historicism can be found in many explanations for Norwegian black metal, both popular and academic (see my discussion and critique in Spracklen, 2006, 2009, 2014a). What we need to do is follow the connections and actors in the network around the second wave of black metal—that is, we need to explore the scene around its key members, the *Helvete* network (so-called because they passed through and were involved in the shop of the same name set up and owned by *Mayhem* guitarist Euronymous). But instead of allowing ourselves to be sidetracked by theories of essential nordicness, or meditations on meaning and transgression, we need to step back and ask the question: how did the music find its way to its genesis? In Latourian terms, drawing on the work Callon (1986) undertook to make sense of the sea-life being investigated by scientists (Latour 1987), how did the riffs and the screams of the archetypical *Mayhem* song *Funeral Fog* enroll allies in their bid to become actualized as agents?

We can begin the actor-network analysis by thinking about the origins of the sounds. The Devil's Interval, a simple chord progression from early European music that sounds spooky, used famously by the early heavy metal band *Black Sabbath*, has come to define heavy metal's sound. Knowledge of how music works is crucial if one is to be a heavy metal musician. It is not enough to look pretty like a boy band. So the black metal musicians had to acquire that knowledge, through a study of *earlier* metal bands, as well as through some form of formal musical tuition (from other musicians, from parents or teachers). One does not become a musician overnight. One needs time, a rehearsal space, and other soft resources such as caring families or other social support, knowing managers and teachers. If the black metal riffs needed the musicians to become musically literate, they also needed the technology of modern rock music to allow them to emerge into the mundane world through electric devices, amplification, and distortion. Crucial to this is the creation of semiconductor electronic transistors and electromagnetic transformers, which are at the heart of amps, guitars, recording devices, and speakers. All metal music is based on an exploration of the limits of the laws of electromagnetism, which were developed by Michael Faraday in his attempt to make entertaining spectacles from public experiments (Guarnieri 2013; James 2011).

The Norwegian black metal musicians positioned themselves as both traditionalists and innovators in their metal music sounds. They were traditionalists because they claimed their music was heavy metal. They were not trying to make hip-hop, or classical music. They were metal fans, making metal music for other metal fans. The musical forms they aspired to were limited by heavy metal's structures, which were limited by rock music. Guitars were plugged in and distorted, drums and electric bass provided the rhythm sections, and musicality was restricted by the scales, time-sequences, and chords used in rock music. They inherited the pantomime theme of Satanism and evilness which will be discussed in more detail. Finally, they employed some of the musical signatures of death metal, such as blast-beats and growled vocals. However, they were also keen to be seen as innovators. Unlike death metal, they introduced screams to their vocal repertoire, and focused on a handful of chords and progressions that sounded spooky and evil. Black metal was as much about being against death metal as it was about being against Christianity. For the Norwegians death metal was stupid music for stupid people, music for poseurs and scenesters, Americans in shorts and sneakers who wanted to get drunk, get laid, and beat people up (Kahn-Harris 2007). The second-wave of black metal, then, was a reaction to the commercialization of heavy metal, the distortion of heavy metal's supposedly authentic ontological state by people who wanted to use it for fun. This was a fundamentalist reaction, a conservative turn, against the sexualization and the emotional and physical core of rock music.

This reaction against sexuality might make us think this is something to do with the Christian culture of northern Europe, the psychological trauma of growing up in a Protestant country with traditional values overlain by the liberal sexuality of secular modernity (Bauman 2000; Lyotard 1984). Christianity is of course an important actor in the network around the second wave of black metal, but its role is more positive than being seen as a source of sexual repression. Christianity's rich mythology and history gave to the Norwegians the very idea of the devil, the idea of sin and Satanic rituals. It gave them a nationalism of good Christians converting bad Viking heathens, a nationalism of small wooden churches built in tidy hamlets, well-known icons of Norwegianness, which burn well. Having these churches wrapped up in its own network gave Christianity a way of co-opting belonging and identity in Norway. But the importance of such churches gave the Norwegian black metal musicians an obvious place to prove their adherence to metal's true Satanic roots. Satan, then, is still an important actor in Christianity's network, and the black metal scene, despite his metaphysical status as a nonexistent metaphor. The musicians wanted to believe.

The Satanism of heavy metal is part of the story of the blues, of rock and roll. Robert Johnson sold his soul to the devil and died in a bar-fight, with a hellhound on his trail (Oliver 1993). *Led Zeppelin* and the *Rolling Stones* played around with the idea of Satanism and the occult. But despite the presence of Satan in rock music and in Christianity, the main devilish actors in the black metal network were Christopher Lee, Vincent Price, and three Geordies. The devil in the heavy metal scene in the 1980s was popularized by the English band *Venom*, who also came up with the name black metal for their primitive, extreme metal. These Geordie musicians did not actually believe in the devil, but they watched lots of films starring Christopher Lee and Vincent Price. Guitarist Jeff "Mantas" Dunn and his band *Venom* drew on the pantomime histrionics that had been a part of rock and roll: the voodoo occultism of Screamin' Jay Hawkins; the camp posing of Little Richard; the madness of Arthur Brown; and the make-up and fireworks of *Kiss*. Through the years in which the black metal musicians were growing up and becoming young adults, the *Venom* version of cartoon Satanism was copied by hundreds of metal bands, and pulp horror films and novels were swapped around by young metal fans who wanted to feel the visceral thrill of the occult, of Satanism, and of the horrible and macabre (Epstein and Pratto 1990).

Alongside the enjoyment of occult horror film and books is the influence of role-playing games on the 1980s metal fan community. Role-playing games such as *Dungeons and Dragons* allowed players to take on roles in quests or adventures bounded by the rules of the game, and controlled by one player who acted as a director or writer. Some of this was due to overt marketing strategies, such as the band *Bolt-Thrower*, so named after a weapon in *Warhammer*, having music distributed with *White Dwarf* magazine. But role-playing games were part of the ontological frames, the Wittgensteinian language games, of alternative-facing young people in this period (Fine 2002). Knowing one's way around a twenty-sided die used to play the games (and remembering to call it a die, not a dice) allowed young men in particular to revel in fantasies of being warriors, wizards, and dragon-slayers, just like Conan the Barbarian and those metal musicians in the band *Manowar* who looked like Conan's friends. Role-playing games were extensions of novels and comic books, pulp fantasy, and science fiction. The fantasy tropes of flagons of ales and big-breasted wenches in taverns appeared on the covers of magazines, games and books, but also metal albums. Role-playing games were an important factor in the huge interest in metal from the work of JRR Tolkien (1937, 1955, 1977), which is expressed throughout the second wave of black metal, especially in the name of the band *Burzum* and the pseudonym adopted by its founding musician Varg Vikernes: Count Grishnakh. Tolkien's Middle-earth is itself a northern European dreamworld, a re-imagined past where the pure races of the elves and the High Men of the Numenoreans are threatened by the evil races—orcs and goblins, swarthy Easterlings and dark-skinned Southrons—of the old enemy's second-in-command Sauron. Tolkien's heathen mythology conflated with the Christian devil fits the heavy metal pantomime Satanism, and gave the Norwegians a way to claim pre-Christian heritage. The racial essentialism at the heart of Tolkien's imaginary world (Spracklen 2011) makes it attractive to those in the second-wave who wished to claim black metal is elitist, anti-Jewish, anti-black, and pro-Aryan.

The final part of the network that allows the black metal riffs to emerge is language. For the musicians surrounding Euronymous and his shop, the importance and meaning of black metal is shaped through intense reading of fanzines and discussions with one another. The English language is particularly gracious in the way it lets the musicians interact with other musicians and fans around the world. The product of imperialism (first British, then American), English in the second half of the twentieth century has become a second language for northern Euro-peans, and for white, middle-class urban elites throughout the world. It is in these communities that heavy metal's rebellious nature finds favor in the 1980s and 1990s (Kahn-Harris 2007). Fanzines are traded from house to house, city to city, country to country, along with copies of demos and other mix-tapes. It became possible for Euronymous and the others to read about music from all sorts of places, and possible for them to pro-mote their music to the people in those far-off places. As well as swap-ping tapes and fanzines, musicians and fans could write to one another as pen pals. There is, then, an English-speaking, English-writing, English-reading network of metalheads debating what death metal is, what extreme metal is, and what the authentic nature of metal is, in the period before and after the rise of the second-wave of black metal. The Norwegians were already publicly critiquing other bands and the death metal subgenre before the crisis points of the murders. Their songs are being written, their ideologies honed, through this interaction. Access to English, and postage stamps and padded envelopes, allows them to engage in posturing over what it means to be a Satanist, what it means to be a black metal musician or follower, before the mainstream metal media discovers them. Even as the churches burn and people die, the relative nearness of Norway to the United Kingdom, one of the two English-speaking countries associated with the hegemony of the modern music industry (Williamson and Cloonan 2007), and one of the two homes of the then-emergent independent extreme metal industry, gives the second-wave bands a helping hand. They get coverage in *Kerrang* magazine, as well as the mainstream press (Kahn-Harris 2007; Spracklen 2006, 2014a). The British and Americans love the story of the second-wave because the right-wing, neoliberal, individualist politicians that have fractured these countries need to show their downtrodden lower classes that liberalism ends in murder and sacrilege. So the stories are told and retold, and the fame of the bands and the musicians grows. They get record deals. They get a measure of fame that has yet to be lost. And the riffs are finally able to get heard.

(NORWEGIAN) BLACK METAL TODAY

In the year of this writing (2015), black metal has become a significant but accepted part of the heavy metal genre. When I first checked on its presence on the Internet for this chapter, a search for "black metal" revealed over 291 million results on Google. Of course, Google searches are notoriously bad for failing to filter out the "noise" (we can imagine here the pages that refer to black metal as part of heavy metal, alongside catalogue descriptions of objects that are made of metal painted black) but even abstracting out that noise there is still a huge presence online of the subgenre of black metal. It is accepted by journalists, musicians, fans, critics, producers, and companies as one part of the "extreme metal" subgenre, with a defined sound, a defined ideology and a defined semiotics. The page on black metal on Wikipedia has approximately 9,000 words, much of it devoted to the Norwegians and the second-wave. The idea that black metal is only about church burnings is seemingly imprinted in the minds of popular culture across the global North, and in the global South, too (Wallach, Berger, and Greene 2011). It is then just another subgenre of heavy metal, a genre of pop music, a form of music that is part of the modern entertainment and cultural industries (Hesmondhalgh and Baker 2013; Kong 2014). Following Horkheimer and Adorno (2002), we might say that black metal, like any form of popular music, is just another business opportunity. Most black metal musicians might struggle to make any money from their music, but they enter into the process of recording and releasing music in the hope that enough people will listen to the music, buy the merchandise, and allow them to become full-time professional artists. Black metal bands have signed deals with major labels, have become headliners at music festivals, and have allowed themselves to be associated with branding opportunities (such as the ubiquitous endorsement deals with the companies that make instruments, pedals, and amps). At the same time, businesses have created marketing campaigns that try to connect to the black metal imagery, such as the Finnish advert for cough medicine that uses *Immortal's* videos as a point of reference.[4] Black metal as an actor in a Latourian network can be seen to be fully compliant in allowing its radical, violent past to become compromised enough for it to be a selling point, while maintaining a safe distance from the transgression of actual murder and arson. Black metal has become a Wittgensteinian "language game," a way of belonging through playing and talking (Wittgenstein 1968).

At the same time, we can see that black metal has managed to negotiate its way into the mainstream of popular culture, and the policy circles where the cultural industries meet the hegemonic power of State control (Spracklen 2012, 2014a). Black metal is just another technology of identity and community formation, one lifestyle choice denuded of any real communicative meaning and purpose. In another place, I have written about the "heat death" of alternative subcultures such as black metal (Spracklen 2014b). What that means is the heat of the ideologies that fired the rapid expansion of black metal globally has all but been cooled down by the waters of instrumentality and commodification. Instead of burning churches and killing each other and random immigrants, black metal musicians seek formal recognition by cultural bodies and regional governments. The band *Enslaved*, for example, take part in arts and cultural projects sponsored by official Norwegian government agencies. Black metal is put in art galleries where its aesthetic is appreciated by middle-class urban hipsters, and its roots are co-opted as part of the Norwegian tourism industry (Spracklen 2012). Black metal's transgressive aesthetic has been taken without permission by the active agency of academics and fashionable people who like the smell of burning churches, but who would never actually burn one to the ground. Black metal might try to fight this cultural appropriation but it does not have the same amount of cultural and economic capital that the hipsters and academics have (Spracklen 2014b). They are the ones who have won the battle to own black metal. *Black Metal Theory*, an attempt to apply the practice of cultural studies to black metal and to bring black metal to cultural

studies, allows academics to write full length papers filled with meditations on cultural theory and philosophy that all say the same thing: we,
the academics, know what black metal is, and black metal is our metaphor for the unknowable or the numinous, or the transgressive, in culture
and in art and in postmodernity. Black metal is discussed by academics
as a legitimate art form, and the agency of black metal is subsequently
lost, the transmission of its ideologies through the network held up by
the hipsters with their clever word play and knowing references
(Masciandaro 2010).

THE IMAGINARY COMMUNITY OF "HEAVY METAL" AND ITS NETWORK

This entropic heat death can be seen in the wider heavy metal imaginary
community. Since the rise of black metal in the 1990s, heavy metal has
been at the forefront of the systems and structures of globalization. Following Stuart Hall we might say that heavy metal's imaginary community has become a space specifically of Westernization, where global
flows of power have been driven by the cultural and political hegemony
of America, which still remains strong even as it economic hegemony is
being tested (Hall 1993). Heavy metal is viewed beyond the West as a
musical form, genre and scene that embodies liberalism, individualism,
and a rejection of conservatism (Wallach, Berger, and Greene 2011).
Heavy metal has become the Trojan Horse for the spread of neoliberal,
secular ideologies, a space for the promotion of a shared urban, young,
educated middle-class to find adventure and belonging. This spread of
heavy metal is shifting its class nature, from being about a marginalized
working class banging their heads and sticking their fingers up at the
man, to a bourgeois, respectable alternative, of the mainstream but at a
safe distance from its center (Hill 2014; Spracklen, 2013). Technological
developments such as the Internet have helped construct this new version of heavy metal's imaginary community, but so has the commodification of popular culture in general (Horkheimer and Adorno 2002; Spracklen, 2013, 2015). Music has become a place where young moderns consume products, invent myths about being rebellious or marginal, while
using music as a way to find a justification for their place in the world
(Bauman 2000). Metal is one part of popular culture, one that still has its
moments of extremity and danger, and one which can still lead to arrest
and imprisonment by corrupt governments clamping down on difference
(Wallach, Berger and Greene 2011). But most metalheads around the
world live in reasonably safe polities, where metal serves up its myths
and memories to reassure its fans that it still has some alternative meaning, even where bands are part of the global entertainment industry, and
fans become politicians and leaders of nation states. It is easy to be a

metalhead, all one needs to do is download the music, read Wikipedia and other sites about the subgenres and the bands, and wear a band t-shirt. If you can grow your hair and have piercings and tattoos then that is fine, because everybody looks like this in the year 2015. You can then be as authentic as someone who has been a metal fan since the 1980s, because the neoliberal ideology says anyone can be anything, and the only barriers to belonging are learning the histories, inventing the memories, and buying the products.

Norwegian black metal is now a brand, one part of the "package" of cut-and-paste heavy metal identities that constitute the heavy metal imaginary community. Its corpse-painted grim-faced men with black leather and spokes, posing in snow-bound forests, are part of heavy metal's popular imagination, part of the folklore of metal. The actual church burnings, killings, and racism of the scene are stories whispered in pubs and bars around the world, between metal fans and whenever they want to impress their rap-listening work colleagues about metal's true transgressive origins. Norwegian black metal is now a technology in the networks of belonging. It provides memories of communicative transgression and a sort of pride; in the extremes, heavy metal has reached fans who would otherwise be mocked for their bombastic cultural tastes. It provides a folk devil that inspires both shock and awe, a devil that is juxtaposed to the mundanity of the mainstream of global heavy metal today. That is, the Norwegians are rolled out and laughed at as the crazy ones who went too far, who did not understand that metal is just a pantomime, a show, an imaginary community for shy people, rich people, people in suits, and people just like you and me.

CONCLUSIONS

The second wave of black metal was the product of the same kind of network of technologies, assumptions, epistemologies, hegemonies, and agents as any other form of heavy metal. We can trace a number of actors present in the genesis story of Norwegian black metal that actually belong to the rise of heavy metal more generally in the 1970s and 1980s. And there are actors in the network who belong to earlier times. For example, the technologies of amplified music could only be used in heavy metal after 200 years of negotiations between scientists, engineers, performers, metal-workers, and the materiality of electromagnetic wave-particles and their conductors. There has been some debate about whether the actual Vikings at the end of the first millennium used natural magnetic sources to find their way (or more accurately to find their place) across the northern seas to places such as Iceland and Greenland, or whether they used some other method to find their way (Ropars, Lakshminarayanan, and Le Floch 2014). Magnetism was a source of wonder for early modern philosophers such as Gilbert as it seemed to indicate the existence of occult forces at work in the universe. The idea that modern-day Vikings have tamed effects of magnetism so much that it becomes possible to create distorted vocals and guitar notes at the flick of a switch (the Latourian black-box being here the switches and circuitry inside the pedals and amplifiers) is ironic but true. Every point of the history of modernity passes through these devices, and every movement in modernity becomes for the second wave of black metal a thing which the actor-network tries to repel. But this is the paradox of the actor-network, because it cannot be anything but a part of modernity, even as it resists it and burns modernity's churches down.

The second wave was merely an extension of the communicative rationality already at work in extreme metal. But the second-wave itself has become a technology and an epistemology that has become a key element of the network of belonging and identity that defines the imaginary community of heavy metal today, becoming more mythical with each retelling.

NOTES

1. This radical view has been inspired partly by the failure of the philosophy of science to come up with a definitive solution to the problem of epistemological realism (see Fuller 1992), partly by the sociological turn in the history of science associated with what is loosely called constructivism (Golinski 1998), and partly by the reassessment of rational epistemology associated with the term postmodernism and the work of poststructuralists such as Lyotard (1984).

2. Collins and Yearley's (1992) disagreements with Latour stem from a radical reading of his actor-network theory, which they claim does not account for the actual practices of working scientists. Collins has argued in the past that science operates through an interchange of ideas and practices between a center (the core set) or centers and the peripheries (Collins 1985). Latour's actor-network theory, claim Collins and Yearley, fails to recognize these asymmetrical relationships.

3. Here I am following what could be described as the Hacking interpretation of Latour (Hacking 2000), interpreting Latour's statements as being statements about representation (epistemology) not reality (ontology).

4. See www.youtube.com/watch?v=3OK1P9GzDPM (accessed 27 April 2015).

REFERENCES

Anderson, Benedict. 1983. *Imagined Communities*. London: Verso.
Barthes, Roland. 1957. *Mythologies*. London: Jonathan Cape.
Bauman, Zygmunt. 2000. *Liquid Modernity*. Cambridge, UK: Polity.
Bloor, David. 1976. *Knowledge and Social Imagery*. London: Routledge.
Bird, Alexander. 1992. *Philosophy of Science*. London: University College London Press.
Callon, Michel. 1986. "Some Elements of a Sociology of Translation: Domestication of the Scallops and the Fishermen." In *Power, Action and Belief*, edited by J. Law, 196–229. London: Routledge.
Chalmers, Alan F. 1982. *What Is This Thing Called Science?* Milton Keynes: Open University Press.

Cohen, Antony P. 1985. *The Symbolic Construction of Community.* London: Tavistock.

Collins, Harry. 1985. *Changing Order.* London: Sage.

Collins, Harry, and Stephen Yearley. 1992. "Epistemological Chicken." In *Science as Practice and Culture*, edited by A. Pickering, 301–26. Chicago: University of Chicago Press.

Craib, Ian. 1992. *Modern Social Theory: From Parsons to Habermas.* Hemel Hempstead: Harvester Wheatsheaf.

Ely, Margot. 1991. *Doing Qualitative Research: Circles Within Circles.* London: Falmer.

Epstein, Jonathon S., and David J. Pratto. 1990. "Heavy Metal Rock Music, Juvenile Delinquency and Satanic Identification." *Popular Music and Society* 14: 67–76.

Feyerabend, Paul. 1975. *Against Method.* London: Verso.

Fine, Gary A. 2002. *Shared Fantasy: Role-Playing Games as Social Worlds.* Chicago: University of Chicago Press.

Friedman, Michael. 1974. "Explanation and Scientific Understanding." *Journal of Philosophy* 71: 1–19.

Fuller, Steve. 1992. "Being There with Thomas Kuhn: A Parable for Postmodern Times." *History and Theory* 31: 241–75.

Glaser, Barney G., and Anselm L. Strauss, 1967. *The Discovery of Grounded Theory.* Chicago: Aldine.

Golinski, Jan. 1998. *Making Natural Knowledge: Constructivism and the History of Science.* Cambridge, UK: Cambridge University Press.

Gramsci, Antonio. 1971. *The Prison Notebooks.* London: Lawrence and Wishart.

Guarnieri, Massimo. 2013. Who Invented the Transformer? *Industrial Electronics Magazine, IEEE* 7: 56–59.

Hacking, Ian. 2000. *The Social Construction of What?* Cambridge, UK: Cambridge University Press.

Hall, Stuart. 1993. "Culture, Community, Nation." *Cultural Studies* 7: 349–63.

Hempel, Carl G. 1966. *Philosophy of Natural Science.* London: Prentice-Hall.

Hesmondhalgh, David, and Sarah Baker. 2013. *Creative Labour: Media Work in Three Cultural Industries.* London: Routledge.

Hesse, Margaret. 1980. *Revolutions and Reconstructions in the Philosophy of Science.* Bloomington: Indiana University Press.

Hill, Rosemary L. 2014. "Reconceptualizing Hard Rock and Metal Fans as a Group: Imaginary Community." *International Journal of Community Music* 7: 173–87.

Hobsbawm, Eric, and Terence Ranger. 1983. *The Invention of Tradition.* Cambridge, UK: Cambridge University Press.

Hoggart, Richard. 1957. *The Uses of Literacy.* Harmondsworth: Penguin.

Horkheimer, Markus, and Theodor W. Adorno. 2002. *Dialectic of Enlightenment: Philosophical Fragments.* Stanford: Stanford University Press.

James, Frank A.J.L. 2011. *Michael Faraday: The Chemical History of a Candle.* Oxford: Oxford University Press.

Kahn-Harris, Keith. 2007. *Extreme Metal: Music and Culture on the Edge.* Oxford: Berg.

Kong, Lily. 2014. "From Cultural Industries to Creative Industries and Back? Towards Clarifying Theory and Rethinking Policy." *Inter-Asia Cultural Studies* 15: 593–607.

Kuhn, Thomas S. 1977. *The Essential Tension.* Chicago: University of Chicago Press.

Latour, Bruno. 1987. *Science in Action.* Cambridge, MA: Harvard University Press.

———. 1988. *The Pasteurization of France.* Cambridge, MA: Harvard University Press.

———. 1990. "Postmodern? No, Simply Amodern! Steps Towards an Anthropology of Science." *Studies in History and Philosophy of Science* 21: 145–71.

———. 1993. *We Have Never Been Modern.* Cambridge, MA: Harvard University Press.

———. 2007. *Reassembling the Social: An Introduction to Actor-Network-Theory.* Oxford: Oxford University Press.

———. 2011. *On the Modern Cult of the Factish Gods.* Durham: Duke University Press.

Latour, Bruno, and Stephen Woolgar. 1979. *Laboratory Life.* London: Sage.

Lipton, Peter. 1991. *Inference to the Best Explanation.* London: Routledge.

Lucas, Caroline, Mark Deeks, and Karl Spracklen. 2011. "Grim Up North: Northern England, Northern Europe and Black Metal." *Journal for Cultural Research* 15: 279–96.

Lyotard, Jean-Francois. 1984. *The Postmodern Condition: A Report on Knowledge*. Manchester: Manchester University Press.

Masciandaro, Nicola. 2010. *Hideous Gnosis: Black Metal Theory Symposium I*. New York: Glossator.

Oliver, Paul. 1993. *Blues Fell One Morning*. Cambridge, UK: Cambridge University Press.

Popper, Karl. 1968. *The Logic of Scientific Discovery*. London: Heinemann.

Ropars, Guy, Vasudevan Lakshminarayanan, and Albert Le Floch. 2014. "The Sunstone and Polarised Skylight: Ancient Viking Navigational Tools?" *Contemporary Physics* 55: 302–17.

Spracklen, Karl. 1996. *Playing the Ball: Constructing Community and Masculine Identity in Rugby*. PhD Thesis: Leeds Metropolitan University.

———. 2006. "Leisure, Consumption and a Blaze in the Northern Sky: Developing an Understanding of Leisure at the End of Modernity through the Habermasian Framework of Communicative and Instrumental Rationality." *World Leisure Journal* 48: 33–44.

———. 2007. "Negotiations of Belonging: Habermasian Stories of Minority Ethnic Rugby League Players in London and the South of England." *World Leisure Journal* 49: 216–26.

———. 2009. *The Meaning and Purpose of Leisure: Habermas and Leisure at the End of Modernity*. Basingstoke: Palgrave Macmillan.

———. 2011. *Constructing Leisure: Historical and Philosophical Debates*. Basingstoke: Palgrave Macmillan.

———. 2012. "Too Old to Raise the Horns? Getting Older on the Metal Scene and the Politics of Intentionality: A Case Study of Second Generation Norwegian BM Bands." In *Heavy Metal Generations*, edited by Andy Brown and Kevin Fellezs, 79–87. Oxford: ID Press.

———. 2013. *Whiteness and Leisure*. Basingstoke: Palgrave Macmillan.

———. 2014a. "True Norwegian Black Metal: The Globalized, Mythological Re-construction of the Second Wave of Black Metal in 1990s Oslo." In *Sounds and the City*, edited by Brett Lashua, Karl Spracklen and Stephen Wagg, 183–95. Basingstoke: Palgrave Macmillan.

———. 2014b. "There Is (Almost) No Alternative: The Slow 'Heat Death' of Music Subcultures and the Instrumentalization of Contemporary Leisure." *Annals of Leisure Research* 17: 252–66.

———. 2015. *Digital Leisure*. London: Palgrave.

Spracklen, Karl, Caroline Lucas, and Mark Deeks. 2014. "The Construction of Heavy Metal Identity Through Heritage Narratives: A Case Study of Extreme Metal Bands in the North of England." *Popular Music and Society* 37: 48–64.

Spracklen, Karl, and Clifford Spracklen. 2008. "Negotiations of Being and Becoming: Minority Ethnic Rugby League Players in the Cathar Country of France." *International Review for the Sociology of Sport* 43: 201–18.

Spracklen, Karl, Stanley Timmins, and Jonathan Long. 2010. "Ethnographies of the Imagined, the Imaginary, and the Critically Real: Blackness, Whiteness, the North of England and Rugby League." *Leisure Studies* 29: 397–414.

Storey, David. 1960. *This Sporting Life*. London: Longman.

Tolkien, Jonathan R. R. 1937. *The Hobbit*. London: Allen and Unwin.

———. 1955. *The Lord of the Rings*. London: Allen and Unwin.

———. 1977. *The Silmarillion*. London: Allen and Unwin.

Wallach, Jeremy, Harris M. Berger, and Paul D. Greene. 2011. *Metal Rules the Globe: Heavy Metal Music Around the World*. Durham: Duke University Press.

Williamson, John and Martin Cloonan. 2007. "Rethinking the Music Industry." *Popular Music* 26: 305–22.

Winch, Peter. 1958. *The Idea of a Social Science*. London: Routledge.
Wittgenstin, Ludwig. 1968. *Philosophical Investigations*. Oxford: Blackwell.

Part 5

Expanding the Community Beyond Previously Thought Borders

NINE

Do Metal Scenes Need Retirement Homes?

Care and the Limitations of Metal Community

Keith Kahn-Harris

What is metal for? This is a question that is rarely addressed directly, but we can at least say—based on the growing canon of metal studies, together with personal experience—what metal *does*: it excites, it transgresses, it creates community and identity, it connects human beings to each other, it provides meaning, and it structures lives. It is much more difficult to research what metal does *not* do, for how can you research an absence? And is it reasonable to point out what is not there? Does metal have to "do everything"?

In this chapter I want to discuss something that metal as a community does erratically or not at all: care. Bound up in my discussion is the question of whether it is reasonable or not to expect or demand that metal communities should provide care. As the conclusion will show, such difficult questions do not have easy answers. Yet they are worth considering as they impact on the bigger question of what metal is for. As such, they also impact on the claims that we can make for metal.

I address the issue of care through a consideration of metal scenes as communities. To use the term "community" to describe metal scenes, we inevitably put them into the same category as a diverse range of other such communities. In this chapter I compare metal communities to the UK Jewish community. Such a comparison is intended not to disparage metal (or the UK Jewish community for that matter) but to illuminate the different things that different communities provide.

BLACK METAL AND THE REJECTION OF CARING

The suicide of Per Ingve Ohlin, aka Dead, vocalist of *Mayhem*, on April 8, 1991, is a well-thumbed chapter in the book of metal history (see for example: Moynihan and Søderlind 1998; Patterson 2014; Pattison 2012). Its significance for the development of the emerging mythology of Norwegian black metal was profound. This was, in large part due to the enthusiastic way in which Euronymous, as the then driving force behind *Mayhem*, exploited the suicide in a very conscious and deliberate way.

Euronymous' tone in the letters that he sent announcing Dead's suicide to the growing global black metal underground was part callous and part celebratory. In one such letter he appeared to revel in Dead's death:[1]

> Goateye is stone dead! He blew his brains out with a shotgun after cutting open all his veins on his wrists and his throat! Brutal as the devil!
>
> Well, the reason for doing this was that he lived only for the EVIL black metal scene, and its lifestyle with rivets, chains, crosses black clothes and hell.
> . . .
> When he discovered that only (with a few exceptions) trendy children listened to us and came to concerts, and that all he stood for with the old evil scene was laid to waste by kids and hardcore-moral-political-idiots; he decided to die.
> . . .
> But I must add that it was interesting to be able to study (half) a human brain and rigor mortis. When I found him I naturally got my camera and took CLOSE-ups of the corpse from different angles, and me and Hellhammer found 2 large pieces of the cranium that we have hung in neck chains. The pictures will be used on the Mayhem album.
> . . .
> No, we will not attend his funeral because Dead would have HATED that. + it is expensive and he will not notice it much anyway. His mother told us that we have to be there but I don't give a fuck, I'm not a fucking therapist. I'm counting on that our bass player will be there, but that is because he is a sentimental wimp-fucker who didn't even have the guts to see the BLOOD. We will probably have a new bass player soon.

It may well be of course, that Euronymous' feelings about Dead's suicide may have been more complex. In any case, other members of *Mayhem* subsequently expressed in interviews that they were shocked at his callous attitude.[2] There is no doubt though that Euronymous' use of Dead's suicide to build the *Mayhem* myth was successful—and the band carried on after his death (and even after Euronymous' own death in August 1993). The myth of Dead's suicide also became embellished over time, with—unsubstantiated—claims that Euroymous cooked and ate part of Dead's brain and used parts of his skull in necklaces possibly started by Euronymous himself.

What of course got lost in this instant myth-making and in subsequent retellings of the story, is Per Ingve Ohlin, the man who became Dead. It is hermeneutically risky to either conflate myth and reality or, conversely, to insist on a separate (and maybe contrary) reality behind a myth. We do not know whether Dead killed himself as a consciously chosen quasi-aesthetic act designed to further the evolving black metal mythos, or whether Ohlin killed himself as an act designed to end intolerable inner pain.

We can, however, have more confidence in knowing what did *not* happen. In life, Ohlin's colleagues in the black metal scene did not, inso-far as we can tell from the still-fragmentary and contradictory historical record, try desperately to attend to the mental health needs of a person at risk of suicide. Nor was there public soul-searching within the black metal scene about whether more could have been done for Ohlin while alive. Within a Scandinavia renowned for its welfare state and in a world of increasing mental health literacy, Ohlin's life and eventual suicide appears to have run its course entirely unanchored from any systematic *care*.[3] It seems that only Ohlin's family, who organized his burial in his native Sweden, may have provided anything approaching care as conventionally understood.

Perhaps this is all stating the obvious. After all, black metal ideology, as developed by Euronymous and of course Dead himself, consciously rejects the idea of care. Norwegian black metal, in the early 1990s at least, exploited the freedoms and support that the Scandinavian social democratic consensus provided, while contemptuously rejecting its value system (Søderlind and Dyrendal 2009). Black metal was to be founded on a rejection of the values of community, mutual support and responsibility, replacing them with values of self-reliance, individual sovereignty, and eliteness (Venkatesh et al. 2015). While this ideology was to some extent moderated by a partially-pragmatic, partially-heartfelt recognition of some kind of common purpose within the black metal scene itself, the idea that the vulnerable should be cared for was foreign to black metal ideology.

Of course it is also important to recognize that Ohlin's involvement in black metal may well have actually brought him many benefits. As Dead he enjoyed cult notoriety and had a purpose to his life. It may well be the case that Ohlin's life was better as a black metal musician in Norway than it could have been as an alienated youth in his native Sweden.

Or perhaps not: human beings have complex needs. A sense of belonging and meaning is only, after all, one part of this complex matrix. In taking the possibility that human beings need care completely off the table, the early 1990s Norwegian black metal scene also took off the table the possibility that someone like Dead could benefit from forms of care.

However, it would be a mistake to see the rejection of care in metal as something confined to proponents of black metal's most extreme ideologues. A few years ago, I witnessed part of the descent into mental illness of an acquaintance in the London metal scene. A well-known, influential and respected figure, he worked within the metal scene itself. Usually, he was a somewhat shy and taciturn figure, not unfriendly, but not forthcoming either. One day, a friend who worked with him, in the course of a telephone conversation, informed me that my acquaintance was "losing it" and that he'd been forced to quit his job. At a gig the next night, I witnessed what losing it entailed: my acquaintance was now loud, excessively friendly, and talking non-stop, not always making much sense. He was full of extraordinary plans, none of with seemed very practical. It was clear that he was going through a manic phase of the sort that bipolar people sometimes encounter. The reaction among our mutual friends and acquaintances was a mixture of amusement and incredulity. There was certainly no attempt, at least that I was aware of, to intervene and help him (although of course those in the grip of manic phases are not easy to help) and even if there was, it was not clear whom to turn to—it's not as though there are metal institutions to help the mentally ill. So a few days later, my acquaintance was found, incoherent, walking at night down the middle of a busy road. He was forcibly institutionalized and after his release went to live with his parents, out of London, his participation in the metal scene subsequently much reduced.

Of course this experience does not necessarily verify any claim that metal scene members are incapable of caring for each other, but looking at metal scenes through the lens of care does bring out important questions of the nature of metal scenes as communities. What sort of communities are metal scenes and how does an examination of the ways caring works or does not work in metal illuminate the nature of these communities?

CARE IN THE JEWISH COMMUNITY

I want to draw a contrast with another community that I know very well. My work on metal has always been carried out in parallel with my work on the British Jewish community (for example: Kahn-Harris and Gidley 2010), in which I have a long history of engagement as a researcher, activist and lifelong member.

There are fewer than 300,000 Jews living in the United Kingdom. While not all Jews are involved in British Jewish communal life, the UK Jewish community is heavily institutionalized. The last systematic survey of the Jewish voluntary sector in the United Kingdom found that there were over 3,000 communal institutions with over £500 million in annual income (Institute for Jewish Policy Research 2003). British Jews rely on and contribute to a wide range of communal services. Many of these institutions are caring institutions, catering for a wide range of welfare needs. In addition, synagogues (like churches and other faith-based institutions) provide care both formally and informally (Harris 1998). The largely middle class and educated membership of the Jewish community is adept at navigating welfare state structures and other sources of care. Moreover, there is a strong Jewish ethic of care. Visiting the sick, supporting the needy, and other forms of care are enshrined in Jewish religious texts as paramount values. When a synagogue member is hospitalized, they are likely to be visited in the hospital. Old people are found places in retirement homes. When someone dies, well-worn mourning practices come into play, ensuring that mourners are not left to struggle on alone.

These forms of care extend to those with mental health issues. I had first-hand experience of this in a synagogue I used to belong to. A single mother I knew, not born in this country, had multiple mental and physical health needs and had great difficulties in living her life and in providing for her two children. The rabbis and other members of the synagogue spent a huge amount of time interceding with welfare services, providing respite care, and financial support. When she died suddenly of a heart attack, one of the rabbis fostered her children.

I want to be clear about what I am not arguing here. First of all, I am not arguing that the British Jewish community is particularly unusual—there are plenty of communities, some religiously- or ethnically-based, some not, that work in similar ways. Nor am I arguing that metal scenes should be like the British Jewish community. The care that the UK Jewish community provides does not necessarily constitute a reproach to Euronymous and the early 1990s black metal scene. What I *am* arguing though is that looking at very different models of community that have sophisticated cultures, networks, and institutions of care does help us in better understanding metal scenes as communities. And comparing metal and other communities in this way can also help to highlight the under recognized need to explore issues of care (or its lack) in metal.

Drawing loosely on the work of Mary Douglas (1982), one can understand community as having two dimensions (and different definitions of community as emphasizing one or other of these dimensions). The first dimension consists of infrastructure, networks, and practices, the mechanisms through which individuals are bound together in practical terms within a common space (Mary Douglas' "grid"). The second dimension consists of the degree to which members identify with a common communal space, the extent to which they understand themselves as being bound together (Mary Douglas' "group").

I suggest that when these two dimensions coincide, when a community is bound together both by infrastructure and identity, we can understand it as *holistic*. By this I mean that it becomes a space in which members can live their *whole* lives, their various needs catered for with only a limited need to have recourse to other kinds of resources drawn from outside the community. Importantly for the purposes of this chapter, such a holistic community would enable caring—it would provide both the resources necessary to attend to members needs in times of difficulty and the sense of mutual responsibility and identification that would lead members to care for others.

The British Jewish community, at its best, is an example of this kind of holistic community. When members are in need, there are a range of institutions to assist them and other members who will see it as their responsibility to mobilize these institutions. Metal scenes do not seem to be holistic communities of this sort. As communities, metal scenes and their members are situated at different places along the two dimensions.

CARE IN METAL SCENES

Euronymous' vision of black metal—which has proved influential (if not unanimously so) in subsequent black metal ideology—was one in which communal identity was eschewed in favor of a celebration of the sovereign, transgressive individual. At the same time though, Euronymous and others who have followed in his footsteps were heavily involved in not just contributing to, but also deepening and strengthening the black metal scene as a set of practices, institutions, and infrastructure. In other words, even if Euronymous and other black metal ideologues might have rejected one dimension of the communal (i.e., identity), they upheld and strengthened the other dimension (i.e., infrastructure).

There are also parts of metal where the reverse is true. American heavy metal band *Manowar*, for example, are renowned for invoking metal as a brotherhood, as a practice that unites metalheads across the globe. Yet despite running their own metal institutions, *Manowar* are only weakly connected into the kind of thick underground infrastructure through which black metal is reproduced. For *Manowar* and others like them, metal is a structure of feeling that transcends practice.

Taken as a whole, most of the time metal scenes and their members are situated between the extremes of both dimensions. Metal scenes have a sophisticated infrastructure, but not one so dense as to become bureaucratic and overly constraining. Metal scenes produce collective metal identities, but not so collective as to prevent individual self-expression. As I have argued elsewhere (2007), metal scenes are reproduced through economies of both transgressive and mundane subcultural capital—with the transgressive being individually focused and the mundane being collectively focused. The delicate equilibrium that is most of the time achieved between these two trajectories also serves to ensure that an equilibrium is achieved most of the time between the two dimensions of community.

This is how metal scenes—and other kinds of scenes too—differ from holistic communities such as the British Jewish community. While one can call a scene a community, it is scene's avoidance of embracing the extremities of both dimensions of community that gives scenes their distinctive character. Scenes are relatively loose kinds of communities that are reproduced by an avoidance of the more constraining tendencies of community. As such, they respond to the simultaneous and contradictory desires for both collective experience and individual autonomy—desires that more traditionally holistic kinds of community find much harder to fulfill.

We can see then that metal scenes limited capacities for caring are trade-offs, exchanged for the fulfillment of transgressive, individualist desires. That does not mean that metal scenes are incapable of providing any kind of care. Rather, an examination of how caring works in metal scenes raises questions about whether the trade-offs are actually worth it.

There are a number of ways in which care is routinized and practiced within metal scenes, but these forms of care are largely confined to the maintenance of scenic institutions. For example, some prominent scene members have, when in difficulties, been supported by scene-wide campaigns. So, before his death in December 2001, Chuck Schuldiner, vocalist/guitarist of the seminal underground band *Death*, was the beneficiary of benefit gigs held around the world to help support his medical care. Once he died, Schuldiner was eulogized and mourned, as have other important metal musicians who have died prematurely such as Ronnie James Dio and Jeff Hanneman. While these are significant expressions of care—even of love—it is important to recognize that Schuldiner et al. were only in receipt of them due to their scenic achievements. Everyday scene members are unlikely to be cared for in these ways. In any case, the benefit gigs organized for Schuldiner were very much the exception rather than the rule. While it is common when important scene figures are in trouble for scene members to express concern (another example being the outpouring of concern for *Behemoth's* singer/guitarist Nergal during his struggle with leukemia), this does not usually translate into anything tangible.

Another form of care that is somewhat more egalitarian, if equally limited, is expressed through the involvement of metal scene members in forms of protest on behalf of oppressed or persecuted members. We can point here to the involvement of metal scene members in the successful campaign to free the West Memphis Three (three Arkansas teenagers who were falsely convicted in 1994 of the ritual murder of three boys) in the United States, or in the Sophie Lancaster Foundation (which is named after a goth teenager who was murdered in 2007, and campaigns against hate crimes and prejudice directed at those from alternative subcultures) in the United Kingdom.

It should be noted however, that the propensity of metal scene members to get behind such campaigns is erratic and certainly much less than in the punk scene where campaigning is a strong part of the scene's identity. For example, the struggles of metalheads in the Middle East, who have in some countries been persecuted and imprisoned (LeVine 2010), while they are sometimes covered in the metal press (Yardley 2012), have occasioned little practical supportive activity. That metalheads may feel a sense of solidarity with their persecuted brethren is not in doubt; that this rarely translates into practical action is equally clear.

Another form of care that has become increasingly important in recent years lies in the development of an ethics of support for labels and bands, focused on buying their product and attending shows ("Support the Underground" remains a popular slogan[4]). Faced with the ubiquity and availability of free online music, buying music and attending shows becomes reframed as a quasi-altruistic act. Without taking away anything from the importance of this ethic, its object is less the support of other scene members for its own sake than it is the pragmatic recognition that scenic institutions such as record labels are necessary for the survival of metal scenes.

When it comes to those metal scene members who are neither celebrated, nor persecuted nor running scenic institutions, it is hard to discern a common pattern in how they might care for other scene members or be cared for in their turn (it is certainly an eminently researchable topic). It is fair to say, though, that whether or not individual scene members do or do not take care of each other, that the practice of doing so is generally not institutionalized within metal scenes. There are, I am sure, counter-examples to the mentally ill scene member I discussed earlier, in which metal scene members intervened and rallied round. The possibility of receiving care depends as much as anything on the specificities of particular individuals and peer groups, rather than on the nature of the metal scene.

The question is, why does this actually matter? Is it not asking too much of metal scenes that they be a source of care? After all, it is hardly as if (with one major exception discussed next) other music scenes are that different. In fact, it is possible that in some respects metal is much more caring than other music scenes—one could point to, for example, metal's longstanding ability to integrate non-western scenes into the global scene, based on the idea of a global metal fraternity. Yet I would insist that the issue of care and its limitations still matters. One can start to see why through looking at the issue of aging in metal.

METAL AND AGING

While post-war music scenes initially appeared to be confined to young people, as the expression of a particular stage in life, it has become clear in recent decades that the connection between youth and popular music is much less essential than it might once have seemed (Hesmondhalgh 2005). Aging within what were previously understood as "youth" cultures is a growing and complex phenomenon that involves complex negotiations between scenes and the "parent" culture (Hodkinson and Bennett 2013). Paul Hodkinson has argued (2013), in the case of Goth culture, that aging scene members are assimilating into wider sociological patterns of adulthood and family, while still retaining some sense of difference from wider society and commitment to the scene.

Metalheads, too, often remain committed to their music into the indefinite future.[5] One can see this in the continued viability of the touring and recording careers of venerable metal acts long after their initial period of success. Some metal bands, *Motorhead* being one example, attract multiple generations to their shows. With metal now in its fifth decade, we are starting to see lifelong scene members emerging into old age. The question is, bearing in mind the issue of care, what sort of old age can they look forward to?

For scene members who have confined their involvement to listening to metal and going to shows, the long-term consequences are likely to be (beyond possible tinnitus) largely positive. Metal can give meaning to a life and, doubtless, comfort in old age. Perhaps even it can energize the geriatric body and endow a sense of agency and power against creeping death. What is much more of concern is the fate of the more involved scene members. I am thinking here of those who have spent years playing in bands, writing or running fanzines and magazines, or managing labels and other institutions. For a very small number, these activities were lucrative enough to enable a comfortable old age and if desired, retirement. For a somewhat larger group, metal activity was an enjoyable add-on to everyday life. For a significant number though, particularly in the more underground metal scenes, a life in metal largely means either scratching a living or deliberately choosing uninvolving low-wage low-status jobs in order to concentrate on metal activity. Metal activity, particularly the metal underground, often involves sacrifice for those who are most active. There are real questions about what fate awaits them in old age.

I was struck by this at a panel put on at the Bowling Green University metal conference in April 2013. The panel featured a number of long-standing scene members from Toledo, most of whom were in early to late middle age. The panelists were indomitable, resilient, and proud. They were also mostly of very modest means. Reaching middle or old age with few savings, no qualifications or transferable skills, and perhaps the health consequences of excessive living and poor diet, is not a recipe for a comfortable retirement. Will the lifetime of pleasure, meaning and companionship that a life spent in metal have brought, compensate for a fraught and impoverished old age? What is certain is that the care they need will not be found in metal scenes. There are no retirement homes for elderly metalheads, no charities supporting elderly metal musicians in distress. A lifetime's subcultural capital accrued within metal scenes cannot be converted into capital outside them. Of course, many will find the care they need outside of metal scenes. Those living in countries with well-developed welfare states can at least expect some kind of dignity and advanced health care. However, the most common source of care is what has always been, but has rarely been recognized such, the great enabler of metal activity: the family.

The importance of family in caring for metal scene members and in the process enabling scenic activity, would be hard to overstate. One striking illustration of this can be found in the 2008 documentary film *Anvil: The Story of Anvil*. The film focuses on Steve Kudlow and Robb Reiner the two original members of the Canadian band. The band formed in 1978 and saw some early success, but by the time the film was made, this success was long behind them. Kudlow and Reiner worked in low paid, insecure jobs and struggled to finance their thirteenth album and a European tour. While the band was remembered fondly by an earlier generation of metal fans, this did not translate into substantive support nearly thirty years on.

Yet *Anvil* kept going. They kept going in part due to a remarkable stubbornness, persistence, and commitment and partly because, with no opportunity for fulfillment in the world of work, *Anvil* was central to their attempt to make life meaningful. However, none of this quasi-heroic persistence would have meant anything without their principle source of support: their families. Both Reiner and Kudlow came from close-knit Jewish families. Their families not only plainly adored them and wanted to keep their dream alive, they also had stable lives and jobs that enabled them to give them the financial assistance that the band needed. What is crucial to remember here is that the families could not be described as metal families—they did not support *Anvil* in order to support metal, but in order to support their loved ones.

The story of *Anvil* is a particularly powerful illustration of a more general phenomenon. Metal scenes and their members are often reliant on the support of families as well as other sources of non-scenic support such as friends, workmates, employers, and even the welfare state. In research that I carried out on metal scenes (Kahn-Harris 2007), it is these sources of support and families in particular that turn up again and again in accounts of involved scene members lives. It is no exaggeration to state that without the care and support that metal scene members receive from outside of metal scenes, then a considerable part of the metal world simply could not function.

WHY CARE MATTERS

So, to ask the question again—why does this matter? It matters because metal's reliance on the non-metal world has important implications for the stories we tell about metal. There is, of course, no shame in pointing out that metal people need care and support just like everyone else does. Yet there does seem to be a certain discomfort in admitting this. For one thing, interviews and articles in the metal press rarely discuss these issues in even the most comprehensive coverage of underground bands. Perhaps part of the reason why Euronymous and other black metal ideologues so emphatically emphasized individual sovereignty is out of a tacit recognition that metal scenes are so reliant on care and support of non-metal people. One could even read Euronymous' callous framing of Dead's suicide as an assertion that it would only be through eschewing care that black metal would truly be able to break free from the world and follow its own ideological logic. Better to kill oneself than to accept the support of those who do not follow the black metal path.

One doesn't have to embrace this ideology to admit that it raises difficult questions. If metal often cannot provide the degree of care and support that its members require throughout the lifespan, then what claims can we make for its wider value? Here, we need to remember Adorno's famous critique of the culture industry (2001). They argued that popular culture and popular music provided an escape from reality, a way of avoiding engagement with the material conditions of existence. This avoidance leaves oppressive and dominating social structures unchallenged, even when popular culture appears transgressive. For Adorno, it is only when cultural forms grapple with the way that the world and social relations are organized, that they become truly valuable.

This is a harsh and reductive standard to hold popular culture and popular music to, but it still has some validity, particularly when strong claims are made about the importance of popular music. Such is the case with metal. Metal tacitly makes big claims for itself by, among other things, frequently dealing with big issues in lyrics, and celebrating the collective and individual puissance of metal (pace *Manowar*). Arguably, the very fact that people can and do sacrifice much for the sake of metal is a kind of affirmation that metal is, somehow, important.

Yet there are aspects of life that metal usually does not and cannot touch. Metal scenes do not cover all areas of existence and all human needs. The need for care is one of these. This is not a trivial limitation. Our need for care stems from our mortality, our fallibility, and our fragility. The question of how to attend to these needs is central to any kind of

judgment about how social systems are organized. If metal is not engaged with this aspect of existence, it is not engaging with fundamental
issues about how the world should be.

None of this invalidates metal a cultural form. The problem of Ador-
nian criticism is that its fundamentalist foundationalism treats anything
that does not engage with the material conditions of existence as upholding the present order and therefore at best a pointless distraction. This
ignores the way culture, metal culture included, can still do important
and even vital things short of shaking the world's material foundations.

That is not to say that metal's limitations are either inevitable or un-
challengeable. There is a rewarding discussion to have about how metal
could develop more systematic practices of care and how it might respond to the needs that are at present largely not met within metal
scenes. I am not arguing that metal needs to develop the kind of welfare
bureaucracy that the British Jewish community has or that metal scenes
necessarily need to become holistic communities. The nimbleness of
metal scenes is worth preserving and it is predicated at least in part on its
non-provision of complex services outside the cultural sphere. At the
very least though, one could envisage the development of some welfare
funds and charities to help scene members in dire need—these have, after
all, existed in the classical musical world for many years. We could also
envisage metal publications drawing attention to the needs of vulnerable
metalheads more than most currently do.

More than these relatively simple and achievable goals, it is also
worth thinking about how metal scenes might be able to cautiously expand their scope to encompass a broader range of existence beyond the
musical. I have argued elsewhere that, with metal confronting what I
have called a crisis of abundance, it is worthwhile thinking about how
metalness can be articulated outside the music (Kahn-Harris 2013). What
might it be to live a metal life, to care in a metal way? What are the
deeper ways of being that are reproduced within metal scenes that can be
broadened out? We could think, for example, about resilience, a critical
metal value, and how it might be applied in the context of care.

There are precedents here. Some punk scenes have long been concerned with developing new ways of living that do respond to a greater
range of human needs than just the need for music (2012). Most famously, the Britsh band *Crass* spawned a number of experiments in anarchist
organization and communal living (Rimbaud 2015). Might there be a
metal equivalent?

CONCLUSION

In pointing out the limitations that metal scenes have with regard to care,
I am not belittling or devaluing metal. I am suggesting that we need to be

more careful in qualifying and specifying the claims we make for the value of metal scenes. Whether or not we think that metal scenes need to provide more systematic practices of care, we can at least be clear about what is and is not possible within the metal way of life.

In some respects, if metal scenes were to continue as they are now as non-holistic communities, it would simply be a reflection of the irreducible complexity of the (late) modern world. In a globalized and ever-more interconnected world, the ability of individuals to confine themselves to any one space and/or identity is ever-more reduced. As such, even those communities that I define as holistic have great difficulty in guarding against the increasing permeability of their boundaries. In the UK Jewish community, fears about assimilation and intermarriage are widespread (Kahn-Harris and Gidley 2010). It may be that the only way that communities can truly ensure that they can care is through processes of self-ghettoization (as with the strictly orthodox Jewish community [Heilman 2012] that, ironically, ends up being anything but "care-full" to those who are marginalized and even persecuted through them).

From this perspective, the price of freedom from oppressive communal structures is lack of care. At the very least, we must recognize that it would be an enormous challenge to institute practices of care in metal without undermining the much-valued freedoms that permeate metal scenes. But while this would seem to lead to the inescapable conclusion that the lack of care in metal scenes is just something we should accept, we also have to face an uncomfortable truth: In Western countries, the public welfare systems that scene members have often relied on are being questioned and undermined. It is often "communities" and voluntary associations that are required to pick up the burden of care that the state relinquishes. If metal scene members have neither a state nor a community to care for them—what then? Is the price of a lifetime's involvement in metal to be an old age spent in poverty and pain?

NOTES

1. Øystein "Euronymous" Aarseth, Letter to an unknown recipient, n.d. Reprinted at surrealdocuments.blogspot.co.uk/2009/05/euronymouss-epistles-pt-6.html. Accessed September 19, 2015.

2. Ibid.

3. Here and in the rest of the chapter, I am drawing in particular on the idea of an "ethics of care" as developed by feminist scholars such as Virginia Held (2005). I am also using the term more generically to refer to contact with welfare services, whether provided by the state or civil society.

4. For example, it is the slogan for the following blog:www.hellnoise.com/ (accessed September 19, 2015). Examples of flyers sporting the slogan can be found in Netherton (2015).

5. One study found that sense of community in metal was correlated positively with age (Varas-Diaz et al. 2015).

REFERENCES

Adorno, Theodor W. 2001. *The Culture Industry.* London: Routledge Classics.
Biel, Joe. 2012. *Beyond The Music.* Portland, OR: Microcosm Publishing.
Douglas, Mary. 1982. *Natural Symbols: Explorations in Cosmology.* New York: Pantheon Books.
Kahn-Harris, Keith. 2007. *Extreme Metal: Music and Culture on the Edge.* Oxford: Berg.
Harris, Margaret. 1998.*Organising God's Work: Challenges for Churches and Synagogues.* London: Macmillan.
Heilman, Samuel C. 2000. *Defenders of the Faith: Inside Ultra-Orthodox Jewry* (2nd edition). Berkeley, CA: University of California Press.
Held, Virginia. 2005. *The Ethics of Care.* Oxford: Oxford University Press.
Hesmondhalgh, David. 2005. "Subcultures, Scenes or Tribes? None of the Above." *Journal Of Youth Studies* 8 (1): 21–40.
Hodkinson, Paul. 2013. "Family and Parenthood in an Ageing 'Youth' Culture: A Collective Embrace of Dominant Adulthood?" *Sociology* 47 (6): 1072–87.
Hodkinson, Paul, and Andy Bennett. 2013. *Ageing and Youth Cultures: Music, Style and Identity.* London: Bloomsbury Academic.
Institute for Jewish Policy Research. 2003. *Long-Term Planning for British Jewry: Final Report and Recommendations.* London: Institute for Jewish Policy Research.
Kahn-Harris, Keith. 2013. Metal Beyond Metal: What Happens Next? Paper presented at the *Heavy Metal and Popular Culture Conference,* Bowling Green University, Ohio, April 4–7.
Kahn-Harris, Keith. 2007. *Extreme Metal: Music and Culture on the Edge.* Oxford: Berg.
Kahn-Harris, Keith, and Ben Gidley. 2010. *Turbulent Times: The British Jewish Community Today.* London: Continuum.
LeVine, Mark. 2010. Freemus Report. *Headbanging Against Repressive Regimes—Censorship of Heavy Metal in the Middle East, North Africa, Southeast Asia and China.* freemuse.org/archives/1540.
Moynihan, Michael, and Didrik Søderlind. 1998. *Lords of Chaos: The Bloody Rise of the Satanic Metal Underground.* Venice, CA: Feral House.
Netherton, Jason. 2015. *Extremity Retained: Notes From the Death Metal Underground.* 2nd edition. London: Handshake Inc.
Patterson, Dayal. 2014. *Black Metal : Evolution of the Cult.* Venice, CA: Feral House.
Pattison, Louise. 2012. *Black Metal: Beyond the Darkness.* London: Black Dog Publishing.
Rimbaud, Penny. 2015. *The Last of the Hippies: An Hysterical Romance.* Oakland, CA: PM Press.
Søderlind, Didrik, and Asbjørn Dyrendal. 2009. "Social Democratic Satanism? Some Examples of Satanism in Scandinavia." In *Contemporary Religious Satanism: A Critical Anthology,* edited by Jesper Aagaard Petersen, 153–70. Farnham: Ashgate.
Varas-Diaz, Nelson, Eliut Rivera-Segarra, Carmen L. Rivera Medina, Sigrid Mendoza, and Osvaldo González-Sepúlveda. 2015. "Predictors of Communal Formation in a Small Heavy Metal Scene: Puerto Rico as a Case Study." *Metal Music Studies* 1 (1): 87–103.
Venkatesh, Vivek, Jeffrey S. Podoshen, Kathryn Urbaniak, and Jason J. Wallin. 2015. "Eschewing Community: Black Metal." *Journal of Community & Applied Social Psychology* 25 (1): 66–81.
Yardley, Miranda. 2012. "The Real Underground: Metal in the Middle East." *Terrorrizer,* September 7,www.terrorizer.com/news/features-2/the-real-underground-metal-in-the-middle-east/(accessed September 19, 2015).

TEN

A Shared Madness

The Joint Ownership of Heavy Metal History and Studies

Brian Hickam

Metal music studies began in earnest with sociologist Deena Weinstein's 1991 monograph *Heavy Metal: A Cultural Sociology* (Weinstein 1991). Thanks largely to a growing array of scholarly events over the past decade, metal music studies has become increasingly transdisciplinary. The scope of metal music studies is anything and everything having to do with heavy metal music and culture: all topics, regions, eras, relationships, and perspectives. The first scholarly conference focused on such subjects was 2008's *Heavy Fundametalisms*, sponsored by Inter-Disciplinary.net (see Scott and von Helden 2010). This gathering brought together scholars from multiple disciplines, countries and points of view. Since the impetus of this conference, metal music studies scholars have been communicating, collaborating, and theorizing in ways that are *cross-disciplinary* (elucidating characteristics of one discipline in terms of another), *interdisciplinary* (transferring methods from one discipline to another), and, sometimes, *transdisciplinary* (intersecting disciplinary boundaries to create a holistic approach).

Subsequent conferences and symposia have brought together musicians, concert and festival promoters, magazine editors, fans, visual artists, scholars, record industry representatives, and others from the global metal community. With the exception of a few events, such as conferences focused on metal and musicology, metal music studies gatherings and publications tend to attract presenters, attendees, and readers from numerous disciplines and backgrounds. Among our audiences, then, exists a wide variety of ways that people frame their understandings of the world. Reciprocal understandings will be essential for these stakeholders (defined below) to collaborate and for metal music studies and its methodologies to coalesce.

"Community" can be defined as "a social, religious, occupational, or other group sharing common characteristics or interests and perceived or perceiving itself as distinct in some respect from the larger society within which it exists" (Dictionary.com 2016). During my four decades of following metal, I have often heard fans note a perceived kinship to other fans which they met only once at a festival, know only from social media, etc. As evidenced by the chapters in this book, the metal community has varied meanings and implications. While we scholars tend to be discipline-specific, and while our experiences as fans within the metal community tend to be limited in various ways, we should strive (as scholars and as fans) to "see the bigger picture." For reasons explained below, we should look to communicate and collaborate with musicians, other fans, and non-metal scholars.

Metaphor, I shall argue, should play a central role in communications. With the foundation of this new field of study still being established, the purpose of this chapter is to examine the communication processes between individuals and between groups, both scholars and non-scholars, and offer broad proposals for the advancement of metal music studies which have been synthesized from the literatures on whole systems theory, stakeholder theory, and metaphor. I encourage scholars to increase their outreach efforts to fans, musicians, and others in the metal community as their understandings of what we do and their contributions to our insights are integral to our efficacy, expertise, growth, and perceived value.

CONSTRUCTING REALITY:
THE TWO STAGES OF OUR TOWER OF BABEL

In the Tower of Babel myth from the Book of Genesis, the designers planned for their tower to touch heaven. This activity brought down the wrath of Jehovah, who disrupted the builders, confounded them with new and different spoken languages, and dispersed these people throughout the world. The Tower of Babel metaphor has been used by authors from many fields to note intra- and interdisciplinary communication problems (e.g., Goodchild 2000, geographic information; Brown 1995, critical race theory and Civil Rights scholarship; Caspi et al. 2000, complementary and alternative medicine; Owen 1992, psychotherapy). The present concern in metal music studies, as our interdisciplinary field integrates approaches from multiple branches of learning and perspectives, builds its initial base, and creates cross-, trans-, and interdisciplinary methodologies, is one of effective communications and common understandings. Knowledge transfer and shared realities are complex processes with which every discipline must struggle. Ideally, metal music studies scholars will do much of our learning vicariously from the histories of other fields and anticipate the inevitable phases of our growth. Tait and Richardson (2010), for example, bring together an interdisciplinary team of authors who take a complex systems view of knowledge, knowledge transfer, and knowledge management. The use of metaphor is one of their primary recommendations for effective collaborative knowledge production, organizational learning, and decision-making in multiple stakeholder circumstances.

As metal music studies researchers create new terms and concepts, we will need to strive to create consensus on each term's and concept's meanings. Otherwise, as Goldstein (2014) relates when discussing chaos and related theories, "misunderstanding can exceed understanding, and language can serve to obscure rather than reveal" (30). Years from now, however, after the various contributing fields of study and perspectives have been synthesized into a consensus of scope and approaches for metal music studies, we'll need to be wary of a second phase in the Tower of Babel model: the miscommunications which stem from specializations within our field. Phillips (2001) cites "highly specialized areas of study," differing methodologies, and lapses in understanding as the primary cause for limitations of progress in sociology (x). Similarly, Hirschheim and Klein (2006) deplore the lack of "sense-making, meaning creations, and negotiations" (103) among Information Systems (IS) scholars when they present at conferences:

> Hence the greatest issue that the IS community faces internally is its fragmentation into numerous specializations (or what we might call "sects"). They need an intellectual synthesis that could emerge from a fruitful discourse. However, we lack a set of shared assumptions and language, and as a result the various subspecializations lack the motivation and capability to communicate with each other. Our large conferences . . . are reincarnations of the Tower of Babel. Fruitful, cross-sectional debate almost never occurs. And it has been like this for decades. (94)

Metal music studies has already witnessed a significant, potential "sect" in black metal theory (BMT). Karl Spracklen in his chapter (this volume) sees fit to critique it; Wilson (2014) argues that it is separate from metal music studies; while Riches (2015), in her book review of Wilson (2014), questions his assertion:

> In the introduction Wilson argues that BMT, and particularly melancology, is not an example of "metal music studies" or other traditional forms of music criticism and sociology. Although I do not wholly agree with Wilson's statement, indeed there are elements of BMT that give it

a different feel and depth in comparison to other scholarly accounts on heavy metal music. (398–99)

Stakeholder theory, as shown below, provides a viewpoint which demonstrates that BMT has more in common with metal music studies than not. It's noteworthy that numerous scholars have presented and published in both arenas. A shared goal of these two nascent fields might be to focus on our mutual concerns and gain inspiration and insights from one another as we build our methodologies.

To clarify, I am not arguing for homogeneity in metal music studies. I am advocating for effective communications. Both diversity and specializations are good. In my view, all metal music scholars need to work together so we can build a proper foundation for our multifaceted discipline. We must first communicate, cooperate, and collaborate. Otherwise, we would be publishing and presenting papers on metal within the frameworks of existing disciplines. As we further specialize within metal music studies, we must strive to communicate our concepts to one another.

INCLUSION AND DIALOGUE

In my view, a dual application of stakeholder theory and whole systems theory to metal music and culture studies, combined with a focus on conceptual metaphor, would facilitate the creation of our foundational concepts, definitions, methodologies, and approaches. Freeman (1984), who is credited as the father of modern stakeholder theory, defines a "stakeholder" as "any group or individual who can affect, or is affected by, the achievement of [an organization's] purpose" (vi). Stakeholder theory originated in management science (Freeman 1984) and has since been applied to numerous disciplines (e.g., Mainardes, Alves, and Raposo 2013, education studies; Lafreniere, Deshpande, Bjornlund, and Hunter 2013, environmental studies; Ray et al. 2014, religious studies; Kok et al. 2015, health education; Khazaei, Elliot, and Joppe 2015, tourism geography). Stakeholder theory and modern whole systems theory have an intertwined history of cross-pollination (see Freeman 1984; Buchholz and Rosenthal 2005; Ulmer, Seeger, and Sellnow 2005; Freeman et al. 2010). As such, the two theories will be combined in my arguments and metal music studies is viewed as an "organization" (i.e., institute, association, or society) within stakeholder theory and an "element" (i.e., facet or constituent) within systems theory.

Freeman (1984) notes that Ackoff (1970; 1974) and Churchman (1968) took inspiration from stakeholder analysis as they "develop[ed] systems theory into a powerful tool for addressing a number of issues in social science" (36). Freeman (1984) states:

The actual word "stakeholder" first appeared in the management literature in an internal memorandum at the Stanford Research Institute (now SRI International, Inc.) in 1963 [and was] defined as "those groups without whose support the organization would cease to exist." The list of stakeholders included shareowners, employees, customers, suppliers, lenders and society. . . . The SRI researchers argued that unless executives understood the needs and concerns of . . . stakeholder groups, they could not formulate corporate objectives which would receive the necessary support for the continued survival of the firm . . . The point of the SRI definition is . . . pure and simple: survival. Without the support of these key groups the firm does not survive, by definition of what we mean by "stakeholder." (31–33)

Equating "the firm" from the quote above with "metal music studies" and discussing whether the survival of metal music and culture studies depends upon our successful integration of the concerns of musicians, fans, and others would best be analyzed in a separate work. I do contend, however, that our discipline is enriched when some scholars incorporate the perspectives of non-scholars.

Whole systems thinking (also referred to as general systems theory) comes from biology via organization development (see Von Bertalanffy 1972, 1975; Laszlo 1972; Ackoff 1974). The metaphorical view of an organization as an organism led to holistic perspectives where the interdependence of elements (i.e., stakeholders) received attention. Anderson and Johnson (1997) define a "system" as:

A group of interacting, interrelated, or interdependent components that form a complex and unified whole. A system's components can be physical objects that you can touch, such as the various parts that make up a car. The components can be *intangible*, such as processes; relationships; company policies; information flows; interpersonal interactions; and internal states of mind such as feelings, values, and beliefs. (2)

Since its introduction in the 1930s and 1940s, general systems theory has spawned numerous schools of thought within systems philosophy.

The goal of general systems theory (GST) is to model the properties and relationships common to all systems, regardless of their specific components, or the academic disciplines in which they are studied. Thus, while physical, biological, or social systems may appear to be quite different in terms of their components and relationships, they all may display certain common properties. The study of these common properties is the goal of GST. (Bailey 2005, 310)

According to Boulding (1985), "social systems arise out of the interactions of human beings and their artifacts" (28). The global metal community can be analyzed as a multidimensional social system.

HEAVY METAL AS SYSTEM

The "artifacts" of heavy metal are its recordings, fanzines, photographs, patches, etc. Various "key groups" within the metal community interact with each type of artifact. With Freeman's (1984) contention that "without the support of . . . key groups the firm does not survive, by definition of what we mean by 'stakeholder'" (31–33), I will highlight the significance of various groups. Noting Ackoff's (1974) GST elements, I have listed in Table 10.1 a list the components, or elements, of the system of heavy metal music and culture, which are also its stakeholders.

Bammer (2014) reviews methods of interdisciplinary dialogue which, collectively, "could accommodate different requirements and preferences for engagement of disciplinary and stakeholder expertise" (390) and adds that:

> Systems thinking allows [any given] real-world problem to be placed center stage and makes it feasible to examine a range of discipline-based and stakeholder perspectives in a coherent and systematic way. It involves looking at the inter-relationships between various aspects of the problem, as well as the broader issues the problem relates to and those interconnections. A systems view about heroin use, for example, involves examining the interactions between users, their families, treatment providers, police, and the community at large, with different foci on crime, social functioning, health, and so on. It also means examining

Table 10.1.   Components of the system of heavy metal music and culture.

Musicians	Record store retailers
Musical instrument manufacturers	Tablature book publishers
Visual artists/graphic designers	"Print" Zine publishers
Costume designers	Reference Sources (e.g., Metal-
Entertainment lawyers	Archives.com; Wikipedia; Rateyourmusic;
Biographers	print encyclopedias)
Archivists	Webzine publishers
Bibliographers	"Tape" traders
Journalists	Recording studios
Reviewers	Filmmakers
Educators	Road crew members
Booking agents	Magazines
Music venues	Online music retailers
Radio stations (broadcast, satellite, and	Groupies
Internet)	Performance rights organizations
Fans	Websites offering video or audio clips
Band/Talent managers	Historians
Concert promoters	Bloggers
Scholars	Others
Engineers	
Record labels	

the broader context of the heroin supply system—the drug cartels, supply lines, and international law enforcement. (397)

A metal music studies scholar, then, who is composing an entry on "fashion" for an encyclopedia might want to incorporate its influence on album cover art, stage performance, filmmakers, webzines, etc. With our list and Ackoff's (1974) characteristics in mind, we note Olds' (1992) contention that a "major implication of systems theory is a challenge to linear notions of causality and a recentering of the locus of causation within a network of interrelated events and process. Intercausality thus pertains to all events, and linear claims of cause and effect cannot be made. This claim is one of the most subtle and powerful in systems perspectives" (125). A "simplified" stakeholder map of metal music and culture studies is shown in figure 10.1.

I will now note Ackoff's (1974) three essential properties of a system, or set, and provide examples from heavy metal:

1. *The properties or behavior of each element of the set has an effect on the properties or behavior of the set taken as a whole.* (Ackoff 1974, 13)

Our "set" or system is the metal community. Metal music and culture scholars, taken as a group (or "element of the set"), analyze any and all of the elements listed above. Together, we study the "set taken as a whole." Each element above, taken as a distinct group, be it band managers or "radio" stations or educators, influences the global metal community. The behaviors and contributions of each element add to the whole. For example, filmmakers impact the "whole"—Rat Skates' (2007) documentary film on the DIY evolution of New York/New Jersey thrash metal; the mockumentary *This Is Spinal Tap* (1984); and all other films about metal.

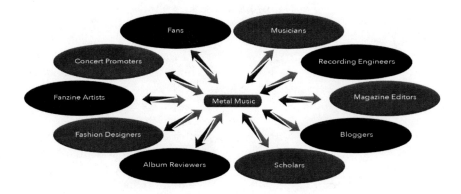

Figure 10.1.   Stakeholders of the heavy metal subculture.

2. The properties and behavior of each element, and the way they affect the
whole, depend on the properties and behavior of at least one other element
in the set. (Ackoff 1974, 13)

Musicians typically depend on engineers, record label executives, and
others to record their music. Retailers, video-sharing websites, music
streaming services, and others determine the music's availability. Book-
ing agents, music venues, concert promoters, band managers, and others
determine which bands perform live and where. Journalists, bloggers,
and others help to review and raise the visibility of bands, musicians, and
festivals. The behavior of every component listed here influences the
metal community and, to varying degrees, one another. The entries
in *Encyclopaedia Metallum — The Metal Archives* (see www.metal-
archives.com), for example, are essential for the work of many scholars,
historians, journalists, and music collectors. This freely available database
is, in fact, like other wikis, the remarkable result of an open system. This
reference tool is dependent on the behaviors of multiple components of
the metal community. Since metal's history is important to many in the
community, such informational tools have a major influence on the
"whole."

I will explore one example in more depth — a recent trend in book
publishing — to better illustrate *property #2*. A few days after Coggins'
(2015) paper presentation on drone metal, fonts, and band logos at
the *Modern Heavy Metal: Markets, Practices and Cultures* conference in
Helsinki, I received a book in the mail which I then recommended to him
as a source for this research. The book (Riddick 2015) is a second edition
and was published not by a traditional book publisher, but by Doomentia
Press, a subsidiary of the relatively small, independent record label and
distributor Doomentia Records (see www.doomentia.com) in the Czech
Republic. I had preordered the book since learning of the first edition
(Riddick 2008a) after it had gone out-of-print. At the time I looked into
purchasing that edition, I discovered that Riddicks' other books (2007,
2008b, 2012) were also out-of-print. These and similar books are highly
desirable for my research and as additions to the *Heavy Metal & Hardcore
Punk Archives*, which has two locations in Ohio (see Hickam 2010, 2014).
Another author, Martos (2015), elected to self-publish his book on metal
album covers (2015, pers. comm.).[1] Three hundred and fifteen fans re-
acted to his Indiegogo campaign request of US $8,310 by providing him
with $19,574 in two months (Martos 2014).

Until 2012, I could largely depend upon myself to learn about new
books on metal. I would search major publishers' and major retailers'
websites, Google, and Worldcat to discover forthcoming, available, and
out-of-print books. Since then, a behavior change in book publishing has
affected my behavior. I am now more dependent on feedback from publishers, book authors, fellow scholars, Facebook friends, etc. The process

of discovery is now more hit and miss and more burdensome. For instance, due to the linear design of the Doomentia website and its lack of a search feature, vinyl records, patches, books, t-shirts, DVDs, magazines, CDs, and other merchandise are interspersed in their order of posting. One must click through the pages of sections for "News," "Distro," or "Releases" in order to learn of the label's and press' offerings. Consequently, I now get email alerts from Doomentia Press. To continue my work as a bibliographer of metal music studies publications (see Hickam 2015), I had to learn of changes from associates in the metal community and alter my behavior. Anderson and Johnson (1997) note that "systems achieve . . . stability through interactions, feedback, and adjustments that continually circulate among the system parts, and between the system and its environment" (4).

Fans also have an effect on other elements and the whole metal subculture when they document its history and fill a void in the literature or oral histories with their subject matter or perspective. Plante (2015, pers. comm.),[2] for example, is a fan and former zine artist, who has spent "every day of the past six years [and the next two or three]" compiling an exhaustive encyclopedia which will be published by Bazillion Points Press. It will be comprised of capsule reviews of "every known 1980s metal demo" by bands, signed or unsigned. As a non-scholar stakeholder, Plante is making valuable contributions to the metal community as most academics do not have the luxury of dedicating so many years to such an enormous task. The contributions of amateur astronomers or bird watchers to scholarly research would be good parallels.

In order to learn of demos and the receptions they received, Plante is using social media to seek copies or originals of all contemporary fanzines (which, he notes, will be the subject matter of a future book). This zine collection will benefit future scholars through his anticipated bequest to the *Heavy Metal & Hardcore Punk Archives*. Author Jason Netherton, in contrast, noted his choice to go with the smaller independent publisher Handshake, Inc. due to Bazillion Points' two-year pipeline for finished manuscripts (J. Netherton 2015, pers. comm).[3] The first edition of Netherton's book is another source that I missed out on as I hadn't yet listened to feedback from the metal community. A cassette compilation, sold in a deluxe package of his book's second edition, quickly sold out (Netherton 2014). Behaviors of authors and publishers affect the behaviors of fans and scholars in these and other ways.

> 3. *Every possible subgroup of elements in the set has the first two properties: each has a nonindependent effect on the whole. Therefore, the whole cannot be decomposed into independent subsets. A system cannot be subdivided into independent subsystems.* (Ackoff 1974, 13)

The "whole" of metal culture is primarily affected by the element of music. Nonetheless, each of the other elements is integral and none could operate in isolation and still be "metal" in nature. Metal clothing fashion, for example, cannot be separated from the other elements of metal culture. If it weren't part of the whole, if it didn't react to the properties or behaviors of metal fans, retailers, musicians, and magazine editors, it would be outside the system. The metal community would not be what it is with an "independent"/unrelated element of fashion. Without the metal t-shirt, leather, denim, patches, chains, and spikes, it wouldn't be the metal culture that we've come to know. Cultural capital in metal would be different. The system and the element are interdependent. Communication between the various elements of our system (the global metal community) allows for shared understandings. Well-described metaphors, then, are a good strategy for facilitating exchanges of ideas between the various stakeholders.

METAPHOR'S UTILITY TO THE GROWTH OF METAL MUSIC STUDIES

As Miller (1982) notes, people's different disciplines, occupations, and experiences result in diverse perspectives on reality and ways of communicating:

> World view points to the conceptual construction which is used by a group to interpret reality. In my view, it is that conceptual framework, the associated images and metaphors, plus the understandings of relationships among them which pre-eminently influence how the members of one discipline think in contrast to the members of another discipline. It is not subject matter or the naming of a single central concept that identifies the essence of a discipline, but the predominant thought model or models. (6)

Scientists often employ metaphors to devise and articulate scientific concepts. Geary (2011) discusses how metaphors are devices used to attain emotional discernment and mental change and highlights ways they are used in successful advertisements, education, and discovery. Feldman (2006) contends that language and thought should be studied more as neuroscience than a system of abstract symbols:

> In general, we see that understanding a sentence involves finding the best match between what was spoken and our current mental state. The brain is inherently a best-match computer; its massively parallel, inter-connected structure allows it to combine many factors in understanding a sentence (or image, etc.). . . . Finding the best match for language input includes evoking metaphors. (13)

The most efficient and effective way for metal music studies scholars to communicate complex theories and concepts to fans, musicians, and scholars in other fields, then, is through the use of conceptual metaphors.

Repko (2008) notes that a "metaphor is a figure of speech in which a word or phrase, a story, or a picture in likened to the idea that one is attempting to communicate" (22).

> Ricoeur (1977) offers a metaphor for cross-disciplinary discourse:
> My inclination is to see the universe of discourse as a universe kept in motion by an interplay of attractions and repulsions that ceaselessly promote the interaction and intersection of domains whose organizing nuclei are off-centred in relation to one another; and still this interplay never comes to rest in an absolute knowledge that would subsume the tensions. (357)

Olds (1992), who cites Ricoeur, takes a systems view of knowledge when she suggests integrating ontological metaphors in order to communicate how perspectives and worldviews relate. Her use of the Buddhist metaphor of Indra's net, which connects disciplines and hierarchies in infinite reflections, complements Ricoeur's (1977) assertion:

> If any metaphor could replace the Gothic cathedral for our time, I believe it would be the image of Indra's net, the cosmic web of interrelatedness extending infinitely in all directions of the universe. Every intersection of intertwining web is set with a glistening jewel, in which all parts of the whole are reflected, mirroring the intricate interconnectedness of all reality and its intercausality. Indra's net captures the web, network, pattern, tapestry, textured imagery of our time, yet perhaps needs to be seen as a more dynamic field of energy, revealing a shimmering and everchanging holarchy, where each part reflects the whole, and where nothing exists apart from the whole. (xiii)

Applying Ackoff's (1974) and Anderson and Johnson's (1997) descriptions of systems and systems theory and Olds' (1992) contention that systems theory is an ideal metaphor for "interrelatedness" or interdisciplinary dialogue, I now review some specific applications from metal music studies. Hickam and Wallach (2011) proposed a metaphor in their recommendation that scholars synthesize the various conceptual frameworks of the disciplines which have contributed to metal music and culture studies to facilitate the creation of methodologies. Our contention was that it is only with distinctive, novel methodologies that scholars will raise our emergent discipline to a well-defined, well-regarded field of study:

> We believe that the metal scholar should be like a Japanese tea master, who must master many arts, including ceramics, architecture, gardening, calligraphy, painting, incense, and flower arranging, in order to become a virtuosic practitioner of the intricate rituals of the tea ceremony. The future metal scholar should strive for substantive knowledge of the fields that have contributed to metal music studies. Metal scholars should also move beyond the mere acquisition of such knowledge. The Japanese tea ceremony has been recognized for its impact upon the Zen

Buddhism that originally influenced its very formation and development. Instead of simply asking what philosophy, cognitive science, ethnomusicology, queer studies, sociology, archival studies, gender stud-
ies, leisure studies or media studies can contribute to metal music stud-
ies, we must also be asking: What can metal music studies contribute to
those academic disciplines? (269)

We were not suggesting that metal music studies' scholars need to be
generalists. Our desired point was that scholarly communication requires
mutual understanding in order to be effective since metal music studies
brings together scholars from dozens of fields, all of which have specific
ways of viewing phenomena. Repko (2008) notes that this will not be an
easy endeavor:

> Mode of thinking means the way of thinking and perceiving reality
> that characterizes a discipline—i.e., its perspective. Identifying and
> blending information from various disciplines about a problem or
> question is difficult enough; harder still is learning how each discipline
> thinks, approaches problem solving, conducts research, and creates
> new knowledge. . . . The disciplines, though difficult to master and
> constantly changing in character, remain invaluable ways to perceive
> and understand the world. (Repko 2008, 19)

A MULTIFACETED, GLOBAL COMMUNITY

Heavy metal music and culture are internationally embraced and sub-
stantial in popularity and size. On July 8, 2015, the *Encyclopaedia Metallum*
website listed the following: 103,804 documented bands (546,636 band
members) from 147 countries; 271,686 albums and 1,940,539 songs;
280,273 registered, active website members and 84,801 inactive members;
84,517 album, concert, and video reviews; and 27,881 record labels
(10,307 of which are active) (Encyclopaedia Metallum 2015a, 2015b). The
musicians, fans, record label executives, authors, magazine publishers,
book publishers, scholars, etc. of metal's global community are well connected with one another (see Bardine et al. 2016; Karjalainen and Kärki
2015; Wallach, Berger, and Greene 2011; Mercer 2009). Several conferences and symposia on metal music studies during the field's eight years
of existence have brought such groups together, including scholars from
dozens of disciplines. Work toward the formation of the *International
Society for Metal Music Studies* (ISMMS) commenced during the 2008 conference in Salzburg. A formal, interdisciplinary planning group was established in early 2010 (see Hickam 2014). ISMMS was founded in an
effort to improve scholarly communication and collaboration and to establish the field within academe. Part of ISMMS' mission is to: facilitate
the scholarly study of the music and culture; document events, oral histories and publications (books, dissertations, book chapters, journal arti-

cles, documentary films, etc.); and preserve such sources in archives (ISMMS 2015). Currently, scholars are developing "metal music studies" methodologies and performing outreach to fans, musicians, and others in the metal community.

In reference to the state of affairs twenty-five years ago, Klein (1990) attests "organizations devoted exclusively to interdisciplinary approaches [were] rare" (48). Present-day scholars continue to debate how to define interdisciplinary work and bemoan the lack of progress in developing interdisciplinary methodologies (see Bammer 2014). Given the passions and high activity levels exhibited by metal music studies scholars in establishing their field and the large number of international stakeholders brought together through social media, scholarly communication, correspondence, and face-to-face events, metal music studies scholars are well positioned to assist with developing interdisciplinary communication tools. The tea master metaphor mentioned earlier relates the need for metal scholars to be interdisciplinary in their knowledge and approach. What is needed for mutual understandings, according to Olds (1992) are metaphors, which will allow a scholar in one discipline to communicate discipline-specific concepts and relationships to a scholar in a different field. Fortunately, compared to other interdisciplinary fields, such as social work or organization development, metal music studies has seen rapid initial growth (see Hickam 2014).

At the *Modern Heavy Metal* conference in Helsinki, Grund (2015) provided a conceptual metaphor, using both text and pictures, for her metal music studies audience. In describing a fan's pleasurable experience of listening to extreme metal, Grund (2015) used an interdisciplinary, Olds-style model based on a metaphor which likens music listening with the digestive system: "I believe that the model provided by counterfactual hearing as it is explicated here is useful for framing discourse regarding a number of philosophical and aesthetic issues relevant to metal, more precisely, extreme metal" (381):

> My rather bold philosophical mission was to propose a "definition" of music that would cover even far out cases such as what would it mean for us to attribute music as a cultural concept that would be meaningful for beings such as androids or space aliens above and beyond that they somehow could "hear" sound. First, we would have to dare to propose some music-making predicates for us humans. My suggestion—and I still am quite fond of this—was *food*. . . . There are many aspects of the category *"foodstuffs"* that make it a prime candidate for at least a plausible music-making predicate for many humans and many kinds of sounds.
>
> . . .
>
> 1. highlighting the role of the hearer and what is required for a hearer to become a listener (i.e., counterfactual hearing)

2. providing the notion of the music-making predicate (possibly predicates) as the linchpin for a kind of metaphorical transferal of the non-sonic into the sonic. (376; emphasis added)

Grund (2015) uses a familiar model to communicate her novel concept of counterfactual hearing. The effective use of metaphors will facilitate dialogue across our respective domains and assist our creation of methodologies distinctive to metal music studies. Through systems thinking and metaphor, metal scholars can see the entirety of metal culture, its many elements/stakeholders. As ambassadors within metal culture, we can encourage fans, musicians, and others to see their integral roles within the system of the global metal community. They would, then, be more likely to: consent to being interviewed; consent to being liaisons for scholars who are outsiders to a particular scene; consent to being translators; consent to offering referrals; and consent to sharing source material.

If popular music historians saw metal music and culture as part of the larger systems of popular music and popular culture, they might see the need to include metal in their publications. As an equally-vital gem in Indra's net, metal would provide a more comprehensive analysis. We would not see metal ignored as often as it currently is and books such as Malone's (2008) "comprehensive" review of the music of southern US culture would do more than provide one passing reference to metal:

> In the 1960s [Howlin' Wolf] was discovered by a younger set of white acolytes in Britain and the United States, and he had incalculable influence on their blues rock, and later hard rock and heavy metal, music. Hard rock and heavy metal singers' menacing macho braggadocio, many of their vocal stylings, and their stage theatrics are descended from Howlin' Wolf—the man, his voice, his music, his lived persona. (Kalra 2008, 193)

If the editor had employed a systems view of southern US culture, he might have included entries for Morrissound Studios, sludge metal, death metal, *King's X*, *D.R.I.*, *Pantera*, *Corrosion of Conformity*, *Death*, *Eyehategod*, *Deicide*, *Morbid Angel*, *Assück*, and other components which music historians like Von Bader (2013) consider to be important.

CONCLUSION

I have proposed applying systems thinking to metal—namely that scholars view the metal community (i.e., "all things metal") as their purview. Metal music studies scholars study this system and are themselves a component of it. The integration of other components of the metal community into metal music studies is improving as we've witnessed increased interest and participation at conferences and symposia from musicians, music industry representatives, students, fans, and others.

Promoting a systems view assists us with attaining cultural capital, buy-in, and participation. This chapter has also emphasized the power of conceptual metaphors for intergroup and interdisciplinary transfers of knowledge that should facilitate mutual understandings among the many stakeholders in the global metal community. We need metaphors to help us understand other stakeholders' views and communicate ours. Metaphor and systems thinking could assist us in communicating the value of metal music and culture and metal music studies to our institutional and professional colleagues (i.e., the non-metal music studies scholars and administrators in our networks)—such as communicating the importance of including metal fans in an analysis of fandom or consumer culture.

Broadening the toolbox of metaphor to the act of framing discourse (e.g., Fairhurst 2011), metal music studies scholars might pay special attention to supplementing their discipline-specific scientific arguments with visual images, metaphor, and narratives/story in order to effectively communicate outside their respective disciplines:

> Language is one of the most sophisticated cognitive skills we possess as humans. It expresses and shapes thought. It contains an implicit classification of experience and is designed to change the neural pathways to the brain, thus changing minds. The changing patterns occur through the use of sounds and symbols. It's a process like that of using metaphors. A metaphor finds connections between things in the mind and new connections enable the mind to see the world differently. (Maltoni 2015)

It is through recognizing the elements of our systems, be it the global metal community or academe, that we acknowledge the tasks before us: building bridges for the benefit of the growth and acceptance of metal music and culture studies. By recognizing and understanding the other systems of which we are a part, we can assess ways to use metaphor to communicate our worth and contributions.

NOTES

1. Martos Ramón Oscuro, in discussion with the author, May 27, 2015.
2. Plante, Robert, in discussion with the author, May 23, 2015.
3. Netherton, Jason, in discussion with the author, May 18, 2015.

REFERENCES

Ackoff, Russell. 1970. *A Concept of Corporate Planning*. New York: John Wiley & Sons.
———. 1974. *Redesigning the Future: A Systems Approach to Societal Problems*. New York: John Wiley & Sons.
Anderson, Virginia and Lauren Johnson. 1997. *Systems Thinking Basics: From Concepts to Causal Loops*. Cambridge, MA: Pegasus Communications.

Bailey, Kenneth D. 2005. "General Systems Theory." In *Encyclopedia of Social Theory*, edited by George Ritzer, 310–16. Thousand Oaks, CA: Sage.

Bammer, Gabriele. 2014. "From Toolbox to Big Science Project: A Bold Proposal." In *Enhancing Communication and Collaboration in Interdisciplinary Research*, edited by Michael O'Rourke, Stephen Crowley, Sanford D. Eigenbrode and J. D. Wulfhorst, 386–406. Thousand Oaks, CA: Sage.

Bardine, Bryan, Gabby Riches, Brenda Walter, and Dave Snell, eds. 2016. *Heavy Metal Music Studies and Popular Culture*. London, UK: Palgrave Macmillan.

Boulding, Kenneth E. 1985. *The World as a Total System*. Beverly Hills, CA: Sage.

Brown, Eleanor M. 1995. "The Tower of Babel: Bridging the Divide Between Critical Race Theory and 'Mainstream' Civil Rights Scholarship." *Yale Law Journal*, 105 (2): 513–47.

Buchholz, Rogene A., and Sandra B. Rosenthal. 2005. "Toward a Contemporary Conceptual Framework for Stakeholder Theory." *Journal Of Business Ethics*, 58 (1–3): 137–48.

Caspi, Opher, Iris R. Bell, David Rychener, Tracy W. Gaudet, and Andrew T. Weil. 2000. "The Tower of Babel: Communication and Medicine: An Essay on Medical Education and Complementary-Alternative Medicine." *Archives of Internal Medicine*, 160 (21): 3193–195.

Churchman, Charles West. 1968. *The Systems Approach*. New York: Dell Books.

Coggins, Owen. 2015. "Experience, Practice, Writing: A Methodological Outline of Drone Metal Research." In *Modern Heavy Metal: Markets, Practices and Cultures*, edited by T-M. Karjalainen and K. Kärk, 354–65. Helsinki, Finland: Aalto University & Turku, International Institute for Popular Culture.

Dictionary.com. "Community." *Dictionary.com Unabridged*. Random House, Inc. Accessed March 5, 2016. dictionary.reference.com/browse/community.

Encyclopaedia Metallum. 2015a. "Browse Bands—By Country." *Encyclopaedia Metallum: The Metal Archives*. Accessed July 9, 2015. www.metal-archives.com/browse/country.

———. 2015b. "Statistics." *Encyclopaedia Metallum: The Metal Archives*. Accessed July 9, 2015. www.metal-archives.com/stats.

Fairhurst, Gail T. 2011. *The Power of Framing: Creating the Language of Leadership*. San Francisco, CA: Jossey-Bass.

Feldman, Jerome A. 2006. *From Molecule to Metaphor: A Neural Theory of Language*. Cambridge, MA: MIT Press.

Freeman, R. Edward. 1984. *Strategic Management: A Stakeholder Approach*. Boston, MA: Pitman.

Freeman, R. Edward, Jeffrey S. Harrison, Andrew C. Wicks, Bidhan L. Parmar, and Simone de Colle, eds. 2010. *Stakeholder Theory: The State of the Art*. Cambridge, NY: Cambridge University Press.

Geary, James. 2011. *I Is An Other: The Secret Life of Metaphor and How It Shapes the Way We See the World*. New York: HarperCollins.

Goldstein, Jeffrey. 2014. "The Tower of Babel in Nonlinear Dynamics: Toward the Clarification of Terms." In *Chaos Theory in Psychology and the Life Sciences*, edited by Robin Robertson and Allan Combs, 39–48. New York: Psychology Press.

Goodchild, Michael F. 2000. "Communicating Geographic Information in a Digital Age." *Annals of The Association Of American Geographers* 90 (2): 344–55.

Grund, Cynthia M. 2015. "The Sound of Metal: A Proposal for the Interpretation of Extreme Metal as Music." In *Modern Heavy Metal: Markets, Practices and Cultures*, ed. Toni-Matti Karjalainen and Kimi Kärki, 374–82. Helsinki, Finland: Aalto University & Turku, International Institute for Popular Culture.

Hickam, Brian. 2010. "Crypts of Eternity: The Archival Preservation of Heavy Metal & Hardcore Punk Music and Culture." Brian Hickam Academia.edu. Accessed October 20, 2015. www.academia.edu/7315515/Crypts_of_Eternity_the_archival_preservation_of_heavy_metal_and_hardcore_punk_music_and_culture.

———. 2014. "Amalgamated Anecdotes: Perspectives on the History of Metal Music and Culture Studies." *Metal Music Studies* 1 (1): 5–23.

———. 2015. "Metal Studies Bibliography: A Publication of International Society for Metal Music Studies." International Society for Metal Music Studies. Accessed July 11, 2015. www.ucmo.edu/metalstudies/metal_studies_home.html.

Hickam, Brian, and Jeremy Wallach. 2011. "Female Authority and Dominion: Discourse and Distinctions of Heavy Metal Scholarship." *Journal for Cultural Research,* 15 (3): 255–77.

Hirscheim, Rudy A., and Heinz K. Klein. 2006. "Crisis in the IS Field? A Critical Reflection on the State of the Discipline." In *Information Systems: The State of the Field,* edited by John Leslie King and Kalle Lyytinen, 71–146. Hoboken, NJ: John Wiley & Sons.

ISMMS. 2015. Mission. *International Society for Metal Music Studies.* Accessed July 11, 2015. www.ucmo.edu/metalstudies/.

Kalra, Ajay. 2008. "Burnett, Chester Arthur (Howlin' Wolf)." In *The New Encyclopedia of Southern Culture: Volume 12, Music,* edited by B. C. Malone, 193–95. Chapel Hill, NC: University of North Carolina Press.

Karjalainen, Toni-Matti and Kimi Kärki, eds. 2015. *Modern Heavy Metal: Markets, Practices and Cultures: International Academic Research Conference.* Turku, Finland: International Institute for Popular Culture.

Khazaei, Anahita, Statia Elliot, and Marion Joppe. 2015. "An Application of Stakeholder Theory to Advance Community Participation in Tourism Planning: The Case for Engaging Immigrants as Fringe Stakeholders." *Journal of Sustainable Tourism,* 23 (7): 1049–62.

Klein, Julie T. 1990. *Interdisciplinarity: History, Theory, and Practice.* Detroit, MI: Wayne State University Press.

Kok, Gerjo, Zamira Gurabardhi, Nell H. Gottlieb, and Fred R. H. Zijlstra. 2015. "Influencing Organizations to Promote Health: Applying Stakeholder Theory." *Health Education & Behavior,* 42 (1): 123S–32S.

Lafreniere, Katherine C., Sameer Deshpande, Henning Bjornlund, and M. Gordon Hunter. 2013. "Extending Stakeholder Theory to Promote Resource Management Initiatives to Key Stakeholders: A Case Study of Water Transfers in Alberta, Canada." *Journal Of Environmental Management* 129: 81–91.

Laszlo, Ervin. 1972. *Introduction to Systems Philosophy: Toward a New Paradigm of Contemporary Thought.* New York: Harper Torchbook.

Mainardes, Emerson, Helena Alves, and Mario Raposo. 2013. "Portuguese Public University Student Satisfaction: A Stakeholder Theory-Based Approach." *Tertiary Education And Management,* 19 (4): 353–72.

Malone, Bill C., ed. 2008. *The New Encyclopedia of Southern Culture: Volume 12, Music.* Chapel Hill, NC: University of North Carolina Press.

Maltoni, Valeria. 2015. "Language and the Lost Art of Letter Writing." *Conversation Agent,* October 27. Accessed July 12, 2015. www.conversationagent.com/2015/10/language-and-the-lost-art-of-letter-writing.html.

Martos, Ramón Oscuro. 2014. *Let's Print And Justice for Art.* Indiegogo, November 3, www.indiegogo.com/projects/let-s-print-and-justice-for-art#/story.

———. 2015. *And Justice for Art: Stories About Heavy Metal Album Covers.* Tampa, FL: Dark Canvas.

Mercer, Mick. 2009. *Music to Die For: The International Guide to Today's Extreme Music Scene.* London, UK: Cherry Red Books.

Miller, Raymond C. 1982. "Varieties of Interdisciplinary Approaches in the Social Sciences." *Issues in Integrative Studies,* 1 (1): 1–37.

Netherton, Jason. 2014. *Extremity Retained: Notes from the Death Metal Underground.* London, ON: Handshake Inc.

Olds, Linda E. 1992. *Metaphors of Interrelatedness: Toward a Systems Theory of Psychology.* Albany, NY: SUNY Press.

Owen, Ian. 1992. "The Tower of Babel: Searching for Core Clinical, Theoretical and Ethical Issues in Psychotherapy." *Counselling Psychology Quarterly*, 5 (1): 67.

Phillips, Bernard S. 2001. *Beyond Sociology's Tower of Babel: Reconstructing the Scientific Method*. New York: Aldine de Gruyter.

Rat Skates. 2007. *Born in the Basement*. Pottstown, PA: MVD Entertainment Group, DVD.

Ray, Donna E, Shawn L. Berman, Michael E. Johnson-Cramer, and Harry J. III Van Buren. 2014. "Refining Normative Stakeholder Theory: Insights from Judaism, Christianity, and Islam." *Journal Of Management, Spirituality & Religion*, 11 (4): 331–56.

Repko, Allen F. 2008. *Interdisciplinary Research: Process and Theory*. Los Angeles, CA: Sage.

Riches, Gabby. 2015. "Reviews: Melancology: Black Metal Theory and Ecology." *Metal Music Studies*, 1 (3): 398–401.

Ricoeur, Paul. 1977. *The Rule of Metaphor: Multi-Disciplinary Studies of the Creation of Meaning in Language*. Toronto: University of Toronto Press.

Riddick, Mark. 2007. *Killustration: The Art of Mark Riddick*. Ashburn, VA: www.Riddickart.com.

———. 2008a. *Logos from Hell: A Compendium of Death and Black Metal Logos*. Ashburn, VA: www.Riddickart.com.

———. 2008b. *Rotten Renderings: The Art of Mark Riddick*. Ashburn, VA: www.Riddickart.com.

———. 2012. *Compendium of Death: The Art of Mark Riddick, 1991–2011*. Vodňany, Czech Republic: Doomentia Press.

———. 2015. *Logos from Hell: A Compendium of Death and Black Metal Logos, 2nd Edition*. Vodňany, Czech Republic: Doomentia Press.

Scott, Niall W.R., and Imke Von Helden. 2010. *The Metal Void: First Gatherings*. Oxford, UK: Inter-Disciplinary Press. PDF ebook. www.inter-disciplinary.net/publishing/product/the-metal-void-first-gatherings/.

Tait, Andrew, and Kurt A. Richardson, eds. 2010. *Complexity and Knowledge Management: Understanding the Role of Knowledge in the Management of Social Networks*. Charlotte, NC: Information Age Publishing.

This is Spinal Tap. Directed by Rob Reiner. 1984. Santa Monica, CA: MGM Home Entertainment, 2000. DVD.

Ulmer, Robert R., Matthew W. Seeger, and Timothy L. Sellnow. 2005. "Stakeholder Theory." In *Encyclopedia of Public Relations*, edited by Robert L. Heath, 809–12. Thousand Oaks, CA: Sage.

Von Bader, David. 2013. "Ten Best Florida Metal Bands of All Time." *New Times Broward-Palm Beach*, April 4. Accessed July 11 2015. www.browardpalmbeach.com/music/ten-best-florida-metal-bands-of-all-time-6421141.

Von Bertalanffy, Ludwig. 1972. Foreword to *Introduction to Systems Philosophy*, Authored by Ervin Laszlow. New York: Harper Torchbook.

———. 1975. *Perspectives on General System Theory: Scientific-philosophical Studies*. New York: George Braziller.

Wallach, Jeremy, Harris M. Berger, and Paul D. Greene, eds. 2011. *Metal Rules the Globe: Heavy Metal Music Around the World*. Durham, NC: Duke University Press.

Weinstein, Deena. 1991. *Heavy Metal: A Cultural Sociology*. New York: Lexington.

Wilson, Scott, ed. 2014. *Melancology: Black Metal Theory and Ecology*. Alresford, UK: Zero Books.

Index

About the Contributors

Esther Clinton, PhD—Visiting assistant professor in the Department of Popular Culture at Bowling Green State University in Ohio (USA). She has written about Heavy Metal music and was one of the organizers of the Heavy Metal and Popular Culture International Conference at Bowling Green State University in 2013. Her work has appeared in *Asian Music, Journal of the National Medical Association, Proverbium*, and in the book *Archetypes and Motifs in Folk Literature: A Handbook*. She coedited a special issue of Asian Music on Indonesian popular music genres, including metal.

E-mail: estherc@bgsu.edu

Brian Hickam, MLIS, MSMOB—Academic librarian for the past twenty years and director of Watson Library at Wilmington College in Ohio. He holds a Master of Library and Information Science and a Master of Science in Management and Organizational Behavior. He is a former president of Ohio's chapter of the Association of College & Research Libraries and is a founding member of the International Society for Metal Music Studies and its affiliated scholarly journal and archive. Brian has published various journal articles, book chapters, bibliographies, newsletter articles, and book reviews, and has curated two exhibits on masks and popular culture. His hobbies include winter tent camping, all genres of music, nature walks, and art museums.

E-mail: Brian_hickam@wilmington.edu

Kathryn Jezer-Morton—Graduate student at Concordia University researching mobile device use habits among immigrant mothers of young children. Contributing ethnographer on the Knight Foundation-funded Indie Games in Libraries working group, she studies the curatorial practices of librarians who run video game clubs. Her writing on the intersections between class, social media, and parenting has appeared on Jezebel.com.

E-mail: kjezermorton@gmail.com

Keith Kahn-Harris, PhD—Sociologist and lecturer at Leo Baeck College, associate lecturer at Birkbeck College, and fellow of the Institute of Jewish Policy Research. He has written widely on contemporary metal culture and is the author of *Extreme Metal: Music and Culture on the Edge*

(2007), and coeditor of *Heavy Metal: Controversies and Counterculture* (2013) and *Global Metal Music and Culture* (2016).

E-mail: keith@kahn-harris.org

Toni-Matti Karjalainen, Doctor of Arts (Art & Design)—Academy research fellow and docent in Aalto University School of Business, Helsinki, Finland. His current research focuses on culture export and cultural narratives, design for branding, design management, and visual storytelling, particularly within heavy metal and rock music. He has published in various academic and popular domains and acted as visiting lecturer in numerous universities, companies, and events in different countries. He organizes the international Modern Heavy Metal Conference in Helsinki and is the Secretary of the International Society for Metal Music Studies (ISMMS) for 2015–2019.

Website: tonimattikarjalainen.info.

Email: toni-matti.karjalainen@aalto.fi

Sigrid Mendoza, MA—Social community psychologist currently completing a PhD at the University of Puerto Rico. She has presented her work on heavy metal studies at the Heavy Metal and Popular Culture Conference and the Annual Convention of the Puerto Rican Psychological Association. She has also worked in the development of *The Distorted Island*, a documentary about the heavy metal community in Puerto Rico. Her research interests include: gender dynamics and feminism, heavy metal studies, ethnography, social construction of sexuality, and cultural studies.

E-mail: mendoza.sigrid@gmail.com

Eric Morales, MA (aka The Beast)—Singer for the Puerto Rican heavy metal band *Dantesco* and owner of Odin's Court record store in the town of Caguas. He is one of the founding members of the local metal scene having been active in it since 1984. He completed a bachelor's degree in history at the University of Puerto Rico's Cayey Campus and a masters' degree in philosophy at the Río Piedras Campus. At the same institution he was part of the "Teatro Lírico" where he trained on classical music and specifically as an opera singer. He has recorded seven albums with his band *Dantesco*. He has also collaborated in other musical projects including *Narval* and *Nimrod* from Chile. He has made numerous guest appearances in albums from international bands, including *Zarpa* (Spain), *Arkanos* (Bolivia), and *Vastator* (Chile). Eric has been a fierce defender of Puerto Rico's metal scene.

Bradley J. Nelson, PhD—Professor of hispanic studies and associate dean of academic programs in the School of Graduate Studies at Concordia University. His research focuses on visual culture, sexual violence, hate speech, and the history of science in Baroque Spain and Latin America, as well as innovations in science pedagogies.

E-mail: Brad.nelson@concordia.ca

Jeffrey S. Podoshen, PhD—Associate professor in the department of Business, Organizations, and Society at Franklin and Marshall College in Lancaster, PA, USA. Jeffrey's area of research relates to dark consumption and dark tourism practice, and he often blends and bridges theory from a variety of disciplines (such as marketing, social psychology, and sociology) in order to explain phenomena and build theory. One of the early pioneers of the use of netnography in social sciences research, Jeffrey utilizes a myriad of mixed method and cutting edge qualitative techniques to distill complex data into more easily defined categories that allows for greater introspection on specific subcultures.

E-mail: Jeffrey.podoshen@fandm.edu

Jihan Rabah—Doctoral candidate and instructor at the Department of Education, Concordia University. Her research interests are grounded in the affordances of digital technologies in learning environments. Her work has been widely disseminated through articles in peer reviewed journals including: *McGill's Journal of Education, Canadian Journal of Higher Education, Canadian Journal for Social Sciences*, and *International Journal of Educational Development*.

Email: jihan.rabah@education.concorda.ca

Paula Rowe, PhD—Social work scholar at the University of South Australia's Centre for Social Change. Her research explores youth identity formation and social transitions through high schooling and into post-school environments, focusing on ways that young people use (sub)cultural interests to build an identity and to develop broader life aspirations. Paula also works with local government as a community planner. In this role, she coordinates community action research projects that foster empowered citizenship and democratic participation for marginalized youth.

E-mail: paula.rowe@mymail.unisa.edu.au

Niall Scott, PhD, MA, BSc, DipTH, DipPGCLTHE—Philosopher, cultural theorist, and senior lecturer in ethics at the University of Central Lancashire in Preston, in the north of England. He is the current chair of the International Society for Metal Music Studies (ISMMS), coeditor of *Metal Music Studies* and editor of *Helvete, a Journal of Black Metal Theory*. He has published widely and spoken internationally on Metal Studies. In addition to this he also researches in the field of bioethics, political philosophy, and on popular culture. His work has featured in the news media—in the *New York Times*, the *Guardian*, and the *Times* newspapers as well as

Metal Hammer magazine. He first met the coeditor for this book, Nelson Varas-Diaz, at the interdisciplinary.net Heavy Fundametalisms conference in Prague, 2010.

E-mail: NWRScott@uclan.ac.uk

Karl Spracklen, PhD—Professor of leisure studies at Leeds Beckett University (UK). He is interested in leisure theory, social identity and community, and leisure spaces. He has researched and written extensively on leisure and music scenes such as goth, folk music, and extreme metal, with over seventy publications to date. He is the Principal Editor of Metal Music Studies.

E-mail: K.Spracklen@leedsbeckett.ac.uk

Méi-Ra St. Laurent—Doctoral student in musicology of popular music at Université Laval (Québec, Canada) under the supervision of Serge Lacasse. Her doctoral thesis covers the musical narrative of black metal music in Québec, and the way the discourse of the scene is not only shaped musically, but also culturally. Her previous studies also included the analysis of extreme metal songs using narratology and musicology, and encompassed the influence of Wagnerian musical elements in the music of symphonic metal bands. Her papers have been published different academic journals including *Metal Music Studies, Intersections: Revue Canadienne de Musique,* and *Sociétés: Revue de Sciences Humaines et Sociales.*

E-mail: mei-ra.st-laurent.1@ulaval.ca

Tieja Thomas, PhD—Research associate with the department of Science, Technology, and Innovation Policy at the Conference Board of Canada. Her research program lies at the intersection of educational technology and citizenship education, and explores how hate, violence, and oppression are manifested and negotiated in online environments. She is a co-Principal Investigator for SOMEONE (Social Media Education Everyday), a project with aims to build curricula for learning across the lifespan to prevent and combat hate appearing online. This is research funded by the Kanishka Contribution Program (Public Safety and Emergency Preparedness Canada).

E-mail: tiejathomasphd@gmail.com

Christopher Thompson, MA—Doctoral student at Uppsala University's Department of History. His areas of research and upcoming dissertation focus on Norwegian black metal, uses of history, and national identity construction.

E-mail: christopher.thompson@hist.uu.se

Kathryn Urbaniak, MA—Research coordinator and instructional designer at Concordia University. Her research interests focus on the intersections of identity, learning, and technology.

E-mail: kathryn.urbaniak@concordia.ca

Nelson Varas-Díaz, PhD—Social psychologist and professor at Florida International University. His music-oriented research addresses the formation of metal scenes in the Caribbean region, focusing on the role of local culture and politics in their development. His work has been published in multiple journals, including: *Metal Music Studies, Journal of International Community Music*, and *Journal of Community Psychology*. He is the producer of the award-wining documentary *The Distorted Island: Heavy Metal and Community in Puerto Rico* (2014).

E-mail: nvaras@mac.com

Vivek Venkatesh, PhD—Associate professor in the Department of Education at Concordia University in Montréal, Québec. He is the director of the SOMEONE—Social Media Education Every Day initiative, and the creator of the Grimposium festival and conference series. Vivek is an interdisciplinary and applied learning scientist who investigates the psychological, cultural and cognitive factors impacting the design, development, and inclusive adoption of digital media in educational and social contexts. Since 2008, Vivek has received more than $1.2 million in funding (as principal or coprincipal investigator) and more than $3.8 million (as coinvestigator) from international, federal and provincial granting agencies.

E-mail: Vivek.venkatesh@concordia.ca

Jeremy Wallach, PhD—Professor in the Department of Popular Culture at Bowling Green State University. He is author of *Modern Noise, Fluid Genres: Popular Music in Indonesia, 1997–2001* (2008) and coeditor of a special issue of *Asian Music* on Indonesian popular music genres (with Esther Clinton, 2013). Jeremy has written extensively on metal music and culture and is coeditor of Metal Rules the Globe: Heavy Metal Music around the World (with Harris Berger and Paul Greene, 2011). He also chaired the organizing committee of the BGSU Heavy Metal and Popular Culture International Conference.

E-mail: jeremyw@bgsu.edu

Jason J. Wallin, PhD—Associate professor of media and youth culture in curriculum in the Faculty of Education at the University of Alberta, Canada, where he teaches courses in visual art, media studies, and cultural curriculum theory. He is the author of *A Deleuzian Approach to Curriculum: Essays on a Pedagogical Life* (2010), coauthor of *Arts-Based Research: A*

Critique and Proposal (with Jan Jagodzinski, 2013), and coeditor of *Deleuze, Guattari, Politics and Education* (with Matt Carlin, 2015).

E-mail: Jjwallin@ualberta.ca

Deena Weinstein—Professor of sociology at DePaul University in Chicago, she specializes in cultural sociology (with a focus on rock music), and social theory. Her books include *Heavy Metal: A Cultural Sociology* (1991), *(Post)-Modernized Simmel* (1993), and most recently *Rock'n America: A Social and Cultural History* (2015). Among her metal-relevant journal articles and book chapters are: "Birmingham's Post-Industrial Metal," "How Is Metal Studies Possible?" "Metallica Kills," "Pagan Metal," "Rock's Guitar Gods—Avatars of the Sixties," and "Just So Stories: How Heavy Metal Got Its Name—A Cautionary Tale." As a rock journalist concentrating in metal, she has also published an extensive array of album and concert reviews and interviews.